BA

MARTHA J. LANGELAN

A FIRESIDE BOOK   PUBLISHED BY SIMON & SCHUSTER

CK OFF!

HOW TO CONFRONT AND STOP
SEXUAL HARASSMENT AND HARASSERS

NEW YORK   LONDON   TORONTO   SYDNEY TOKYO   SINGAPORE

FIRESIDE
Simon & Schuster Building
Rockefeller Center
1230 Avenue of the Americas
New York, New York 10020

Designed by Songhee Kim
Manufactured in the United States of America

10 9 8 7 6 5 4 3 2 1

Library of Congress Cataloging-in-Publication Data
Langelan, Martha J.
    Back off! : how to confront and stop sexual harassment and
harassers / Martha J. Langelan.
        p. cm.
    "A Fireside book."
    Includes bibliographical references.
    1. Sexual harassment of women—United States—
Prevention. I. Title.
HQ1237.5.U6L36   1993
305.42′0973—dc20   93-11153   CIP
ISBN 0-671-78856-6

ACKNOWLEDGMENTS

Back Off! reflects the work of countless women. From the beginning, the D.C. Rape Crisis Center offered exceptionally generous support, sponsoring the project and providing research and administrative assistance. Part of the proceeds from *Back Off!* will fund the Center's ongoing work to end sexual violence, including confrontation and self-defense classes.

More than two hundred women responded to our request for success stories. Courageous, resourceful, inspiring—your resistance strategies are a gift to women everywhere. *Back Off!* is your book. It is an honor to present even a few of your successes here; I wish we could publish them all.

Women across the country also took the initiative to circulate flyers, publish the request in newsletters, write articles, distribute announcements at conferences, and otherwise spread the word. You got news of the project out to women around the world: Success stories came in from coast to coast and from as far away as Thailand, Germany, and the Netherlands. It was a stunning demonstration of the women's network in action. Thank you, one and all.

Credit is due to many of our foremothers as well: to the women of the U.S. civil rights movement who used early forms of confrontation to challenge racism in the 1950s and 1960s; to the feminist martial arts instructors who began teaching assertiveness and women's self-defense workshops in the early 1970s; and to the women of the Community Action Strategies to Stop Rape (CASSR) project in Columbus, Ohio, who originally developed the techniques for confronting street harassers as part of their rape-prevention program. The feminist community of Washington, D.C., helped me to extend those techniques to apply to harassers on the job and elsewhere, and the members of the Nonviolence Collective at the Washington Peace Center shaped my understanding of successful resistance to power abuse.

Two women in particular deserve public recognition for their historic role in the struggle to end sexual harassment: Catharine MacKinnon, whose ground-breaking analysis defined harassment as illegal sex discrimination and enabled women to begin winning sexual harassment cases, and Anita Hill, whose testimony before the U.S. Senate broke the silence once and for all.

I owe a very special personal debt of gratitude to Crindi Loschinkohl and Debbie Chalfie, both members of the original CASSR project. Ten years ago, they taught me how to confront street harassers. My life has never been the same, and *Back Off!* could never have been written without their analytical insight, friendship, and support.

The thousands of women who have participated in my self-defense classes and confrontation workshops over the past decade can also take a large share of the credit for creating this book. The men in my corporate antiharassment seminars have contributed some enlightening insights as well; some have been refreshingly honest about sexual harassment and creative about what men can do to stop it.

Thanks also go to Barb Hanson for first suggesting that I write about the strategies that work and to Catherine Bernard, Leslie Breed, Debbie Chalfie, Catharine MacKinnon, and Debbie Morris for offering valuable comments on the manuscript. Helga Abramson, Nana Badu, Gina Cattalini, Radhika Chari, Sylvia Cole, Mary Farmer, Jennifer Hamilton, Janet Heisse, Christine Jahnke, Marsha Krassner, Anne Laurent, Pat LeoGrande, Crindi Loschinkohl, Annie McCombs, Melanie McLaughlin, Lauren N. Nile, Becky Otter, Patricia Petrash, Denise Snyder, Nkenge Toure, and Lisa Wolcott provided advice, research, administrative help, translations, publicity, networking, and encouragement at every turn. Their excitement about the project was a joy; their assistance made *Back Off!* a much better book than I could ever have produced alone.

My agents, Leslie Breed and Elizabeth Outka, and my editor, Betsy Radin, loved the idea of a book about women's success stories and did a magnificent job of turning the idea into a reality. In addition, Ray Weil and Shelton Jackson at the U.S. Department of Transportation generously allowed me time to write, in the form of a flexible work schedule and a brief leave of absence.

Creating *Back Off!* has been an intense experience—exhilarating but sometimes exhausting. To my mother, Severine Langelan, who kept telling me I could do it; to my aunt, Helen Doyce, who sent her own success stories along with her encouragement; to my sister, Rosalie Langelan, who sang to me; and to my partner, Bill LeoGrande, who donated a computer, kept me fed, fixed what broke, and just kept on bringing me those mugs of tea at midnight: Thank you from the heart.

TO SEVERINA GURZYNSKA LANGELAN
WHO HAS NEVER LET FEAR KEEP HER SILENT

CONTENTS

by Catharine A. MacKinnon

In this book, women confront their sexual tormentors on their own and win. Telling their stories in their own voices, women speak of stopping the abuse, alone and together, physically and verbally, spontaneously and by design. It is a tale of solidarity and sell-out, of turning powerlessness into power, of facing down bullies, of small but real victories in a war thought lost, of getting what we need to go on. Each woman—and everywoman—walks out of these pages with her report from the front, a "letter from a war zone"* that is the everyday life of women everywhere.

Confrontation is a form of direct action, of fighting back in the world as if women were entitled to inhabit more than just an inner island. Women's responses to harassment have always been part of their strategies for living through men's aggression. But they have usually been calculated to save men's egos, to minimize their anger and dangerousness. Reports of even this much "uppity" behavior—as isolated and privatized as men's abuse of women—have traveled underground, whispered in survival circles from Laundromats to assembly lines to board rooms. This book ends that. Here, women have claimed living space; women have stood up in public; women have gone self-respecting. This book marks a crucial moment where pacification and coping stop and change begins.

This book shows women unbound, women uncircum-

---

* Andrea Dworkin, *Letters from a War Zone* (New York: Dutton, 1988).

scribed, women writing their own scripts and confronting men on grounds women define. A lawsuit, by comparison, is a formalized confrontation based on a script someone else wrote, a ritualized and circumscribed form of action. At the same time, the approach that produced this book is the same as the one that produced the idea that sexual harassment should be legally actionable: taking harm to women seriously and acting against it, as if you were entitled to. When it is illegitimate to fight for your own dignity, legally or socially, you are invisible and expendable, the sludge of humanity, to whom anything can be done and nothing will be done about it. The law of sexual harassment has begun to move the legal system beyond its previously formal, passive, mechanistic notions of equality. Sexual domination has been taken more seriously. These confrontations claim the same ground in social life. Confronting sexual harassment, in law or life, is taking hierarchy, history, and harm seriously. Both bear witness, refuse to be silenced, and claim that women live here, too.

Since about 1974, women have been coming to me with their accounts of what we now call sexual harassment, and I began trying to figure out what to do about it. In recognizing sexual harassment as a legal claim, the legal system has given legitimacy to women's resistance to sexual violation and has provided a mechanism of accountability for their violators. But the point has always been to *stop* them. Proceedings before courts and administrative agencies can be long, slow, expensive, grueling, cruel, misogynist, and manipulated. Adjudications are more than nothing but so often not enough. And because equality is guaranteed to women only at work and school, places where men will acknowledge at least formally that they do not own us, sexual harassment is seen as discriminatory only there—not at home or on the street, for example. Early on, we began devising other than legal ways to stop the abuse and keep women's jobs or doctors or homes *and their sexual integrity and human dignity, too.* Court is a last resort anyway. So we began to develop what this book makes into a term of art: techniques of confrontation.

The contents of this book are part of the engagement between law and life. Formally outside the law, Anita Hill confronted Clarence Thomas in his confirmation hearing for the Supreme Court. It was the sexual harassment confrontation of all time, moving the issue forward in a way no law or legal proceeding has or could have. But there would have been no Anita Hill without women like Pamela Price and Mechelle Vinson—women who confronted the law with legal claims of sexual harassment when there was no law against it—also black women with clarity of vision, strength of purpose, and indominability of spirit. The facts of their cases tell their stories. This book tells the stories of women like Anita Hill who live after them, in a world their stories helped create, a world in which sexual harassment is recognized as *not* one of life's little joys.

This book reminds you of what you know from your own life. As such, it is an act of mobilization, of consciousness, of organizing. It reminded me that when I was in law school, I ran a daily gantlet of men hanging out around the bar on the corner of my block in a bombed-out area of New Haven. The men kissy-kissed the air, made what I identified (having been raised in a farming area) as dog- and pig-calling sounds, belched, yelled invitations in English and Spanish, and occasionally howled in an indeterminate tongue. After trying everything else, I made up yellow cards that stated, in English and Spanish: "You have just offended a woman. This card has been chemically treated. Your prick will fall off in three days." Then I walked the gantlet slowly, looked each man personally in the face, and gave him a card. Looking completely startled, some shook my hand. Others mumbled, "Thank you." Ever after—for, I assure you, years—when they saw me coming they became engrossed in their shoelaces or the pigeons on the roof, or went inside for a drink. Every woman has stories like this and better, and this book has them all.

Many of the experiences documented here are framed by the total absence of legal remedies for sexual abuse in many areas of social life. One from my own illustrates. Three young boys in a car apparently did not like one of my more creative driving maneuvers—it stayed their forward progress perhaps five seconds, thus threatening their ownership of the road. They screamed "slut" at me several times as they screeched away. I pulled an even more creative maneuver in order to follow them in what became a high-speed chase. After first losing them, I searched them out, cowering behind a line of trees at the back of a supermarket parking lot. Not having planned what I would do at all, I jumped out and started taking down their license plate number. The driver's terrified looks became torrents of apology: "Gosh, lady, we didn't mean anything wrong . . ." was about as far as he got. "Don't you *ever* say that to *any* woman *ever* again," I exploded—one of the few times in my life I have been truly angry. Upon which, the other kid in the front seat injected brightly, "He thought you were his sister. He meant to say, you're, she's, a whore." This was not a promising line of defense. After ten minutes of my reading them out on the meaning of all this, on their use of debased terms for women's body parts and oppressed conditions as insults, and who did they think they were, they all solemnly promised they would never do it again and begged me not to tell their parents. It took me about four hours to cool off.

My friend Andrea Dworkin later remarked dryly that we were lucky not to find my body in a ditch. She was right. Marty Langelan's informants, and her discussions, balance an affirmation of women's judgment and audacity with a realistic view of the risks we run. These days, women are shot so kids like these can joyride in their cars. But these are also days in which organized bigots are claiming a free-speech right to this sort of abuse, even in areas of social life where laws of equality do exist. What is a woman supposed to do?

The longer I litigate, the more I respect self-help remedies, even in areas in which clear legal remedies do exist. One of my oldest friends from law school, now a law professor, was told his sister's landlord said she could continue to live in his building but she would have to move in with him. Instead of filing a complaint for sexual harassment in rental housing, an avenue clearly available there, my friend went to the landlord and told him that he had friends who would break his kneecaps for a beer, no telling what they would do for a six-pack, and if he so much as showed his face to his family ever again, some inventive medical intervention would be necessary to put his body parts back in their original positions. His sister kept her apartment. It is interesting that even those of us who have knowledge and access to the law often choose direct action when we and ours are on the line.

This book is full of such strategies, most of them by women who are direct targets, a few by others in solidarity with them. They work. The fact is, the law does not have much experience with sexual harassment and women have a lot. Concerning sexual harassment, as much else, women have more to tell the law than the law has to tell women, and this book tells it.

This book has what Pandora probably had in her box: the truth about the ugliness and horrors we have seen; imaginative, explosive, inspiring, transformative strategies for resistance; spirits of a new order. Loose this and who knows what will happen. This book is applied theory at its best; it is experience we can use. I would give it to any woman who comes to me for legal advice. The stories are personal, political, vivid, gripping, and invigorating; the analysis is strong and helpful; the practical advice is perceptive, accessible, and responsible. The women in this book make me proud to be a woman. Marty Langelan has done as much as you can do with a book: move us forward in the fight for freedom.

PART
one

THE CULTURE AND HISTORY
OF HARASSMENT AND RESISTANCE

Sexual Harassment: The Beginning of the End

I'm twenty-four and work in Washington, D.C. Last July, I was on the L4 bus, heading home. The weather was hot and sticky, and it had been a long day at work. People were standing packed shoulder to shoulder in the aisle. I think lots of women and girls have probably had the experience of men using that kind of crowded-bus situation to feel us up— once a guy slid his hand up under my skirt, real quick, all the way up to my crotch. Gross! I was so shocked I just stood there. Usually, my friends and I just try to move away as fast as we can, to get out of the creep's reach, although it can be hard to get away when the bus is jammed full.

But this time, the most amazing thing happened. A woman about four feet in front of me suddenly reached around behind her. She was completely calm, but she gripped this guy's arm, held his hand up in the air, and in a loud, clear, commanding voice—carried all through the bus—she said, "What was this hand doing on my ass?" She held on to his arm, held his hand right up there.

The man who'd harassed her—three-piece suit, looked like some junior executive type—didn't even try to deny it. Everyone knew his hand had been exactly where she said it was. He turned bright red, looked guilty as hell, and jumped off the bus at the first stop.

The women on the bus loved it. I thought, "Wow, that's terrific, I know what I'm going to do from now on! I bet he thinks twice before he feels up another woman."

In the 1990s, women are putting harassers on notice. The cultural standards of our society are changing: Women are refusing to tolerate sexual harassment in any form. Harassers can no longer count on women retreating helplessly or acting like fearful, embarrassed victims. Men who rely on the protection of anonymity are in for a shock; their victims may turn around on the spot and hold them publicly accountable for their actions. Women have begun to use "confrontation" techniques—a powerful new way to stop sexual bullies. Women today are not only speaking up and filing charges but taking decisive, personal action against sexual harassment on the job, on the street, in the university, in the neighborhood, and, yes, even on the city bus at the end of a long, hot day.

The change has been a long time in the making. Sexual harassment has been a dirty little secret for generations, an unacknowledged barrage of intrusive, threatening male behavior that has limited women's freedom and violated even their simple human right to ride a bus or walk down a street in peace. Women have always tried to stop harassment or work around it, usually with great frustration. Elena, a strong, smart woman now in her eighties, recounted some of her actions over a lifetime of harassment:

- I was sixteen. My girlfriend and I accepted a ride from two young men we knew who had always been polite to us. Instead of taking us home, they drove into a forest preserve and tried to assault us. We managed to escape by telling them that my uncle was a police detective and they'd never see the light of day again when he got through with them. Thank God, it worked.
- I went for a job interview and was ushered into a private office. The interviewer came in and closed the door. He sat down beside me and started to fondle me. I jumped up and yelled, "Keep your hands off me!" and raced out of the room. The employees in the outer office just smiled at me as I left. So much for that "job opportunity."

• When I was about forty-five, I went to a bank for a personal loan. I filled out the loan application, and the loan officer said he was willing to give me the loan—provided that I had sex with him. I called him a son of a bitch but was too embarrassed to make an issue of it at the time. I didn't get the loan.

Typical harassment? Yes. In these three incidents, and many more, Elena kept her integrity and refused to be intimidated. But even the smartest women had no effective remedies, no way to hold harassers accountable for their actions.

For many years, there was not even a name for this invasive behavior; it was only twenty years ago that women began to label it "sexual harassment." In the workplace, women have been dealing with harassment ever since the beginning of the Industrial Revolution (and even before then, in the agricultural workforce), but it was not until the 1960s that the first U.S. federal statute against sex discrimination at work was passed. Even then, it was difficult, and often impossible, to file charges of any kind. Reviewing the research on sexual harassment, the National Council for Research on Women found that the legal mechanisms for processing complaints were usually ineffective, while the emotional and financial costs to the victim were often devastating.[1]

Throughout the 1970s and 1980s, women struggled to find new ways to stop sexual harassment. Twenty years ago, a generation of women began to turn their analytical skills to the issue of sexual violence, including sexual harassment. In small meetings and feminist consciousness-raising groups across the United States, women began to talk about their experiences and take a systematic look at the hidden epidemic of rape, battering, and harassment in their own daily lives.

Out of those early discussions came the first rape crisis hotlines and women's martial arts workshops. Rape survivors began to come forward. By 1975, women had begun to develop new self-defense strategies and assertiveness training seminars, as well as some rigorous research on sexual violence—along with many new community institutions such as rape crisis centers, battered women's shelters, and women's martial arts programs. The first public speak-out on record against sexual harassment took place in Ithaca, New York, in the spring of 1975. In the 1980s, battered women and incest survivors spoke out, breaking through more layers of societal denial and creating a deeper public awareness of the extent of sexual violence. And women began to win the first sexual harassment cases in state and federal courts, using the new legal theories pioneered by Professor Catharine MacKinnon and other activists. In 1986, the U.S. Supreme Court finally recognized harassment as a form of illegal sex discrimination.

As the lawyers tackled harassment in the courts, women also began to develop creative ways of dealing with street harassers. In the 1970s, some women handed out special business cards that read: "You have just insulted a woman. This card has been chemically treated. In three days your prick will fall off." Women in Santa Cruz started identifying rapists on public posters and organizing group actions to challenge them on the street. And in 1977, a group of feminists from Women Against Rape in Columbus, Ohio, began a new project: Community Action Strategies to Stop Rape (CASSR). With a grant from the National Institute for Mental Health, CASSR developed a community-based rape prevention program. CASSR combined assertiveness training with a careful analysis of street harassment and rape, and came up with confrontation as a way to help women overcome the socialized passivity that contributes to their vulnerability to attack. In 1980, CASSR sponsored a national conference on its successful strategies, including the first practical guidelines for confronting harassers.

By 1981, the Washington, D.C., Rape Crisis Center and other antiviolence groups began to incorporate these powerful, nonviolent techniques into their self-defense courses and community education programs. Feminist self-defense instructors started teaching harassment confrontation classes and expanding the strategy to apply not just to street harassers but across many different settings. By the time Anita Hill faced the Senate Judiciary Committee in the fall of 1991, many women were beginning to succeed, not only with sexual harassment lawsuits but with direct-action confrontation techniques that stopped harassers in their tracks.

Now, in the 1990s, more and more women are using all of the tools at their disposal—lawsuits, administrative procedures, publicity, and direct confrontation—to handle harassers. Women are standing up for themselves, breaking out of the old patterns of victimization. We are in the midst of a cultural breakthrough, a real change in women's ability to take action. It is the beginning of the end for harassers.

CHANGING THE CULTURE

Sexual harassment is not some vague, abstract concept, impossible to define. It is a pattern of behavior with a long and ugly history. What kinds of behavior do women consider offensive and discriminatory? Here's a partial list compiled from women who've taken self-defense classes over the past few years:

Wolf whistles
Leering
Sexual innuendo
Comments about women's bodies
Tales of sexual exploits
Graphic descriptions of pornography
Pressure for dates
Hooting, sucking, lip-smacking, and animal noises
Sexually explicit gestures
Unwelcome touching and hugging
Excluding women from meetings
Sabotaging women's work
Sexist and insulting graffiti
Demanding "Hey, baby, give me a smile"
Sexist jokes and cartoons

Hostile put-downs of women
Exaggerated, mocking "courtesy"
Public humiliation
Obscene phone calls
Displaying pornography in the workplace
Insisting that workers wear revealing clothing
Inappropriate gifts (for example, lingerie)
Inappropriate invitations (for example, to go to a hot
    tub or nude beach)
Discussion of one's partner's sexual inadequacies
Lewd and threatening letters
"Accidentally" brushing sexual parts of the body
Pressing or rubbing up against the victim
Leaning over or otherwise invading a victim's space
Sexual sneak attacks (such as grabbing breasts or
    buttocks on the run)
Indecent exposure
Soliciting sexual services
Demanding sexual services
Stalking a victim
Sexual assault

There is no excuse for any of this behavior. But, for generations, this is what women have been expected to tolerate, in shame and silence, as the price for holding a job, taking a class, or just walking down the street. Some of the same behavior (bigoted jokes, exclusionary tactics, personal insults, sabotage, physical assault) is also used in incidents of racial, anti-Semitic, and homophobic harassment, for the very same purposes: intimidation and humiliation, power and dominance.

How frequent is this behavior? So frequent that it is a typical and inescapable part of most women's lives.

Millions of men never harass women. But so many do, in so many different locations, that it is almost impossible for women to avoid the experience. According to the National Council for Research on Women, 50 to 85 percent of U.S. women can expect to encounter some form of sexual harassment during their academic or working life.[2] Women in relatively powerless positions (students, service workers, clerks) are particularly vulnerable, but women at the highest professional levels also get harassed. In 1991, Dr. Frances Conley, one of the first female neurosurgeons in the country, resigned from her senior faculty position at Stanford Medical School, citing pervasive sexual harassment from other surgeons as the reason she was leaving. Even women lawyers get harassed; a 1989 study in the *National Law Journal* found that 60 percent of the three thousand women attorneys at the top 250 U.S. law firms had experienced sexual harassment.

Discouraging as these statistics are, harassment at school or on the job is only a small part of the picture. Many women report that they are far more frequently harassed on the street and in the community—at the gas station or the local shopping center, for example—than in the workplace. In this environment, what can women do to avoid harassment? Never hold a job? Never go to school? Never walk down a city street or through a public park? Even a woman who never leaves her own home can be the target of sexual harassment, in the form of obscene phone calls, threatening mail, and sexual assault. Sexual harassment infringes on women's freedom and women's lives at the most elementary level. Like air pollution, harassment is pervasive—sometimes better, sometimes worse, but almost always present in our communities. There is no way for women to escape this abusive behavior, except to stop it, decisively, with an environmental cleanup campaign.

And that is precisely what more and more women are beginning to do.

The cultural breakthrough came in October 1991, when the Senate confirmation hearings for Supreme Court Justice Clarence Thomas set off a storm of public debate on the issue of sexual harassment. Law professor Anita Hill's allegations of gross misconduct by Thomas riveted the nation, exposing the dynamics of harassment in a stunning public drama. The Senate Committee's actions—first ignoring the charges, then assailing Hill's character, motives, and mental stability in the public hearings, and finally confirming the nominee despite the many unanswered questions about his behavior—unleashed an enormous wave of recognition and anger among women.

Millions of women found something familiar about Hill's testimony, something that echoed their own experiences—from the abuse of power involved and the fear of retaliation she felt, right down to the bizarre things harassers actually do and say, including absurd comments about pubic hair on Coke cans and sophomoric boasts about their own genital equipment. However, it was not the tale of harassment alone that triggered the nationwide response. Millions of women found it just as painfully familiar to witness the way Hill was treated by the white, upper-class panel of male senators sitting in judgment. Like Hill, many women knew how it felt to be first harassed, then insulted and disbelieved by the men in power who should have exercised some enlightened authority and moral judgment.

At that historic moment, something in the underlying structure of society shifted and cracked open. A cultural taboo crumbled. Instead of shame and silence, millions of women who had been harassed responded with honesty and anger. In the aftermath of the Hill-Thomas hearings, stories of women's own experiences with sexual harassment came pouring out as women began to talk openly about the incidents that humiliated and enraged them—the underground plague of sexual harassment that has cost women jobs and education, created ulcers, derailed women's careers, and demolished their self-esteem. From that moment on, there was no going back.

Almost every woman has a story. Most have several. Women were suddenly aware of just how much harassment they had been putting up with, one by one, over and over again—on the job and on the street. The magnitude of the problem was undeniable, and neither public institutions nor private employers had taken serious action to protect women's rights. Women had little confidence that formal complaints or lawsuits would solve the problem; the institutional authorities they had to deal with were, in many cases, just as sexist and unprincipled as the harassers themselves. In some instances, senior officials *were* the harassers. It was a moment of great clarity, for millions of men and women alike: the free ride for harassers was over. The behavior was epidemic, and organizations that failed to take responsible action were about to find themselves in deep trouble.

More women than ever are now challenging both the harassers and the men in charge who still "just don't get it." Women have had it with institutional coverups and excuses. For example, when Lieutenant Paula Coughlin stepped forward to report what happened at the Navy pilots' 1991 "Tailhook" convention in Las Vegas, she ran into months of stony resistance at first, both from fellow officers and from the admirals up the line. There was no question about the harassment itself. *The New York Times* reported: "In the packed hallways, drunken gangs of aviators would surround unsuspecting female guests stepping off the elevator and pass them down a gantlet, grabbing at their breasts and buttocks, and stripping their clothes."[3] More than eighty women were attacked, many of them Navy officers.

This was not an isolated incident; it was a predictable type of behavior in any organization—in this case, the U.S. Navy —that had an institutional culture based on sexism and machismo. In 1989, male classmates chained a female midshipman to a urinal at the U.S. Naval Academy; in April 1992, five Navy aviators were accused of raping a woman at a bachelor party in Virginia. After the Tailhook incident, one of the Navy officers assigned to investigate the charges added insult to injury by propositioning Lieutenant Coughlin himself. At the same time, the U.S. Army was having problems of its own; multiple reports of U.S. military women being raped by their own officers and fellow soldiers during the Gulf War began to come out.

But this time, the context was different. Lieutenant Coughlin did not give up. She went public in June 1992, nine months after the Tailhook assaults. What has changed, since Anita Hill broke through the barricades, is the cultural climate of acceptance. The tired old sexist excuses that have been used for generations—boys will be boys, women should know better than to be there, and all the rest of the usual evasions—will no longer get either harassers or institutions off the hook. For the first time, as a result of Lieutenant Coughlin's action, the Navy's failure to take action on sexual harassment actually cost the Secretary of the Navy his job. The admiral who shrugged off the initial, morning-after report of the Tailhook assaults was demoted. At least two other Navy admirals have now lost promotions, in other harassment incidents. And, because harassment can no longer be swept under the rug, the U.S. Congress held formal public hearings on the Gulf War rapes, instead of hushing them up.

Like women in the U.S. military, women in civilian jobs are also challenging the underlying sexist culture that condones and supports harassment. Five women working at the Stroh's Brewery, for example, have now filed a lawsuit linking the harassment they experience on the job to Stroh's sexist and racist advertising. Stroh's marketing campaigns, these women believe, are producing a direct effect on the workplace culture, encouraging a hostile working environment that is rife with verbal abuse of women, crude sexual posters (including some of Stroh's own ads), and pornography throughout the brewery. Top-level management decisions about advertising are sending a clear message to brewery workers about the status of women, the lawsuit argues, and Stroh's own women workers are bearing the brunt of it.

Transitions are never easy. Some men will dig in their heels to defend the macho culture of their organizations—whether a brewery or the U.S. military—and their age-old "right" to harass. Some women will even support them, because there is always some hostility and backlash when a cultural change of this magnitude shakes the social bedrock. Long-standing sexist assumptions about male and female behavior are crashing down. Some public institutions and private companies (and some obstinate individuals) will go through grinding dislocations—an organizational or personal earthquake—before they finally come to terms with the fact that the culture has shifted profoundly.

In the midst of this transition, the legal and institutional remedies available to women are improving rapidly, but women can still face an uphill battle when they actually file sexual harassment charges. It is still true, even in the 1990s, that most women who are harassed will never report it officially. It is not hard to understand the reasons for their reluctance. Anita Hill's public ordeal at the hands of the Senate Judiciary Committee was an object lesson to women about the punitive reactions they can expect from some men in power. Responding with great dignity, Hill kept both her temper and her job—but most women do not have the economic protection of university tenure and a Yale law degree. "If that's the way they treat a law professor," many women have asked, "can you imagine what they would do to me?"

Women are well aware of the steep personal costs they can face: the loss of privacy; the risk of retaliation, hostility, and disbelief; the pain of further humiliation, insulting personal speculation, "instant expert" psychologizing, and blame-the-victim reactions (sometimes even from other women); the threat of economic reprisals; and ultimately, in some instances, even the danger of escalation and physical violence. All of these risks are real. According to one study, two factors alone are enough to keep 90 percent of harassment victims from coming forward: fear of retaliation and fear of loss of privacy. In total, researchers estimate, only 3 percent of women who are harassed ever report it or file charges.[4]

Millions of women face a dilemma: silence only protects the harasser, but what is the alternative? The expense and emotional burden of an official company investigation or a lawsuit can be considerable. And in many cases (street and neighborhood harassment, for example), useful legal remedies still do not exist. Passive acceptance is no answer; continued harassment is intolerable. What can women do, when remaining silent is unthinkable and filing charges is not an option?

Women need an additional remedy, a strong, effective, direct-action strategy to go hand in hand with the changes they are creating in the law and in corporate and institutional procedures. Confrontation is a way to name the behavior, hold the harasser accountable for his actions, and disrupt the power dynamics of harassment. It is neither passive nor aggressive; it does not involve appeasing the harasser or yelling obscenities back at him. Confrontation gives women a set of strong, honest, nonviolent tactics that work.

Filing administrative charges or lawsuits is one important way to stop harassment; direct confrontation is a related strategy. In fact, for a woman who can file charges, using confrontation to identify and challenge the harasser's actions will strengthen her case if she later goes to court. By legal standards, a confrontation clearly defines the behavior as unwelcome and illegal from that point forward. At the same time, confrontation often makes legal action unnecessary; it can stop harassment instantly. Learning to confront is a powerful and very satisfying antidote to victimization.

DEFINING THE PROBLEM FROM WOMEN'S PERSPECTIVES

Women of all races have been involved in the development of direct-action strategies to stop sexual harassment. The D.C. Rape Crisis Center uses a definition of sexual harassment from the African-American Women's Committee for Community Education: "Sexual harassment is the use of words, gestures, bodily actions or other means of verbal and nonverbal communication to insult, degrade, humiliate, or otherwise dehumanize women." Women of color—African-American, Asian-American, Latina, and Native American—often experience a combination of sexual and racial harassment, sometimes within a single incident, and they have played both a historical and a contemporary role in creating strategies for resistance. As one of the editors of *Essence* magazine commented recently, "If anyone has stories to tell, it must be Black women. For centuries we've devised creative and innovative tactics to fight oppression and survive."[5] And, as a defense strategy, confrontation works well against sexual, racial, anti-Semitic, homophobic, and many other forms of harassment.

In addition, union women have begun to put sexual harassment on the agenda as a significant workplace issue, and some union organizers are now teaching their members how to confront. The American Federation of State, County, and Municipal Employees (AFSCME) urges women to take immediate action and hold the harasser accountable for his behavior: "Object. Speak to the harasser and be specific about what behavior you find objectionable. Speak to other women in the work area." AFSCME also recommends—correctly— that women keep a log of incidents, tell their supervisors, tell their union stewards, file grievances, file formal charges with the company and the state human rights agency, and in cases of assault, file criminal charges. Like AFSCME, the United Food and Commercial Workers Union (UFCW) counts a large number of women among its members. UFCW advises its workers, "Fight back! Don't ignore the problem. It won't go away by itself." UFCW defines harassment explicitly as an issue of workers' rights: "Sexual harassment isn't just a personal threat. It's economic blackmail and it's a violation of civil rights. . . . It's not flattering. It's not your fault. It's against the law."

Some church groups are also encouraging women to take action to stop sexual harassment by ministers, priests, rabbis, and other religious leaders. The Center for the Prevention of Sexual and Domestic Violence, an interdenominational organization, notes that sexual contact between a minister and a member of the congregation is a violation of professional ethics: "There is a difference in power between a person in a ministerial role and a member of his or her congregation. . . . Meaningful consent can occur [only] when two people are relatively equal in power and when fear, coercion or manipulation are completely absent from their relationship." These religious experts urge women, "Pay attention to your feelings and trust yourself. . . . Remember that you might not be the only person to whom this has happened and that your action can help both yourself and others." The same power dynamics and ethical considerations apply in any professional relationship: doctors, lawyers, therapists, social workers, teachers, coaches, real estate agents, accountants, law enforcement officers, and others should be held to the same standard of behavior.

The National Council for Research on Women characterizes harassment more generally as "the inappropriate sexualization of an otherwise nonsexual relationship, an assertion by men of the primacy of a woman's sexuality over her role as worker or professional colleague or student." That definition clearly applies to the actions of academic and workplace harassers, but it can also be extended to harassers on the street. A man who yells, "Baby, give me some ass," or mutters, "Nice tits!" to a stranger on the street is transforming what should be an ordinary situation—two people passing on the sidewalk—into a sexualized encounter. His action is coercive in itself (forcing the woman to respond, if only with tension and teeth-gritting silence); often it includes a real sexual threat as well. Women are subjected to this kind of invasive, involuntary sexualization in a hundred different settings, both on and off the job, from men of all economic classes. As the Council also notes, "Harassers are found in all types of occupations, at all organizational levels, among college professors as well as in the business and professional world, and among individuals who live otherwise exemplary lives."[6]

Federal, state, and local statutes define sexual harassment officially as a form of illegal sex discrimination. Here is the legal definition, from the federal Equal Employment Opportunity Commission (EEOC):

Unwelcome sexual advances, requests for sexual favors, and other verbal or physical conduct of a sexual nature constitute sexual harassment when:

1. submission to such conduct is made either explicitly or implicitly a term or condition of an individual's employment;

2. submission to or rejection of such conduct by an individual is used as the basis for employment decisions affecting such individual; or
3. such conduct has the purpose or effect of unreasonably interfering with an individual's work performance or creating an intimidating, hostile, or offensive working environment.

The first two categories in the EEOC definition are called *quid pro quo* ("this for that") harassment, meaning that an employer or supervisor is forcing the employee to provide sexual services or tolerate other forms of sexual harassment in order to get or keep a job, a promotion, or an assignment, for example. That kind of explicit on-the-job tradeoff is relatively infrequent. Most cases of abusive behavior in the workplace fall into the third category, called *hostile-environment* harassment. Not only supervisors but coworkers and subordinates (or even clients and customers) can create a hostile environment for women that amounts to illegal sex discrimination. As Debbie Chalfie notes in Appendix B of this book, women have now extended the original law on workplace harassment to apply to similar situations in education and housing. And although the law does not yet address harassment in the community at large, it is clear that harassers' behavior has the same effect in any location. Men who decide to engage in sexual harassment can just as easily transform a park, a street corner, or a public basketball court into an equally "hostile environment" for women.

Confrontation works as a powerful direct-action response to both *quid pro quo* harassment and hostile-environment harassment, on the job, in education, and in housing. It also works as a means of stopping offensive, sexist behavior in areas where the law does not yet reach—on the street, for example, or at the local bar or the neighborhood ballfield. Confrontation is a strategy women can use for themselves, without waiting for official approval or relying on institutional or legal procedures. It is a careful, principled form of nonviolent direct action, designed to defeat harassers, in any location, who engage in almost any kind of intrusive, threatening, or unwelcome behavior.

Ever since Anita Hill stood before the Senate Judiciary Committee and the nation, more and more women have been standing up in public and telling the truth about harassment. Women today are rapidly revising the old cultural definition of harassment as "normal" and "acceptable" behavior. They are demanding both institutional accountability and personal integrity, claiming their right to live and work without sexual abuse, even in traditionally male settings.

A strong, clear confrontation is more than just a good personal defense against this kind of sexual abuse—it is also a strategy to undermine the larger social practice of harassment, to transform the social environment in ways that make it very hard for harassers to continue to abuse women. Thanks to legal strategists like Catharine MacKinnon and courageous individuals like Anita Hill, Paula Coughlin, and the many other women who have now come forward to change the cultural climate, lawsuits and administrative complaints are becoming an increasingly effective way to compel corporations, universities, and other public institutions to take action to stop harassment. However, those are not the only places where harassment happens, and the ability to file charges is not the only tool that women need. Confrontation is the other half of the tool kit—the logical, necessary, direct-action component of the campaign to defend women's human rights, hold harassers accountable for their actions, and finally clean up one portion of the sexism in the environment. Confrontation is an essential part of women's overall social, legal, cultural, and political effort to end sexual harassment. And it works.

What's Going On Here? Why Do Men Harass Women?

Sexual harassment is a women's issue. It affects millions of women's lives, from childhood forward, on every level—from the most personal intrusions that set women's adrenaline racing, to the larger structure of our culture and society, where harassment shapes the environment for women every day. Harassment colors women's decisions at a level so deeply internalized that it may be almost unconscious: what to wear, what routes to take, where to sit or walk or stand, how to get through the day at work, how to get past a construction site or maneuver around that gang of teenage boys in the parking lot. It begins early—when women taking self-defense classes at the D.C. Rape Crisis Center are asked, most report their first serious incident of gender-related harassment by neighborhood boys before age eight, and their first major encounter with sexual harassment by adult male strangers by age ten or eleven. For women in their teens, twenties, and thirties, harassment is at a peak; it can become a daily experience on the job and on the street. It diminishes but does not stop with age; sixty- and seventy-year-old women also report sexual harassment and modify their behavior to avoid harassers in public places. Women are harassed by strangers and by men they know, in cities, suburbs, and rural areas, indoors and outdoors, at all times of year, and at all times of day.

Because it is so common, harassment is an issue for women everywhere—but it is not a women's problem. It is a *male* social practice, a widespread, destructive pattern of male behavior. The problem belongs to those who choose to create the situation—the men who commit harassment. Ultimately, it is men's responsibility to stop sexual harassment, since it is they who are abusing power. In the interim, however, women have no choice but to understand this social practice and deal with it as effectively as possible. Any responsible strategy for ending sexual harassment must begin, therefore, with a systematic analysis of the structure of sexual harassment and the functions it performs for men: the purposes it serves, the ways they learn to do it, the benefits they receive, the personal rewards and motivations, and the historical, social, and economic structure behind this social practice.

THE STRUCTURE OF HARASSMENT

Sexual harassment is about power. The dynamics of harassment involve a complex interaction of power and gender; to analyze sexual harassment as a social practice, we need to take a close look at sexuality and power. A particular incident of harassment may or may not include any explicitly sexual behavior, but it always involves some form of abuse of power. For example, when a harasser sabotages a woman's work or slashes the tires on her car, he is not engaging in any kind of romantic sexual action. He is engaging in aggression. So is the street harasser who rates a woman's body as she walks by, the coworker who won't keep his hands off her, and the landlord who won't repair the plumbing because she hasn't been "nice enough" to him. Not one of these actions is "sexual" in an affectionate or friendly sense, although they are all forms of sexual harassment. What kind of sexual behavior is actually going on here?

It is important to be clear about the "sexual" aspect of sexual harassment, because sexuality is so often used as a justification for this social practice. Confusion about the difference between sexual invitation and sexual harassment is common. Moreover, confusion about the dynamics of sexuality and power in sexual harassment can prevent women from reacting to harassers with strong, effective countermeasures.

Many men—from garage mechanics to U.S. senators—continue to believe that sexual harassment is a practice based on simple sexual attraction. They see it as an expression of male interest, a turn-on, and a form of flattering sexual attention for women—a sometimes vulgar but essentially harmless romantic game, well within the range of normal, acceptable behavior between the genders. It is not a reciprocal form of behavior (women rarely harass men in this way) but, after all, our culture expects men to take the sexual initiative. By this reasoning, sexual harassment is just part of the overall social pattern of sexual attraction and "courtship" between men and women.

In one way, these men are right: harassment is a common, albeit one-sided, behavior pattern in gender interactions, a perfectly ordinary, well established, daily social practice. But when it comes to the "sexual" component of harassment, men who claim that harassment is simply a friendly sexual game are deluding themselves (at best) about the real meaning of their behavior.

If harassment really is just a sexual "courtship" behavior, it is a spectacularly unsuccessful one. As a means of generating sexual interest on the recipient's part, it is not only ineffective, but consistently counterproductive: women react with disgust, not desire, with fear, not fascination. Any rational male, acting on a genuine desire to interest a possible sexual partner, would quickly come to the realization that his best bet is to abandon this disastrous approach.

Moreover, no human action with such a dismal rate of success is likely to become a widespread social pattern of behavior. Specific behavior becomes a general social practice only when it works—not when it fails. Because sexual communication is so important, most human societies (and most species, for that matter) have developed remarkably efficient courtship rituals. There are infinite varieties of courtship behavior among human beings, mammals, and other animals, but none has a failure rate remotely approaching the failure of harassment as a sexual attractant.

How, then, do we explain the fact that harassment is such a commonplace pattern of behavior among human males?

Logically, there are only two possibilities: either (1) millions of men, acting on authentic sexual interest, are irrationally continuing to engage in a bungling, self-defeating form of "courtship" that angers and repels the very women they wish to attract; or (2) harassment serves some other purpose —it must be a successful male behavior in some other sense, to have become so widely adopted as a gender-based societal norm.

When the alternatives are posed that clearly, there is only one possible conclusion: harassment is not courtship behavior of any kind. It is not clumsy courtship, or rude courtship, or joking courtship, or "misunderstood" courtship. It is not meant to appeal to women; it is behavior that serves another function entirely. Like rape, sexual harassment is designed to coerce women, not to attract them.

The difference between invitation and harassment is the use of power; when the recipient has no choice in the encounter, or has reason to fear the repercussions if she declines, the interaction has moved out of the realm of invitation and courtship into the ugly arena of intimidation and aggression. Labeling sexual harassment as an inept form of courtship is a convenient fabrication to mask the abuse of power involved, a way to cloud and obscure the real dynamics of harassment. It's time to get rid of the mystification: sexual harassment is an expression of power, intended to control the recipient's behavior.

As coercion, harassment is exceptionally effective. All sexual harassment is, at root, an exercise of power: the power to command a woman's attention on the street; the power to force her to walk three blocks out of her way to avoid a construction site; the power to make her so acutely uncomfortable that she drops out of a class; the power to compel her to provide sexual services if she wants to keep her job; and, ultimately, the power to define whole sections of our geography and social structure, from public street corners to high-wage "male" technical jobs, as gender-controlled territory where women can venture only at their own risk.

Furthermore, *all sexual harassment is based on real, mate-*

rial power. The fear women feel when they are harassed is not the product of an overactive, "hysterical" imagination. Men are able to harass because they have three types of concrete power: (1) straightforward economic power over women on the job; (2) status or role-based social power over women, in the case of ministers, teachers, coaches, and other authority figures; and (3) gender-based social power on the part of almost all men. Even men who have no real economic clout and hold no position of authority still have gender-based power, rooted in long-standing cultural patterns of male dominance and backed up by the threat of violence and the ability to rape.

Behind the harasser's behavior there is always a real threat. Because, objectively, he does have one or more of these forms of material power, he has the capacity to do serious harm to his victim, in one way or another: economic reprisals, public humiliation, sabotage, assault.

For the woman who is harassed, therefore, there is always an underlying sense of tension about the harasser's agenda: How far is he going to go? How much power is he willing to use? The initial incident may be only the tip of the iceberg. Will he escalate the situation? Retaliate if she says no? She has, at that moment, no way of knowing what his ultimate intentions are; she is likely to react with a level of tension and fear that reflects the full underlying threat, not simply the immediate, surface interaction. Uncertainty about the harasser's agenda means that even a minor episode of harassment can have a major impact in disrupting the victim's life.

What is the harasser's agenda? Sexual harassment serves many functions for men, both sexual and nonsexual. Men who harass women are willing to use whatever power they possess—economic, role-based, or gender-based—to dominate their victims and achieve their objectives. For *sexually predatory harassers,* the motive is sexual access—harassment is sexually arousing in itself, or a means to force a woman to provide sexual services. *Dominance harassers* are looking for sexual power—female deference and intimidation are the goal, and actual sexual arousal or access may be only secondary. *Strategic and territorial harassers* usually have an economic objective—they apply sexual harassment as a way to exclude women and protect their turf.

In short, it comes down to sex, power, and territory (money, when high-wage jobs are at issue). These are all powerful motives for human behavior. Harassers act for all three of these reasons—sometimes in combination. It's clear why women respond with fear: The stakes are high. This is not trivial behavior, either for the victims or for the harassers themselves. There are strong psychological motives, conscious or unconscious, behind even the most routine street harassment.

All three kinds of harassment—predatory, dominance, and strategic—involve a sexual component, targeting women because of their gender and using women's sexuality against them. All three involve the abuse of power, in one way or another. And all three can do substantial damage to women's civil rights and economic opportunities. Because each of these kinds of sexual harassment is a common social practice, we can analyze harassers' behavior with some precision.

PREDATORY HARASSERS

Although harassment is certainly not a friendly sexual game, some men do use harassment for explicitly sexual purposes. The sexuality involved is unilateral, not mutual; for the recipient, it is coercive, not freely chosen.

In the simplest form of *sexually predatory harassment*, the harasser finds sexual excitement in the act of harassment itself. The flasher or obscene phone caller gets a sexual thrill from his behavior, for example. He may never touch his victims, but he freely uses them for his sexual purposes, without their consent and without regard for the damage his behavior produces. This is sexual-pastime harassment, a one-sided, intrusive sexual interaction based on the sexual use of unwilling victims.

The relationship between sexuality and power is complex, but for some men, the abuse of power is itself a sexual turn-on. The fear and anxiety that flashers or obscene phone call-ers create in their victims are part of the sexual reward they experience; like rapists, they get off on the practice of sexual victimization.

For some harassers, sexually predatory behavior goes be-yond a sexual pastime, into full-scale sexual extortion and rape. Our culture, like many others, eroticizes dominance and submission and defines the "conquest" of women as sexy and exciting. One of the most basic themes in pornogra-phy, for example, is the portrayal of men as sexual masters and women as sexy victims, whose graphic victimization is, in itself, sexually stimulating to the viewer. Some rapists respond sexually not to images of nude women, but to im-ages of women tied up, torn, battered, and bleeding. Vio-lence itself can be a turn-on for the assailant. In our society, the spectrum of aggression and violence that some men find "sexy" is very broad. Sexually coercive harassment ranges from the use of personal intimidation to obtain sexual ser-vices, to threats of economic reprisals, to actual rape.

Even men who stay, personally, on the milder side of that spectrum—who do not find physical violence against women sexually exciting and have never committed a rape—may not think twice about using their power in sexually coercive ways. In one typical study of college males, for example, psychologists Donald Mosher and Ronald Anderson found that the men they tested were no strangers to coercive tac-tics: 75 percent admitted using drugs or alcohol to have sex with a date; 69 percent had used some form of verbal manip-ulation or intimidation; more than 40 percent had used anger as a weapon to pressure a woman to comply; 13 percent had threatened physical violence; and 20 percent had actually used violence.[1] Sexually coercive harassment is not an iso-lated phenomenon; it is part of the spectrum of force, the range of coercive behavior and power abuse, that some men are willing to use to gain sexual access to unwilling partners.

When this kind of sexual extortion occurs on the job or in the university, it can be prosecuted as *quid pro quo* harass-ment: a supervisor, employer, teacher, or professor who forces a woman to provide sexual services in order to get or keep her job, get a promotion, or get a good grade in class is committing a form of sex discrimination that has been defined as illegal and actionable. Women are also beginning to win cases against men who take advantage of their positions, rather than economic or academic power. For example, coaches, ministers, landlords, and other men who use their positions of authority to engage in sexual coercion have also been found legally liable. Some predators specifically target young women—first-year women in college, for example, or women on their first job. The pressure to be adult and sophisticated makes these young women especially vulnerable. The more a young woman tries to be "cool" and not "overreact" to the harasser's sexual encroachment, the easier it is for a predatory harasser to manipulate her into complying. Although this kind of sexual harassment is illegal, many women never report it.

The same kind of power abuse and sexual extortion also occurs in many private encounters. Sexual predators who have no official economic, academic, or role-based power over a woman often resort to the gender-based social power they control to demand sexual compliance. Current rape laws do not acknowledge the extent of personal coercion that can be involved in "consensual" sexual interactions, but a woman's "consent" under pressure is clearly not a reflection of her own free choice and desire. Predatory harassment in private interactions includes an entire spectrum of emotional, psychological, and physical extortion, from the use of anger, threats, and intimidation, all the way up to date rape, acquaintance rape, and marital rape. How many women have engaged in sexual activity not because they wanted sex, but because they feared what their partners would do if they refused? Being harassed into "consenting" is a far cry from mutual, enthusiastic sex.

The motive of the coercive harasser is sexual conquest; harassment is the tool he uses to exercise power and compel an unwilling sexual partner to capitulate. But some men use harassment to gain sexual access in a very different sense.

One of the most sinister forms of sexually predatory harassment is *rape-testing*. A significant number of acquaintance and stranger rapes are preceded by an intrusive verbal or physical interaction, as the rapist selects his victims. Many rapes are planned; the assailant has watched the neighborhood or campus, timed women's entries and exits, and identified potential candidates for assault. Rapists are not looking for a fair fight. They have learned that sexual harassment is a good way to gauge the likelihood that a woman will fight back in an assault; if she is passive and timid when harassed, they assume she will be passive and terrified when attacked. So this kind of rapist moves in on his potential victims, standing too close to one at a bus stop, using verbal harassment with another, to see how each of the women will respond. If she is a classmate, a customer, or other acquaintance, he may test her with inappropriate sexual touching or personal comments that are out of line, to see whether she will defend herself or call him on his remarks. Like any skillful predator, he sizes up his prey. And, with chilling precision, he uses harassment to do it.

All three forms of sexually predatory harassment are widespread: some men get off on the behavior itself, some engage in harassment to coerce sexual services, and some use harassment as a rape-testing device. However, as persistent as this behavior is, predatory harassment may *not* be the most frequent form of sexual harassment.

DOMINANCE HARASSERS

Many men harass women not for sexual access but for motives of personal sexual power—as a way to bolster their egos (at women's expense), assert their status, and reassure themselves that their masculinity commands respect and female deference. This is *male-dominance harassment*. It is a social practice based on gender and power, not a demand for sexual services. Judging from women's own accounts, this is by far the single most common form of harassment. For these men, harassment is not necessarily a sexual turn-on, in and of itself. The average street harasser, for example, does not expect his victim to comply sexually—he would be astonished if she did. His motive is status, not sex; he is looking for an ego-boost, not necessarily an erection. Harassing women gives him a simple, direct surge of sexual power.

On a personal level, many men routinely use this kind of sexual harassment to meet their own emotional needs for respect and prestige: when he harasses, he's a big man, he can compel a woman's attention (even against her will), he can intimidate, he can make a woman jump. Many sexist men feel a strong, almost painful psychological tension between the male supremacist ideal of manhood—the bold, conquering hero, always in control—and the reality of their own lives, where the boss is on their back all day, the kids don't listen, and even the dog won't obey them. As a means of enforcing deference, harassment works for men both individually and in groups. Harassing women on his own, without other males around, a man can feel personally powerful, no matter how powerless the rest of his life may be. Harassing women in front of other sexist men, he can not only reaffirm his own masculine standing but uphold the status of the entire male group. Group harassment is a form of negative male bonding—building sexist male solidarity by exercising collective masculine power over women.

In this context, harassment is not a matter of using aggression to obtain sexual access, but a sexually aggressive way to maintain both the individual harasser's prestige and the larger social structure of male dominance. He is simply using the social practice of sexual harassment, on a casual, daily basis, to reassert his standing in the gender hierarchy and put women in their place.

Of course, the cumulative result of several million men deciding to meet their emotional needs for dominance, ego reassurance, and male bonding in this way is a society that constantly bombards women with the message that, because of their sex, they are subordinate. The threat that women can be punished if they get out of line is always present, openly or implicitly. For women, who are already dealing with the sexism of institutional discrimination, low wages, occupational segregation, underrepresentation in government, and other forms of inequality, the repeated experience of male-dominance harassment, large and small, serves to underscore and maintain the concrete, daily reality of their subordinate status. Harassment produces an environment that is dense with male power.

Male-dominance harassment is a routine, daily social practice, emotionally rewarding for men and disempowering for women. On the job or at school, a group of men engaging in dominance harassment can produce the type of "hostile environment" that has been recognized as illegal sexual harassment by the law. Once again, however, this behavior is not limited to the workplace or university. Women encounter dominance harassment in an enormous range of public and private settings, from the office, to the park, to the local hardware store. On a societal level, the actions of millions of harassers who are meeting their emotional needs at women's expense add up to something much larger: a daily, hourly, unrelenting enforcement mechanism that restricts women's freedom, maintains the social structure of male supremacy, and enforces the overall social norm of male dominance and female submission.

STRATEGIC AND TERRITORIAL HARASSERS

Both sexually predatory harassment and male-dominance harassment are ugly, aggressive behavior—sexist, unethical, and (in some settings) illegal. However, some men also use sexual harassment as a deliberate intimidation device to maintain their social, economic, and political privilege. *Strategic harassment* is not simply the combined effect of individual harassers acting out their sexual or emotional needs: this is planned, self-aware behavior. Strategic harassment can be applied to meet all kinds of objectives: to keep women out of the machine shop or out of the brokerage firm; to dissuade women from majoring in engineering or studying electronics; to drive women out of everything from coal mines to college courses to corporate headquarters. Harassment is a way to control access to jobs, education, public institutions, and many other kinds of community facilities.

Some strategic harassment is quite literally territorial. Men often use harassment to guard their privately owned institutions, making the corporate convention, the factory assembly line, the uptown golf course, or the neighborhood bar such a hostile, sexist environment that they can force most women to back off. And sometimes, with astounding arrogance, men even employ harassment to claim *publicly owned* space—parks, basketball courts, public streets, government jobs, and university classes—as distinctly male territory, which they then ferociously defend from women.

In these situations, sexual harassment has relatively little to do with sexual arousal per se, and everything to do with power, gender, and women's freedom. These men use sexual harassment precisely because it is such an effective intimidation device.

Strategic harassers go after their own coworkers. Women in traditionally male occupations or educational fields are at especially high risk of harassment from both colleagues and supervisors. One young geologist, for example, survived three years of incessant harassment from her professors and fellow geology students in graduate school, only to be told point-blank, during her first job interview with a major mining company, that she would not be hired unless she agreed to sleep with the firm's principal clients. She did not take the job. But the problem was endemic: women geologists were not welcome anywhere in the industry. After a few years of severe harassment with another firm, she quit geology altogether, took a 40 percent pay cut, and became a high-school science teacher. Public institutions are not immune. For example, one-third of the women at the U.S. Naval Academy, 40 percent at the Air Force Academy, and 64 percent at West Point have experienced serious sexual harassment, as have at least 42 percent of the women holding civilian federal jobs.[2]

At the crudest level, the goal of strategic harassment is to force women out, to protect a male monopoly on jobs, educational opportunities, community facilities, or other economic resources. Sometimes, however, sexual harassment is applied even more selectively: with cold-blooded calculation, blue-collar or white-collar men may target a specific female colleague to undermine her performance and eliminate her as a competitor. More than one talented, highly capable electrician, painter, or pipe-fitter has found her work sabotaged by her coworkers overnight; more than one superb doctor has quit the specialty she loved, under a relentless barrage of harassment; more than one top-notch attorney has left a law firm in disgust; and more than one highly skilled Senate staffer, too effective for her own good, has been harassed right off Capitol Hill.

When corporate goals are at stake, strategic harassers also go after their business opponents. High-ranking women on industrial negotiating teams have had the unpleasant jolt of being targeted for harassment precisely when they are succeeding. Suddenly, a male counterpart across the negotiating table will begin to use sexual innuendo, blatant comments about women's sexuality, or invasive body language, as a tactic to throw his opponent off balance and regain the strategic advantage. He is not interested in sexual access or the ego rewards of male dominance—he wants to manipulate the outcome of the deal. The same maneuver has been used against women on official government business. More than one senior U.S. official, taking a tough stand in international meetings, has suddenly encountered a display of exaggerated hand-kissing, comments, and other verbal harassment designed to single her out and undermine her authority. In these situations, harassment is an effort to disable a formidable female opponent. By emphasizing her sexuality and her subordinate status as a female, the harasser attempts to undercut her authority as a corporate or government official. If he succeeds, he may not only break her stride and shake her confidence, but disrupt the delegation and distance her male colleagues from her—which will undermine her performance even further. Strategic harassment is a way to fight dirty when a woman is too effective.

From the men who run the local plumbers' apprentice program, to the future officers at West Point, to the gentlemen of the U.S. Senate, men of all class backgrounds are skilled in the use of strategic harassment as a tactic to exclude and disempower women in male environments. "Male turf" of every kind is vigorously defended, and strategic sexual harassment is an exceptionally effective weapon.

On every level, from the most personal and emotional to the most coldly strategic, every form of sexual harassment is about the use and abuse of power. As a social practice, sexual harassment is a well developed pattern of behavior, based on gender and power, which men routinely use for many different purposes: to obtain sexual stimulation, force sexual access, and select victims for sexual assault; to meet ego- and status-based emotional needs, disempower women, and reassert male dominance; and to limit women's access to both public and private resources, drive women out of traditionally male jobs, and undermine female competitors and opponents. Harassment is a widespread male practice not because it works as a romantic courtship ritual, but because it works so successfully as an exercise of gender-based power.

All men benefit from the social and economic effects of sexual harassment, in that it keeps women subordinate, disempowered, and excluded. Women lose far more than the right to stroll safely through a park on a sunny day: harassment sets hard boundaries on women's hopes and dreams for the future, as well as their present choices. For example, strategic harassment not only drives out the women who dare to venture into high-wage male jobs today, but sends an unmistakable message to their younger sisters: keep out—don't even think about trying to enter this profession. Sexual harassment is an extremely efficient social control mechanism.

HARASSMENT AS GENDER-SPECIFIC BEHAVIOR

As a result of both the unequal distribution of power in society and the very different cultural norms established for male and female behavior, the perpetrators of sexual harassment are rarely female, just as the targets are rarely male. Still, not all harassment follows gender lines. Men can and sometimes do sexually harass other men; women, on very rare occasions, have been known to sexually harass men or other women.

In the overwhelming majority of cases, however, sexual harassment is in fact a gender-specific behavior with respect to the sex of both the perpetrator and the victim. The National Association of Working Women reports that an estimated 90 percent of harassment cases involve men who have harassed women, 9 percent are same-sex (straight men harassing gay men, for example), and only 1 percent involve women who have harassed men.[3] In short, when we talk about sexual harassment, we are talking about a pattern of actions committed by men, against women. Men of every class, race, region, occupation, education, size, shape, and age can and do engage in sexual harassment. Women of every class, race, region, occupation, education, size, shape, and age can be—and frequently are—harassed. Each of the three major structural categories of harassment—sexually predatory harassment, dominance harassment, and strategic territorial harassment—is a specifically male social practice.

But not all men harass women. In light of the many benefits men can achieve from harassing women, why don't all men do it? Rather than explaining why some men harass, we need to explain why many men do not.

Personal motivations play a role here. Some men genuinely like and respect women; they do not harass because they know women well, understand what sexual harassment does to women's freedom, and care about women's lives. In some cases, men who refuse to harass are acting on principle; they are committed to social change, including justice and equality for women. They do not harass women because they consider it morally and ethically wrong. And some men are personally unaggressive; they would never dream of using coercion or engaging in any form of unprovoked aggression, against either women or men. Harassment is outside their range of behavior, not necessarily as a matter of principle, but as a simple matter of temperament.

Moreover, some men have learned about the realities of harassment the hard way. Even in a sexist culture, many males understand firsthand that sexual harassment is aggression, not a harmless game or a clumsy form of courtship. Men who have been on the receiving end of racist, anti-Semitic, or homophobic harassment know that this kind of power abuse is vicious and destructive: For bigots, verbal and physical harassment is a hate crime. It can be aimed at any member of a despised target group, on the street or on the job, and, like sexual harassment, is usually part of a larger pattern of economic discrimination, political exclusion, and social violence. For sexist men, harassment is a hate crime against women. Because they understand these connections between bigotry, power, and harassment, many men refuse to harass women.

And finally, in some cases, the environment can act as a check on abusive male behavior. Most public areas are male territory; the harasser usually approaches his victim privately, one on one, but he does so at the job site, on the street, at the school or the park or the shopping center—in a public arena where men can claim and exercise some authority. However, there is one kind of public environment where women report that harassment is relatively rare. In stable, settled neighborhoods where women have some authority on the local level, sexual harassment is much less common. There is no social protection or anonymity for the harasser in this kind of setting, and the social network of neighborhood women can often succeed in enforcing a different set of behavioral norms.

Picture a tightly knit, urban, ethnic community, in Baltimore or Pittsburgh, perhaps, where neighbors know each other well and people watch what goes on in the neighborhood: if Mrs. Padrewski's boy hassles Mrs. Kovak's daughter, the word will be up and down the block the next day. There are real costs for the harasser: his entire family is embarrassed, and every woman on the block may let him have it when she sees him.

In this environment, women who talk to each other and stand up for each other can create a mechanism of public accountability that will all but eliminate harassment on the block. For the harasser, the rewards simply aren't worth the risks. He'll have fifteen angry women on his case if he tries it here, including his own mother, sister, and grandmother. It is not a matter of changing male attitudes (a long-term project), but of establishing an accountability mechanism, here and now, that controls certain kinds of behavior by changing the social reward structure. The men may still be sexist in many other ways, and may feel entirely free to harass women elsewhere—but within the boundaries of this kind of neighborhood, women have seized social control of the environment and created small oases where one form of sexist behavior, sexual harassment, is neither condoned nor tolerated. Neighborhoods like this are increasingly rare in our mobile, individualistic society, but women's success in making even a few neighborhoods harassment-free can shed some useful light on larger societal strategies for ending sexual harassment in other environments.

From men who do not harass women, we can also draw another important conclusion about the nature of sexual harassment. That so many men choose not to engage in harassment makes it clear that this behavior is neither biologically determined nor inevitable. And, in fact, not all harassers are male.

Women are capable of committing sexual harassment, although they rarely do so. Women can abuse power and engage in sexual aggression, but in terms of real power, relatively few women are in a position to force men into unwanted sexual activity, engage in dominance harassment, or use sexual harassment to accomplish economic objectives.

With respect to coercive sexual behavior, relatively few women, so far, have managed to overcome their cultural and psychological conditioning enough to even desire a sexual interaction that is based on unilateral power abuse, rather than need or affection. Few women get off on obscene phone calls, and almost no women commit rape. Power abuse is not a sexual turn-on for most women; even the most sexually aggressive women generally seek *willing* partners.

On a broader level, harassment is not part of the cultural

pattern of typical female behavior in this society (or most others). There are endless arrays of culturally prescribed and socially enforced norms for female behavior, from makeup and high heels to trained helplessness and passivity, but nowhere in the entire constellation of acceptable female behavior in our culture is there a norm that prescribes engaging in sexual harassment. Women who do so—on the job, on the street, or elsewhere—are cutting across the grain of their entire culture. The very meaning of the behavior is different when a woman does it. A woman flasher, for example, conveys a message of sexual invitation, not threat. The meaning of a direct proposition differs dramatically by gender—one study found that only 17 percent of women would take a proposition on the job as a compliment, but 67 percent of the men surveyed said they would consider it flattering to be sexually propositioned by a woman at work.

For women, harassment does not work as a means to assert gender dominance; women who engage in vulgar, abusive behavior are scorned, not empowered by the male responses they get. Strategic harassment also seldom works; few public or private institutions are controlled by women, and it is a rare woman who is in a position to harass men out of a job, a training program, or a neighborhood park.

In short, in a sexist society neither a woman's sexual comments nor her behavior has the same cultural meaning as a man's. She may be able to abuse power in other ways, but she can rarely use sexual harassment as an intimidation tactic. Female harassers are few and far between, not because women are necessarily morally superior to men, but because nothing in their culture or material power base supports or condones such behavior on their part. For men, on the other hand, harassment is a behavior they begin learning in childhood.

LEARNING TO HARASS

Sexual harassment is learned behavior—a particular form of aggression that is functional and pleasurable for men and

effective in controlling women's freedom, mobility, and economic opportunities. In many cultures, virtually all public
space—the workplace, the school, and the street—is de facto
male territory; the harassment of women and girls who venture into those male arenas is not only socially acceptable,
but standard, expected behavior for men.

Boys learn how to harass at an early age, by watching the
patterns of male behavior in their own community. When
they first try it for themselves (usually by age seven or eight),
they find that it makes them feel good; they like it. They can
successfully intimidate many of the girls around them, and it
feels like fun; it's a new skill, a new ability to make things
happen.

That taste of power is a heady reward for young male children, since they are already beginning to chafe under the
restrictions imposed by the adult (female) world. Because
women are still responsible for almost all childcare, young
children usually perceive women as the authority that is cur-
tailing their freedom. Mothers, teachers, and female caregivers are the ones saying no, giving orders, intruding on
their privacy, and setting limits on their behavior. For male
children, the issues of gender and power are already linked.
They already know that males are "supposed" to have power
and authority: from male heroes in action films to men in
the neighborhood, children see men exercising power over
women, and women deferring to them. The stories they read,
the television shows they enjoy, even the cartoons they
watch, emphasize the primacy of maleness: the Ninja Turtles
are all male, the Smurfs and other cartoon characters are 99
percent male, and the few female characters rarely play any
decisive role in the action. Even Santa Claus and Barney
the Dinosaur are male. In a male supremacist society, being
under the power of women does not sit well with male children.

By second or third grade, many boys have already learned
that cutting up in class and being disruptive are effective
countercontrol tactics. By "misbehaving," boys can manipulate the situation and exercise some power of their own,

overriding the teacher's agenda and compelling her attention. Harassment of the girls on the playground and in the neighborhood is part of the same process, as boys begin to develop their skills in asserting power over females.

The dynamic is not explicitly sexual at this stage (in the sense of actual sexual activity), but it is gender-related. Harassment serves a variety of social and psychological functions. It can be used to compensate for feelings of inadequacy generated by the girls' better social skills, coordination, and school performance at this stage of childhood development. It can be used—fiercely—to claim the treehouse or other turf as the boys' own space, off-limits to girls. And, even at this age, it can be used to enforce male dominance.

On almost any unregulated schoolyard or playground, for example, the boys usually dominate the central space and most of the equipment; the girls cling to the edges and corners. How do girls get that message about ownership of public space? How do boys enforce it? Watch what happens if a group of girls attempts to move into the boys' territory—to take over the basketball hoop, for instance. The boys' reaction is instantaneous—the gender-based insults fly, and the threat of physical force is not far behind. It is in fact rare for girls to even try that kind of incursion. Usually, by age eight, they have already ceded that public territory to the boys. The males' ownership of the playground has become part of the social norm, internalized by both male and female children and, all too often, by their teachers and parents as well. The inequality becomes invisible, normal, and the power dynamics behind it go unspoken. Young boys have already learned how to use harassment to control public resources; young girls are already learning the limits on their freedom.

Slightly older boys may begin to try out their harassment skills on adult women, to test their gender-based power. It is not uncommon for groups of ten- or twelve-year-olds to target adult women on the street. Boys usually start out playing this "game" in small gangs, not only because they feel more comfortable in groups at this age, but because they are not quite sure yet just how far their power will carry.

For an adult woman who is suddenly surrounded by a pack of jeering preadolescents, the experience can be terrifying. Her adult status does not guarantee her safety, and she may rapidly find herself losing control of the interaction. She has the benefit of age but the handicap of femaleness; they have the advantage of numbers and masculinity, underscored by the perceived threat of violence they can already convey. If they succeed in intimidating her, they've won something that matters: status, prestige, power. Hostility and sexuality are inextricably linked in this behavior. Preadolescent boys testing their gender-based power against adult women are exploring what it means to exercise coercion, to create fear, to seize control from an adult. More specifically, they are exploring a definition of manhood hinged on power, differentiating themselves from females/victims and defining their masculinity in terms of aggression and control over women.

For her, it's likely to be a very unnerving experience of powerlessness and fear: "My God, they were only children! It was awful!" For the boys, on the other hand, it's a satisfying exercise in control and male bonding, direct reassurance that their status and power are real, that their maleness must be taken seriously. The psychological rewards are very deep.

As with any other form of social behavior, learning to harass takes practice. In some U.S. junior high schools, the latest male "game" during class breaks is to rush up to female classmates in the hallways, grab their breasts with one or both hands, then run. The boys keep score—which girls they grabbed, how many they managed to grab, and how large their breasts were. This "game" of sexual predation is a violation of the girls' bodies, physical boundaries, and personal freedom; they've lost the right to defend their physical integrity or walk from one class to the next without harassment, in their own schools. The game is entirely one-sided. Girls do not dash through the halls, grabbing boys' genitals and ranking them by size. Only boys play predator, and only girls are the targets of attack.

In any other context, this kind of aggressive sexual touching would legally be considered assault. But girls have no real training in how to analyze or deal with such behavior in the context of junior high school. We've taught them to beware of strangers, but these are boys they know. Very few parents or teachers are addressing the underlying reality—the sexual hostility, aggression, and inequality—embedded in this "game" of predator and prey.

Some girls feel assaulted, but quickly learn from their peers that it is not cool to object to being grabbed. Some feel humiliated, but expressing anger is not an option; they blush and giggle with embarrassment instead. Many respond with avoidance tactics, clutching their books to their chests and running to their next class to try to minimize the risk they face. Some are already so damaged in their sense of self, and so desperate for male attention, that they see this predatory behavior not as the assault it is, but as a form of flattery—any attention from the boys, however demeaning or invasive, is better than none. Very few girls believe that they have any ability to stop the game, or any right to do so.

And because our culture has largely condoned and accepted sexual harassment as normal male behavior (boys will be boys, we say with a shrug), at no point in childhood or young adolescence are boys likely to have this kind of behavior challenged in any strong, serious way. If the girls shriek and hate it, that's part of the fun of sexual aggression. If adults disapprove of the behavior, that just makes it a more daring game to play. There are no penalties enforced for engaging in these assaults. At what point are the girls told that they have rights they can defend, that their bodies belong to them, that harassment is anything but inevitable? At what point are the boys told that their behavior has serious consequences, that it damages girls' self-esteem and interferes with their ability to learn, violates their rights and their sense of self—that it is harassment, it is hostile, it is illegal, and it will be stopped?

The "game" of adolescent sexual harassment is far from playful. Allowing boys to harass with impunity reinforces their sense of sexist male entitlement and encourages them to hone their skills as sexual predators. Moreover, when parents and teachers dismiss such attacks as childish male pranks and abandon girls to deal with the harassment on their own, they are training another generation of women in the corresponding stereotypes of learned female power-lessness and passive victimization: this is the way it is, put up with it however you can.

In fact, to label such aggression a "game" or prank is to define it solely in terms of the adolescent males' own self-centered perspective. Accepting that definition uncritically means ignoring the girls' experience of harassment as an invasive, disempowering display of male power; ignoring adults' responsibility to analyze the real dynamics of power abuse in their children's lives and intervene when necessary; and ignoring the significant role that adolescent harassment plays in reproducing the larger societal patterns of male dominance and female submission—the practice of sexism.

As the success stories in Chapter 5 demonstrate, girls can stop harassment. They can stop it on their own sometimes, with direct confrontation, and they can stop it if the adults around them take their rights seriously and back them up with some sanctions, to offset the psychological rewards of harassment with some real penalties.

But most boys are never confronted for committing harassment, either by their victims or by adult authority. As a result, in their experience, harassment is a form of behavior that has many psychological rewards and few, if any, costs. So teenage males go on to routinely harass girls and women on the street, testing the limits, trying out the extent of their power. Usually, they find out that there are no effective limits: with a word, a look, a gesture, they can make women of any age scurry away quickly, in nervous, angry silence. Women pretend to ignore it (as they've been taught to do since girlhood), but their body language tells the truth: the jaws clench, the shoulders stiffen, the relaxed stride vanishes instantly. The boys laugh and strut as they watch the women react to their sexual aggression. They know the women cannot, in fact, ignore their presence. They control the street corner; they can command fear. They have learned their lessons well, as they begin to reap the rewards of male power in a sexist society.

WHAT DO HARASSERS HAVE TO SAY FOR THEMSELVES?

Adult males go on to develop their own areas of specialization. Some become flashers or obscene phone callers, some are routine street harassers, some feel up women riding on public transportation, some become landlords who use sexual extortion on their tenants, some harass women on the job, at the mall, at school, or in the local bar—and some may even do all of the above.

It's clear that some men harass just for the hell of it. From their point of view, it's fun, it's entertaining, it's a way to amuse themselves. The destructive effect of their behavior on women's lives is of little or no concern; they may not even recognize that their behavior has any negative impact on their victims. Routine male-dominance or sexual-pastime harassment is just their idea of a good time. Summarizing the results of a German study (one of the few actual surveys of street harassers), Cheryl Benard and Edit Schlaffer report:

> What is going on in the minds of men who do this? Not much, judging from their difficulties in articulating their intentions. . . .
> Pressed for an explanation of their behavior, most of the men initially were at a loss. It alleviates boredom, it gives them a feeling of youthful camaraderie when they discuss women with other men; it's "fun" and it "doesn't hurt anybody," they often added a little defensively. The notion that women dislike this was a novel idea for most men, not because they had another image of the woman's response but because they had never given it any thought at all.[4]

Like other women who have informally asked harassers the same question, Benard and Schlaffer found a number of men who were firmly convinced, despite all evidence to the contrary, that women enjoyed the harassment they received. The arrogance and self-serving delusion of sexist males can be breathtaking in scope: "One 45-year-old construction worker portrayed himself as a kind of benefactor to womanhood and claimed to specialize in older and less attractive women to whom, he was sure, his display of sexual interest was sure to be the highlight in an otherwise drab existence."[5]

On the other hand, some men acknowledge that their harassment is in fact a form of sexual aggression. Benard and Schlaffer found that, in their sample, "a minority, around 15 percent, explicitly set out to anger or humiliate their victims. This is the same group that employs graphic commentary and threats."[6] For these men, there is no confusion about the real meaning and impact of their behavior; harassment is a direct, hostile expression of gender-based dominance and aggressive sexual threat.

The research also provides some evidence about the importance of negative male bonding. About 20 percent of the men surveyed in the German study said that they harassed women only in the company of male friends—a figure consistent with U.S. women's experience in anecdotal reports, and with the findings of the U.S. Merit Systems Protection Board about group harassment of women in the federal workforce. For these men, sexual harassment is a way to demonstrate their machismo to their male companions and reinforce their solidarity with other men, in a deliberate and reassuring display of public power over women.

Race and class can also enter into the equation. Some migrant workers (African and Arab, in the German study), some white working-class laborers, and some black and Hispanic harassers in Washington, D.C., have said that they specifically target white women or well-dressed upper- and middle-class women for abuse, as a way of expressing hostility to the racial or class privilege the women represent.

There is nothing casual or unaware about this type of harassment. Men who engage in race- or class-based harassment make no pretense that it is intended as flattering sexual interest.

As a political strategy to end racism and economic exploitation, sexual harassment is obviously ineffective (women have been harassed for centuries, without putting a dent in racism or class divisions). Instead of undermining race or class privilege, such harassment usually has the opposite effect: it supports the status quo by reinforcing the targeted women's own racism or their stereotypes about working-class men. It is also cowardly—harassing women is much easier and safer than challenging men in positions of power or actually engaging in any real action for political change. At bottom, the "race and class revenge" rationale is only one more elaborate, self-serving excuse for men to boost their own egos and sense of status by harassing women—a low-risk way for relatively powerless men to feel powerful. This is dominance harassment, with a political twist. For harassers like these, gender-based power may be the only kind of power they command; regardless of class or race, they can still intimidate half the population.

While street harassers defend their behavior on many different grounds, harassers who control some real economic power or positions of authority often use a different defensive tack: flat-out denial. The power these men exercise in the world at large gives them a sense of entitlement and a belief that they have almost absolute protection from the consequences of their behavior toward women. They rarely admit that they are engaging in sexual harassment and rarely see any need to justify their actions. Instead, they count on their status to silence the women they victimize; if need be, they will use their authority to try to discredit any woman who dares to speak up. As Anita Hill found, when a woman steps forward to accuse a powerful, highly placed harasser, both he and the men around him may circle the wagons and let loose with a barrage of charges that she is "crazy," "a woman scorned," "fantasizing," or "vengeful." Denial has been a successful defense for powerful harassers for generations, but it no longer works quite as well as it used to. One high-level federal official, for example, continued to adamantly deny that he had ever harassed anyone, even after twenty women came forward to attest to his behavior. He was shocked when they managed to win a lawsuit and hold him accountable for the sexual abuse he had committed.

At all social and economic levels, many harassers are unable or unwilling to explain their actions. For them, sexual harassment is standard male behavior, unexamined and unremarkable. The few who have thought about it tend to take refuge in self-serving excuses or denials. They would much rather believe in convenient myths about "innocent sexual attraction" than acknowledge that they are engaging in sexual power abuse, dominance behavior, strategic social control of women, or outright sexual extortion.

For women, however, it is essential to understand the framework of harassment. Analysis is not a luxury; it's a matter of self-defense. Women are much less likely to be caught off guard, to be taken in by excuses, or to feel compelled to tolerate abusive behavior when they can recognize the harasser's motives, identify the power dynamics involved, and analyze what's really going on. Understanding sexual harassment as a social practice is the first step toward ending it.

THE SOCIAL HISTORY OF SEXUAL HARASSMENT

Like any social practice, harassment occurs in a historical context; the kinds of power men can exercise over women and the cultural norms for male and female behavior affect the way harassment is practiced by men and the way it is experienced by women.

Because our culture is changing, women no longer experience sexual harassment with quite the same sense of helplessness that their mothers and grandmothers felt. Women today have more economic power, more political clout, more legal rights, more institutional remedies, and more direct-action strategies to use. Thanks to the women's movement, they are also speaking up about their experiences, defining harassment from the recipient's point of view instead of accepting the old male excuses that trivialize and dismiss this pattern of power abuse. As women's own power increases, they are less and less likely to see harassment as inevitable or natural, or to feel that they have to put up with it in any form.

But if women's perspective has changed, the harassers' behavior still hasn't.

Much of the harassment women encounter today can be traced, historically, to earlier patterns of male behavior and earlier forms of male economic and social power. The functions of harassment, the kinds of power it is based on, the motives of the harassers, and many of the specific forms of the behavior itself are not new. The technology may have changed—women now report getting obscene and threatening computer messages—but modern harassers deserve no credit for creativity. They did not invent their behavior, although they themselves may be entirely unaware that in many cases they are following some very old patterns of gender- and status-related power abuse.

One of the earliest recorded incidents of sexual harassment comes right out of the Bible: the story of Susanna and the Elders, in the Book of Daniel. Walking alone in her garden courtyard, Susanna was cornered, propositioned, and threatened by two elders who were powerful Hebrew judges. When she refused their sexual demands and began to shout for help, these two predatory harassers falsely accused her of adultery. Although Susanna protested her innocence, they had the weight of authority on their side; she was tried and convicted on the strength of their testimony, and sentenced to death. Daniel came to the rescue, cross-examining the elders and proving that they had lied. Daniel made his reputation, Susanna was freed, and the two elders were sentenced to the same punishment they had intended to inflict on her.

Even today, harassment is often veiled in silence, and sexual harassment is certainly not the kind of behavior that male historians, diarists, journalists, and other sources have been anxious to record for posterity. But because harassment has been such a common form of male behavior, evidence of the practice has seeped into historical documents in many different areas. And that record, partial as it is, provides some telling insights into the social practice of harassment today.

For example, although most routine harassment falls within the category of male-dominance behavior, many men continue to seek sexual access to women over whom they have some form of economic power. They are not reluctant to use the threat of economic reprisals to force women to comply. The notion that good sex is mutually and freely chosen, not extorted, is apparently still an alien concept. Some employers, supervisors, and managers act as if they had a sexual right to any woman who is economically under their control.

These men are re-enacting a pattern of sexual property rights that has a long and dishonorable history, dating back well before the Industrial Revolution, to the Middle Ages. The "droit du seigneur," the right of the first night, gave each medieval lord the right to take first sexual access to any female serf who married on his land holdings. Under the feudal system, both land and serfs belonged to the lord; new brides were a form of sexual property, and he had an economic right to sexual access. The practice was enforced in areas of France, Germany, Italy, Poland, and Great Britain. In some regions, the bride or her new husband could buy the lord off with payment in the form of cash or crops. This custom enabled many couples to purchase their way out of legal "first-night" rapes, but the financial payment also constituted a formal, public recognition of the landowner's economic right to the woman. Employers and managers who harass their workers today are, in effect, still operating on the premise that they have that kind of economic right to their employees as sexual property.

When coworkers, rather than supervisors, systematically harass their women colleagues, they are usually operating on a different kind of economic premise. They do not have the same degree of economic power that an employer or manager has, but they do have the power to move beyond casual male-dominance harassment to the individual or collective use of strategic harassment, to protect their monopoly on the jobs, training programs, or other economic resources at stake. The harassers who decide to drive the first woman carpenter off the construction site or force that young woman attorney to quit before she comes up for law firm partner are being tediously unoriginal. Territorial harassment is an ancient intimidation tactic to defend male economic privilege. There are hundreds of examples, dating back centuries. In 1835, for example, printers in Boston launched an all-out campaign to force women out of typesetting jobs. In 1819, journeyman tailors in New York even went on strike to prevent master tailors from hiring women.[7]

Racially based harassment also has a long history. In the United States, for example, the practice of men of color harassing white women for racial motives is relatively rare. It is far outweighed, historically, by the practice of white men assaulting black women with almost total license. During the centuries of slavery, African-American women used every resistance technique they could devise to prevent sexual abuse; with impressive ingenuity and determination, they sometimes succeeded. Ultimately, however, they had little or no recourse against any form of harassment that slaveowners and other white males chose to inflict, from unwanted sexual touching to rape and incest. The legal rights of the slaveowner, combined with the violence at his disposal and the economic power he commanded (the threat of selling the woman or her children), gave slaveholders nearly absolute power to engage in sexual violation.[8] Hispanic women in the Southwest, Native American women, and Asian women on the West Coast, although not legally slaves, often faced the same kind of sexual predation, with almost as little recourse. In some respects, the pattern continues today; combining racism with sexism, some white men still feel very free to abuse women of color, and very few whites are prosecuted or convicted for harassing or assaulting black, Hispanic, Asian, or Native American women.

Like race-related sexual aggression, class-based harassment of women is not a new phenomenon, but the dynamics,
again, usually reflect the real distribution of power. Historically, many of the harassers have been men with high economic status or positions of authority (rather than relatively
powerless men using harassment as revenge for economic
exploitation), and most of the victims have been working-
class women.

Like women of color, the hundreds of thousands of white
women (often immigrants) who worked as domestic servants
and companions in the homes of the upper and middle class
throughout the seventeenth, eighteenth, and nineteenth centuries faced a silent epidemic of sexual harassment—up to
and including rape—from their wealthy and respectable
male employers. They often had to fend off sexual assaults
from his sons and acquaintances as well. Louisa May Alcott,
the author of *Little Women*, was a victim of domestic harassment. She was the primary financial support for her father
and her siblings and worked at a variety of menial jobs to
keep the family out of poverty. At one point, Alcott found a
position as a paid companion to a middle-aged upper-class
woman; it was a better job than most, but the woman's
brother harassed Alcott so incessantly that she was forced to
quit.[9]

Whether women in domestic service resisted or complied
with their harassers, they usually lost their jobs in the process. Women had no effective birth control, no unemployment insurance, and no legal recourse against their
employers. Refusal could mean dismissal without a "character" (a good employment reference), which made finding a
new domestic position very difficult. There were almost no
professional jobs open to women, and very few alternatives
for domestic workers.

Housemaids who got pregnant as a result of sexual coercion by their employers found themselves out on the street
almost overnight, often moving from domestic labor to prostitution in order to earn a living. As Constance Backhouse and
Leah Cohen have noted, the historical evidence suggests

that the single most common prior occupation of nineteenth-century prostitutes was, in fact, domestic service. "Ironically," Backhouse and Cohen remark, "this knowledge of the pattern-of-employment shift from domestic service to prostitution itself increased the frequency of sexual harassment perpetrated against domestic servants," as public opinion leaped to the conclusion not that men of prominent community standing were systematically exploiting the women they employed, but that domestic workers were "immoral" as a class and free game for sexual use.[10]

Women working in the early factories and textile mills were up against the same kind of sexual coercion from mill owners, managers, and foremen. Overseers could fire women for any offense, real or fictitious, a setup that provided considerable latitude for sexual abuse. In October 1846, *The Factory Girls' Album*, a magazine that published material by women workers, ran the following commentary on the perils of factory life:

Hundreds of operatives who work in our mills are scarcely paid sufficient to board themselves. . . . The consequence is, they become discouraged—lose confidence in themselves, and then, regardless of consequences, abandon their virtue to obtain favors. A goodly proportion of those in large cities who inhabit "dens of shame" are first initiated into this awful vice in manufacturing places. Soon after . . . they become known, and are compelled to leave their work in the mills. . . . [Women] run the risk of being ruined in a manufacturing village.[11]

Despite the Victorian prose, it is clear that sexual extortion was going on in the mill towns. The "favors" for which women traded their "virtue" were usually jobs, and sometimes as little as a meal. In the 1840s, women in the New England mills were working thirteen-hour days, for an average wage of two cents an hour. They could barely cover the cost of a shared room in a boardinghouse, let alone regular meals. During the same period, the *Nashua Gazette* published a letter that characterized the overseers as "the male tyrants of the cotton mills" and described their behavior more bluntly: "The thousands of unprotected white females of Lowell [are] slaves to the overseers of a dozen or two of cotton mills, who hold not only the bread, but the characters of those girls, in the palms of their hands, and can do with them as any passion may dictate or any caprice suggest, with perfect impunity of the law, and safety from all consequences to themselves." Even writing a letter was obviously risky: this one was signed only by "A Factory Girl in the Nashua Corporation."[12]

Women were economically powerless but not passive about this abuse. Sarah Bagley, a pioneer labor leader who worked in the Lowell mills for eight years and edited the labor journal *Voice of Industry* for a brief period, urged her coworkers to resist and report harassers:

[A]buse of trust however trivial, insolence from whatever source, and whether from the agent, the overseer or petty tender, in the capacity of under clerk, from the Bank managers, men in authority of the city government, or gentlemen of the professions . . . we will punish as it merits, without stint or reserve. . . . [S]hrink as from the abyss of infamy, from the steady gaze or stealthy touch of the *fiend* in human form, who for a paltry momentary job, would rob you of bliss for life, and destroy a lone girl's happiness, away from friends and home. Give us the names of all such even making the attempt, and the scorching memory of their crimes shall follow them.[13]

There is no record that the women mill workers ever actually published the names of their harassers and extortionists, but Sarah Bagley deserves considerable credit for coming up with the strategy.

Like domestic and factory workers, nineteenth-century women salesclerks also faced harassment on the job. Wages were low, clerks were easy to replace, and refusing to comply with the sexual demands of male supervisors and floorwalkers could put a woman's job in immediate jeopardy. The power of male supervisors was virtually unchecked. Managers could and routinely did require saleswomen to stand for twelve or more hours a day; when state laws finally required seats for the women, the larger stores put in chairs but the managers fired women who sat down. Women shop clerks typically had to ask for passes from their male supervisors just to go to the toilet. A manager who chose to amuse himself with harassment and petty power abuse could withhold the pass and prevent women from using the toilets at all.[14] In this environment, sexual coercion was rampant. In 1926, Maud Nathan wrote, "Floorwalkers in the old days were veritable tsars; they often ruled with a rod of iron. Only the girls who were 'free-and-easy' with them, who consented to lunch or dine with them, who permitted certain liberties, were allowed any freedom of action or felt secure in their positions."[15]

Demographic history also provides some very suggestive evidence of the extent of sexual harassment. Historians have documented a marked increase in the rate of births to unmarried women during the Industrial Revolution. Most have uncritically assumed that the trend was due to an increase in *voluntary* sexual contact outside marriage, under conditions of increasing urbanization. Few historians have even considered the role of sexual harassment in those rising birth statistics. How much of the increase in out-of-wedlock pregnancy was a direct result of the extent to which women domestic, factory, and sales workers were forced to provide involuntary sexual services to their employers? Having a child outside of marriage was an economic disaster for most women in that era—not a risk they were likely to choose willingly.

At the same time that men in positions of authority were regularly exploiting women and engaging in wholesale sexual coercion, the public (male) perception of working women as promiscuous, immoral, and readily available for sexual access was widespread both in the United States and abroad. It was a very convenient rationale for sexual harassment. Mary Bularzik recounts the story of Rosa Cohen, working in the New York garment district at age twelve and becoming bilingual the hard way. The first English sentence Rosa learned was, "Keep your hands off please."[16]

Working-class women were routinely subjected to sexual propositions from strangers, and upper- and middle-class men were among the worst offenders. For example, in London in 1862, the Victorian diarist Arthur Munby recorded a conversation with a young factory worker, who explained that she had "many times been solicited by well-drest men to go home with them or meet them after dark for an evil purpose"—most recently, less than two hours earlier, by a white-haired gentleman ("He were sixty if he were a day, and a fine man as you'd like to see") who first asked about her weaving machine, and then "he took on wi summat quite different." When the man propositioned her directly, she told him to "get oot, ye auld rascal!" Munby's diary notes, "She added that she did not believe there was one of the factory girls in the building who had not been insulted in the same way."[17]

Similarly, a young woman who sold oranges for a living on the streets of Victorian London told the painter W. P. Frith that the worst harassment she experienced came not from street toughs and working-class men but from "swells." "Gentlemen," she explained, "is much greater blackguards than what blackguards is."[18]

Like harassers today, men have historically relied on their economic power, their positions of authority, and their gender-based power (including the underlying threat of violence) as the basis for their ability to harass and intimidate women. Their motives, to the extent they can be documented, appear to be essentially similar to the motives of harassers today: forcing sexual access, enforcing male dominance, and applying strategic harassment to drive women out of male occupations. There is even some evidence that eighteenth- and nineteenth-century rapists may have engaged in rape-testing.

What has changed, in some respects, is the degree of power that men can exercise over women. As a result of feminism, civil rights, and labor laws, most employers and supervisors today no longer wield unlimited power over their women workers. More women have some economic power of their own; every step toward pay equity makes women less vulnerable. With new awareness of their rights, new techniques for confronting harassers, and new legal avenues to address sexual harassment, more women than ever are also willing and able to challenge harassers, even those who have economic or role-based power. In addition, more women than ever are studying self-defense and martial arts; women who can defend themselves against physical assault can begin to reduce their vulnerability to harassers as well as rapists.

However, even as women begin to make some inroads on the real, material bases of male power behind harassment, the social practice of harassment continues. Male-dominance harassment may be more common than ever, as millions of ordinary sexist men, feeling powerless on the job, ineffective, and unrespected, resort to harassment as part of a larger social backlash to defend their crumbling macho status. Coerced deference from the women they harass may be their last vestige of macho "entitlement" in an impersonal corporate society—a society that still holds out the male-supremacist ideal of personal male power but delivers very little real power or prestige to the average working-class or middle-class male.

In addition, sexually predatory harassment still occurs with appalling frequency; in particular, working-class women of all races are still the objects of sexual extortion, both on and off the job. And of course, even today, labeling lower-class women (especially low-income single mothers) "immoral" very conveniently serves to mask the real extent of the sexual aggression they experience at the hands of men who abuse power. Barely disguised code words about the alleged morals of "welfare mothers" convey the equivalent racist message about women of color.

Strategic harassment is still a common tactic as well, used by upper-, middle-, and lower-class men in an enormous range of settings to disempower women and protect male turf from female encroachment. In both motive and method, these harassers are engaging in the same pattern of behavior they used as boys in their efforts to keep girls off the playground equipment and out of the treehouse. Personally, they've been practicing the techniques for years. Jeers, taunts, invasive behavior, verbal and physical abuse, posting pornography as a territorial flag of male possession, sabotaging women's work, using threats of violence and sometimes actual violence to keep women out—these are all standard tactics that some men, threatened by the prospect of working and competing with increasing numbers of women as equals and colleagues, are still using to defend their treehouses. But this time, denying access can cost women jobs, careers, income, pensions, educational opportunities, and the fundamental right to earn a living—even the simple right to walk down a city street. It's not just the treehouse anymore. And this time, women won't put up with it.

Sexual harassment is a pattern of male behavior learned in childhood as a normal part of a sexist culture. It is a well-established and specifically male social practice that serves to enforce male dominance and female submission, perpetuating the overall social structure of male supremacy. As a social practice, harassment can be analyzed: it has a social history, an identifiable structure and power base, clear functional purposes, and a broad array of social, psychological, and economic rewards for men. It is a pervasive, socially accepted, and effective pattern of behavior, but it is not universal, it is not a biological imperative, and it is not inevitable.

Social practices change when the conditions that support them change. They change when they no longer succeed in serving their purpose. They change when the costs of the behavior begin to exceed the rewards.

Women may not be able to transform the entire social structure in a single generation, but they can tackle the specific practice of harassment. Women can erode the male control of economic and social power that serves as the material basis for harassment; in fact, they are already doing so. With a combination of lawsuits and direct action, women can also redefine the societal norms that legitimize harassment as "natural," inevitable behavior—and, in the 1990s, they are doing that decisively. With both individual and collective action, women can begin to raise the costs of sexual harassment in ways that men have never dreamed of. When harassing women no longer produces the expected male rewards—when it becomes, instead, a high-risk behavior for men—women will be able to stop sexual harassment.

The Roots of Successful Resistance: Civil Rights, Self-defense, and Nonviolence

> *There is no need to fear the strong. All one needs to know is the method of overcoming them. There is a special jujitsu for every strong man.*
>
> —*Yevgeny Yevtushenko*

The effort to end sexual harassment is part of a long tradition of creative activism and social change, and the confrontation techniques we use today did not spring up out of a vacuum. Confrontation brings together in a systematic way two important strands of women's history—a centuries-old pattern of nonviolent political activism and the more recent innovation of feminist self-defense—to address the specific social practice of sexual harassment today.

In the midst of violence, individual women have demonstrated astonishing resourcefulness. More than a century ago, for example, feminist and abolitionist Lucy Stone (1818–93) came up with a brilliant tactic during an antislavery speaking tour. At a time when abolitionists were being killed, an angry mob stormed the stage in Cape Cod where she and Stephen Foster were to speak. As the crowd surged onto the platform, Stone told Foster to go ahead and run; he took off. Then she faced the thug who was leading the mob, took him by the arm, looked him in the eye, and said decisively, "This gentleman will take care of me." To his complete bewilderment, he escorted her to safety. But she didn't stop there. As he walked her through the riot, she persuaded him to let her speak. He gathered up the mob and kept order with a club, while she spoke, standing on a tree stump. She even collected twenty dollars from the crowd (a lot of money in those days) to pay for the damage they'd done to Stephen Foster's clothing.[1] Doing the unexpected is one characteristic of a successful nonviolent confrontation—and in the face of impending disaster, Stone's action was a superb example.

Women have shown the same kind of courage and creativity in devising new, nonviolent forms of political action. As the Australian feminist and author Dale Spender notes, it is in some ways ironic that Mahatma Gandhi is considered the originator of nonviolent resistance. By his own admission, it was from the British women's suffrage activists that he learned the power of systematic, unrelenting, creative nonviolent resistance as a political strategy.[2] Gandhi successfully used nonviolence campaigns as a political tool, first in South Africa and then in India from 1919 until his death in 1948, but it was women who provided the model.

Women have been developing nonviolent strategies to stop aggression and injustice, and taking direct action based on those strategies, for a very long time. Some of the earliest literature in the world features women applying effective nonviolent action. In 412 B.C., Aristophanes wrote a play, *Lysistrata,* celebrating a successful women's peace organization with a nonviolent antiwar strategy that was probably already ancient when he described it. (In the play, the women of Athens and Sparta, led by the heroine, Lysistrata, occupy public buildings and boycott sex to force an end to the twenty-one-year Peloponnesian War. They prevail, and Lysistrata dictates the terms of the peace agreement.)

History is full of examples of successful nonviolent direct action by women. During the American Revolution, when British troops hoarded the food supplies in New York City, women liberated the warehouses without firing a shot and distributed the food to the public. A few generations later, abolitionist women like Sojourner Truth (c. 1797–1883) and the Grimke sisters (Sarah, 1792–1873; Angelina, 1805–79) were demanding the right to speak in public meetings. They broke all the conventions of "ladylike" behavior to document and condemn the institutionalized violence of slavery. Harriet Tubman (c. 1820–1913) and an entire network of Quaker women began taking direct action to help hundreds of slaves escape to freedom on the underground railroad. That kind of activism has been the backbone of every social-change and antiwar movement since. During the U.S. war in Vietnam, women organized everything from draft-board sit-ins to door-to-door neighborhood canvassing drives to national antiwar marches, to mobilize public opposition and bring the war to an end. Quaker women helped to found and run a new "underground railroad" to carry war resisters to Canada.

Women have played a particularly important role in the U.S. civil rights movement. We think of the 1960s as the era of civil rights activism, but in the 1890s, Ida B. Wells-Barnett launched and led the national campaign to stop lynching, even after her office was destroyed by a racist mob and she herself was threatened with death. One of the very first sit-ins in the movement took place in the late 1940s, in Washington, D.C., when three young African-American women from Howard University sat down at a lunch counter a few blocks from the White House to challenge the injustice of segregation in the nation's capital. In 1955, it was Rosa Parks, a forty-three-year-old seamstress and activist, who began the famous bus boycott in Montgomery, Alabama, that launched Martin Luther King's career. And it was the sustained effort of hundreds of courageous, determined women in the churches and the community that made that boycott work despite economic reprisals and repeated threats of violence. Less than a decade later, Ella Baker was the strategist behind the founding of the Student Non-Violent Coordinating Committee (SNCC), the group responsible for organizing the volunteers who headed south in the dangerous and successful voting rights campaign of Freedom Summer, 1964.[3]

In every generation, women have been activists, philosophers, innovators, and organizers, developing nonviolent direct-action tactics both as a personal, pragmatic method of dealing with aggression and as a political strategy to challenge social patterns of violence and injustice.

There are many kinds of power abuse and many forms of nonviolent action. It was the U.S. civil rights movement that first began to apply a carefully structured verbal confrontation technique as part of a systematic nonviolent campaign for social justice. Elements of the confrontation technique were part of the training the Freedom Summer volunteers received: speaking from principle; naming violent or racist behavior simply and directly; holding a violent or abusive sheriff or Klan member personally and publicly responsible for his actions; forcing him to make a conscious, personal decision to stop, or continue, his unjust actions. Women have been extending the technique ever since, practicing and implementing it in many different ways.

In the United States, racism was codified in "Jim Crow" laws until the 1960s. It is still embedded in both institutional and social behavior. In a society where institutional discrimination as well as sexist and racist harassment have been a common part of the daily experience of African-American women and other women of color, confrontation has been a tool for resisting many forms of oppression in women's lives. Here, for example, is Rosa Parks's own account of the famous confrontation that ignited the modern civil rights movement on December 1, 1955:

THE MONTGOMERY BUS BOYCOTT

Having to take a certain section [on a bus] because of your race was humiliating, but having to stand up because a particular driver wanted to keep a white person from having to stand was, to my mind, most inhumane. . . .

I happened to be the secretary of the Montgomery branch of the NAACP as well as the NAACP Youth Council adviser. Many cases did come to my attention that nothing came out of 'cause the person that was abused would be too intimidated to sign an affidavit, or to make a statement. Over the years, I had had my own problems with the bus drivers. . . .

On December 1, 1955, I had finished my day's work as a tailor's assistant in the Montgomery Fair department store and I was on my way home. There was one vacant seat on the Cleveland Avenue bus, which I took, alongside a man and two women across the aisle. There were still a few vacant seats in the white section in the front, of course. We went to the next stop without being disturbed. On the third [stop], the front seats were occupied and this one man, a white man, was standing. The driver asked us to stand up and let him have those seats, and when none of us moved at his first words, he said, "You all make it light on yourselves and let me have those seats." And the man who was sitting next to the window stood up, and I made room for him to pass by me. The two women across the aisle stood up and moved out.

When the driver saw me still sitting, he asked if I was going to stand up and I said, "No, I'm not."

And he said, "Well, if you don't stand up, I'm going to call the police and have you arrested."

I said, "You may do that."

He did get off the bus, and I still stayed where I was. Two policemen came on the bus. One of the policemen asked me if the bus driver had asked me to stand and I said yes.

He said, "Why don't you stand up?"

And I asked him, "Why do you push us around?"

He said, "I do not know, but the law is the law and you're under arrest."[4]

Rosa Parks's calm, resolute confrontation was a direct personal challenge in a society whose segregation was enforced by an all-white crew of bus drivers, an all-white police force, and the law itself. She understood the need to stand up to the social practice of racism, even when it was officially sanctioned by the state, and she was ready to name injustice and confront it with dignity and power. "Why do you push us around?" is the quintessential question every harasser needs to be asked—"Why do you commit this injustice?"

Her clarity in presenting that powerful question was not a

fluke. It reflected a lifetime of thought and commitment, a habit of insisting on the basic principle of respect, even in the face of Jim Crow laws and the white power establishment. Mrs. Parks later commented, "My resistance to being mistreated on the buses and anywhere else was just a regular thing with me and not just that day."[5]

By posing that simple, honest, direct question of principle, she turned the tables in the encounter and forced one Alabama police officer to make a profound personal choice of his own: to enforce an unjust law, or not. He could not justify his action. Face to face with the meaning of his own behavior, he gave her an honest answer—"I do not know"—but his courage was no match for hers. He sided with injustice and the status quo, and made an arrest with historic repercussions.

Like racism, sexism is both a personal and a political form of power abuse. Day after day, in a hundred thousand different places, one man at a time decides to engage in sexual injustice and power abuse. He does it because he likes it. He does it because he can. He does it because he has the power to exploit women economically, through sexual coercion on the job, or socially, through the power of his position or the threat of physical assault. His behavior is condoned not by formal Jim Crow laws but by powerful and pervasive societal norms—the notion that men are predators and women are the prey, the excuse that "boys will be boys," and the massive weight of cultural habit in a society where the daily practice of sexual harassment is still all too often considered acceptable. The ideology of sexism and male supremacy is doubly pernicious where sexual harassment is concerned: it not only excuses abusive male behavior as normal, but tells women that they are powerless to change it.

Every time a woman faces sexual harassment, she has to make a personal choice about how to react to the abuse. She has to stop and decide how severe the risk is, what agenda he has in mind, what she should say or do, what effect it might have. She is forced to deal with a range of powerful emotions—from simple annoyance at the intrusion, to deep anger, humiliation, and fear of escalation. At any time, any place, a man who chooses to harass has the power to yank her up face to face with her fear of physical assault or her fear of economic reprisals. He can set her adrenaline pounding as she walks through a public square or down a corridor at work. He can cost her her livelihood, her education, and her ability to sleep at night. The harasser who targets a woman invades her life on a deeply intimate, personal level.

But because harassment is a pervasive social practice, it is a political as well as a personal problem. Many men never harass women, but the cumulative behavior of those who do systematically denies women the right to walk down that street, take that class, do their jobs, or even enjoy a public park in peace. The individual harasser is part of a social structure of sexist behavior and male abuse of power that denies women some of their most fundamental civil liberties. Not many human rights are more basic or more ancient than the right to walk, to learn, and to work.

No right exists in the abstract. If current social conditions prevent significant numbers of people from freely exercising a right, that right has effectively ceased to exist. Poll taxes, Jim Crow laws, and bogus literacy tests, backed up by racist violence, eliminated the right to vote for generations of blacks in the American South. And sexual harassment—one man at a time, one incident after another—costs women their most basic human rights today. Jobs, education, housing, religion—no aspect of women's lives is immune to destruction when harassers strike. When the minister harasses, women lose the right to worship in the congregation of their choice. When the landlord is the harasser, women lose the right to their own homes. In any just society, the freedom to walk down a public thoroughfare, to study, to work, to live and worship where one chooses, is not negotiable; these rights are not a matter of debate. But in the United States at the end of the twentieth century, the epidemic of sexual harassment means that, for women, these are rights that are in no way guaranteed. At the whim of a harasser, these rights can cease to exist. If politics are about the distribution of power and freedom in society, sexual harassment is profoundly political.

To reclaim and defend their human rights, women need a resistance strategy that works on both the personal and the political levels. Confrontation operates on the personal level as a specific means to break through the harasser's destructive behavior. It disrupts his abuse of power, gets the individual woman out of the situation, and shifts the balance of power in the interaction—leaving the woman feeling strong and self-respecting, instead of angry and victimized, and the harasser feeling vulnerable, instead of powerful and successful. On the political level, harassment curtails women's freedom. Confrontation transforms the status quo by increasing the risks of harassment for each harasser, changing the power dynamics between men and women, slowly and steadily, one incident at a time. Confrontation challenges the fundamental gender assumptions and behavioral patterns of a sexist society.

A woman who engages in a clear, principled confrontation confounds not only the harasser's sexist expectations, but the entire social pattern of male dominance and power behind his decision to harass. She does not act like a docile, compliant victim and does not passively accept the status quo. Faced with sexist aggression, she does not relinquish her rights—she reclaims them as a matter of principle. In the process, she makes it personally difficult for the harasser to continue his behavior; she also creates the beginnings of a new social structure, one in which harassment is no longer a cost-free game for men. And because most confrontations take place in public settings, she educates everyone else around her as well. A good confrontation can be a dramatic piece of street theater, with a clear and compelling message for the audience. Each time a woman confronts, she turns up the pressure on the old social structure, weakens the old patterns of expected behavior and the old social norms that excuse and condone harassment. Like the aggregate effect of harassment, the cumulative effect of women's acts of confrontation can change the social and political structure.

Where harassment abridges freedom, confrontation expands it.

Why does confrontation work? Why does it succeed in stopping sexual harassment? It combines the most effective characteristics of personal self-defense and nonviolent social change—the personal and the political—in a single powerful and disciplined act of resistance.

FIGHT SMART: CONFRONTATION AND SELF-DEFENSE

Feminist self-defense theory sets forth four criteria for judging tactics to deal with sexual violence: (1) Does the tactic accurately address the realities of women's lives? (2) Does it build on women's own strengths and expand their abilities? (3) Does it extend women's mobility? (4) Does it promote independence and increase women's freedom?[6]

All too often, advice meant for women's protection restricts women's freedom. Advising women never to go out alone at night, for example, fails immediately on two counts: it limits women's mobility (can't go out at night) and curtails their independence (can't venture out alone). It also ignores the reality of two important facts about women's lives: many women have no choice but to go out alone at night, to work, to night school, or to family and community commitments; and many sexual assaults—both acquaintance and stranger rapes—occur not out on the street, but in women's own homes. However well-meaning, this kind of advice severely limits women's freedom of action, without significantly increasing their safety.

Confrontation, however, meets all four criteria. It is based on a very practical, accurate, behavioral analysis of the power dynamics of sexual harassment and the role that harassment plays in women's daily lives. It builds women's verbal strengths and expands their self-defense abilities. It increases women's mobility by giving women a set of tools they can use to deal with everything from an all-male job site to the gang of harassers in the local park. It not only promotes women's independence but empowers women, individually and collectively, to reclaim some of their most basic human rights and freedoms. On every count, confrontation meets the analytical standards for a successful defense strategy.

As a practical matter, *the element of surprise* is a significant advantage in stopping aggression. Most rapists do not expect women to know how to fight back, and most harassers do not expect their victims to turn and confront. In both cases, a woman who resists aggression decisively has the benefit of surprise on her side. She is breaking through societal norms that define women as helpless victims, and she is taking advantage of the assailant's own stereotyped notions of women as easy prey. Her unexpected action throws him off balance and leaves him unsure about what will happen next. Instead of overpowering her easily, he is suddenly faced with the possibility that *he* may be at some risk.

The ability to react immediately is a strong defense tactic in its own right. For example, the first few minutes of a sexual assault are critical; that is the moment when the assailant has the least invested in the attack, can most easily be taken by surprise, and is most likely to be defeated if the woman decides to fight back. Strong, immediate verbal and physical resistance is the single most successful self-defense strategy in stopping rape (see Chapter 12). The same is true of sexual harassment. A woman who can confront immediately, in no uncertain terms, has an excellent chance of breaking off the harassment at the outset and preventing its recurrence. Like self-defense or martial arts, confrontation training equips a woman to analyze a situation, size up the potential aggressor, know her options, and be mentally and physically ready to act.

Another fundamental principle of self-defense is *using the defender's strengths against the assailant's weak points.* Although many petite women are excellent martial artists and very powerful fighters, women's smaller average physical stature can be a disadvantage in physical hand-to-hand defense. Consequently, many specific self-defense moves are designed to help women "fight smart"—to use leverage points and tactics that target the assailant's vulnerable areas, rather than trying to overcome him with brute strength. Confrontation tactics apply the same key principle in cases of sexual harassment, targeting the harasser's most vulnerable points: his desire for respect and his indefensible behavior. Size is no disadvantage when it comes to confronting harassers; if anything, the average woman has the verbal edge.

Confrontation also succeeds as a defense strategy because it *reduces the level of violence* in our society. The purpose of any feminist self-defense tactic is not to beat the assailant into submission, but to stop the attack as quickly and efficiently as possible, prevent the assailant from harming his victim, and give him a reason to think twice before he tries that kind of aggression again. Confrontation stops the assailant, instead of escalating the violence.

Like other highly efficient self-defense tactics, confrontation is also designed to produce *maximum effects with a minimum of engagement*. It uses a quick, clear verbal statement, backed up by appropriate body language, to flip the power dynamics. The effect is usually immediate; there is no need for a prolonged physical encounter or an intense discussion with the harasser. Emotionally, a good confrontation allows a woman to be done with him and go about her business (instead of simmering with anger all day), while it leaves the harasser unsettled and disoriented.

Confrontation stops harassment by applying many of the basic lessons that have come out of feminist research on self-defense over the past twenty years. In cases of rape-testing, confrontation can sometimes even stop rape, by breaking off the attack before it happens.

CONFRONTATION AND NONVIOLENCE

But confrontation is more than just an effective self-defense strategy. It is also a potent tool for social change. As a social-change mechanism, confrontation works for the same reasons that other forms of nonviolent resistance work. A group of demonstrators might use nonviolent direct action to protest an unjust law and seek new legislation. A woman who confronts harassment is doing much the same—using direct action to protest an unjust societal norm and to change the unwritten, but equally powerful, standards of socially accepted sexist behavior.

Anthropologists define these kinds of cultural norms as "laws" in a very real sense.[7] Societal norms involve rigid unwritten codes that define appropriate behavior for both men and women—speech patterns, body language, physical appearance, mannerisms, and actions. When a woman confronts a harasser, she is committing an act of civil disobedience, defying the unwritten cultural law that says that he has a right to harass and she must passively accept that abuse.

Whether it's a picket line or a prayer vigil, a boycott or a sit-in, whatever the specific tactics chosen, every successful nonviolent act of resistance has four essential characteristics:

- A clear public statement of a moral or ethical position
- Very specific behavior on the part of the participants
- A time and location chosen to emphasize and reinforce the message
- A process, used to plan and carry out the action, that reflects certain basic human values[8]

In many instances, the extent to which these nonviolence standards are met will determine the success of the tactics. That is true of organized political protest actions, and it is true of confrontations with harassers.

Expressing a clear moral or ethical position means communicating three things explicitly: the moral principle one's action is based on; the injustice one is challenging; and the specific remedies, changes, or responses one is seeking. In a confrontation, the moral principle is respect and human dignity: women's freedom is at stake. The injustice is sexual harassment, in any and all of its forms. And the remedy is an immediate change in the harasser's behavior.

When a woman names the harasser's behavior at the beginning of a confrontation ("Stop making those kissing and sucking noises at women on the street," "Take your hand off me right now"), she is stating the fact of his aggression in the most specific way possible. Usually, the more explicit the statement, the better. "I don't like the way you stare at my chest when you talk to me," is much more powerful than, "You make me uncomfortable sometimes." There is no defense for his behavior; naming it clearly makes the injustice clear.

When she follows up by holding him accountable for his actions ("That's harassment: stop harassing women!"), she is articulating the moral principle: her right to respect and freedom. Speaking on behalf of women generally ("I don't like it; no woman likes it!") also underscores the principle involved; this is not just an incidental whim or personal preference. It is perfectly appropriate to speak in moral or ethical terms and to name the principle explicitly: "This is about respect! Women have a right to work here without being harassed."

And when the confronter demands that the behavior stop, she is laying out the remedy she seeks in no uncertain terms. Women who confront harassers demand not only that they stop the injustice immediately, but that they cease and desist in the future: "Back off right now. Don't you ever do that to a woman again."

In fact, the verbal structure of a confrontation is a textbook example of effective nonviolent resistance. The confrontation statement contains all of the essential elements—principle, injustice, remedy—in short, direct, powerful language. Because it is so clear, it usually leaves the harasser shaken. And because his behavior is utterly indefensible, having it named out loud is very unnerving for him.

The shock value alone is effective, but making it a matter of principle adds considerably to the impact. People do not like to be told that they've violated principles that they themselves hold dear. Most men are very conscious of their status in the social and workplace hierarchy; they demand respect for themselves, their position, and, of course, their manhood itself. The most sexist men—the harassers—do not extend that principle of respect to women; women are the "other," the object, the prey, not equally human. In terms of respect and status, men who support sexism see women as ranking at the bottom of the male hierarchy, or outside it altogether.

Men who are insecure about their manhood and prestige often try to compensate for their insecurity and reinforce their sense of status by acting macho, using women to bolster their egos, and treating women like doormats. If all else fails, they can always reassure themselves of some status, they think, by putting women down. Because harassing women has been such an easy way for men to feel powerful and keep women in their place, it is a comfortable, normal part of the repertoire of the sexist male. That combination—a deep emotional need for respect and power for himself and an easy, reassuring habit of abuse and disrespect toward women —is the standard psychological package behind most harassers' behavior.

Consequently, it is doubly effective when the "doormat" uses a well-structured confrontation statement to challenge the harasser, explicitly and calmly, on the basis of that same fundamental principle: the essential right to respect. But she is upholding the principle in a way that uses his own sexist assumptions against him, to turn the power dynamics of the interaction upside down. *She's* not supposed to demand respect. He expected to feel powerful when he harassed her, but what he actually feels is shocked and confused. In his sexist world view, no one respects a man who's forcefully challenged by a woman. Now here she is, loud and clear, making it obvious that he is being an unprincipled bully and a jerk: she's holding him accountable, telling everyone within earshot exactly what he just did. Suddenly he's on the wrong end. Because of his harassment he's losing on his own terms, in status and prestige. To his astonishment, he's also just lost control of the interaction.

The contradiction she forces him to face, between his own need for respect and control and the realization that his behavior is crashing down in failure, is extremely uncomfortable. The more sexist the man, the more excruciating and disorienting the encounter is for him. If the confrontation is public, the awareness that there is an audience watching his conspicuous failure adds to his psychological pain. The emotional turmoil and sense of failure he feels are strong incentives to back off and reconsider. An individual confrontation rocks the psychological ground he's standing on, and a confrontation by a group of women is even more devastating.

To make that happen, confronters need to use not only the verbal message of a confrontation (naming the principle, the injustice, and the remedy) but all the power of the nonviolent techniques developed in social-change movements. The second basic characteristic of any successful nonviolent action—*specific behavior* on the part of the activists—is an equally critical component in a successful confrontation.

Honesty is a crucial part of that behavior. Nonviolent resistance is sometimes described as "speaking truth to power," and Gandhi used the term *satyagraha*—"truth force"—to describe the importance of honesty in producing the impact of nonviolent action. One of the essential elements of a good confrontation is the use of completely honest, accurate statements, with no verbal padding, no idle threats, no insults, and no excuses: speaking the strong, simple truth to a man who is abusing his power. That behavior alone—cutting through the fog of sexism, fear, and denial to speak from the core of the woman's own experience and lay the harasser's abusive behavior bare in the full light of day—is very powerful. Remember the child who said the emperor had no clothes?

In addition, the behavior taught in nonviolence training sessions, for activists who are considering civil disobedience and other kinds of protest actions, includes the following:

- Self-respecting, nonvictimized and nonvictimizing body language (neither submissive nor aggressive)
- Eye contact with the opponent
- Language that does not include slurs or insults of any kind
- A strong, firm, steady tone of voice
- Holding one's ground calmly (don't give in to panic or anger)

- Refusing to label the opponent as "the enemy" (criticize the behavior, respect the person)
- Calming techniques to keep oneself centered, including support from friends and a willingness to face one's fears honestly
- Creativity (don't be afraid to do the unexpected)

Developed and tested over many years of practice, these behavioral elements are a defining characteristic of successful nonviolent social-change campaigns. They convey a strong, principled presence and increase the impact of the action.

Every one of these elements is important in confronting sexual harassment. The guidelines for confrontation require women to think carefully about all of the behavioral components of the confrontation. In more complex situations (for example, a persistent harasser in the workplace), it is often useful to plan and rehearse the confrontation beforehand, with supportive friends, just as one would plan the details of a march, a picket line, or any other protest action. The more fully a woman can incorporate the appropriate nonviolent behavior into her action, the more effective her confrontation is likely to be.

The third key aspect of nonviolent direct action—*choosing a strategic time and location* to emphasize and reinforce the message—is also important in making a confrontation work. Nonviolence theory suggests that confronters need to be clear about their objectives and creative about their options in designing both individual and group confrontations.

For a one-shot harasser on a public street, the time and place are easy. A straightforward confrontation statement, on the spot, is generally appropriate and sufficient. In cases of severe or prolonged harassment, however, the time and location of the confrontation are factors the confronter can determine. Whenever possible the choice should be hers, not the harasser's. These are strategic decisions, not random elements. Each woman should review the possibilities, think creatively, and choose the setting that will best meet her objectives. Deciding when and where to confront an abuser gives her an additional measure of control over the interaction and helps her to plan a difficult confrontation more precisely. When the harasser is someone who is abusing a position of authority, confronting him in front of his peers or community can be effective. Even if the victim decides to confront in private, her allies should always be present, or at least within earshot. In at least one instance, a waitress decided to confront a persistent harasser in front of his wife and mother (that worked quite well). Annie McCombs's success story, "A Summer Evening in the Rose Garden" (Chapter 13), is a good example of how decisions about time and location can reinforce the impact of a confrontation.

And finally, under the fourth criterion of nonviolent action, any successful act of resistance should reflect some *fundamental human values*, in both the planning and the implementation of the action. The purpose of all nonviolent action —marches, vigils, confrontations, principled resistance of all sorts—is to prevent people in positions of power from violating the basic human values of justice, compassion, equality, and respect. Men who engage in sexual harassment are violating every one of these values.

Power abuse is power abuse—on any level. When governments violate these values, human rights groups hold them accountable. The strong, disciplined confrontation techniques women use to stop sexual harassment are strikingly similar to the strategies that Amnesty International and other organizations use to confront governments around the world that violate human rights:

- Speaking the simple truth, uncensored and unafraid —naming the behavior explicitly and publicizing the government's actions, by documenting human rights abuses in clear, straightforward public statements and reports
- Naming the abusers and holding them personally and publicly responsible for their actions, from violations of civil rights to unjust imprisonment, political torture, and executions

- Demanding publicly and unequivocally that the abuses stop, with no excuses or exceptions
- Speaking out as a matter of principle, on behalf of *all* people, to condemn violations of human rights
- Marshaling allies, applying the pressure of visibility and public condemnation, and using every other nonviolent sanction possible—from "freedom writer" letter campaigns to United Nations resolutions to economic sanctions—to increase the costs, for the government, of continuing to violate human rights
- Ultimately, through the weight of consistent, relentless, principled public action, creating a political environment in which governments in general find that the political and economic costs of violating human rights outweigh any short-term advantages they might hope to achieve

Amnesty International, Human Rights Watch, and similar political organizations have saved thousands of lives over the years, freed thousands of political prisoners, held dictators in check, and helped to bring governments down. From the overthrow of Duvalier in Haiti and Marcos in the Philippines to the dismantling of the old regime in the Soviet Union, nonviolent action and public confrontation have forced political change.

Human rights organizations use the tools of confrontation to create an international climate in which governments' violations of human rights cannot be ignored and are no longer tolerated. Women who confront harassers are using the same powerful tools to defend women's human rights and create a new social and political environment—a climate in which sexual harassment, as a fundamental violation of women's freedom, cannot be ignored and is no longer tolerated.

To be effective, the confronter's own behavior must incorporate the basic human values she seeks to uphold. Confrontation works best when it is most principled. A confrontation is not a temper tantrum. It is a careful, planned, ethical act of resistance to a pervasive form of power abuse. Confronting out of uncontrolled rage, engaging in abusive verbal violence to humiliate and punish the harasser, or sabotaging him behind his back are forms of emotional venting, not social change. They contradict the principles of both nonviolent action and effective self-defense. Revenge is not a moral principle, and revenge is not the purpose of confrontation.

At the same time, it is important to recognize that confrontation is not simply a matter of moral persuasion. As the theorist and nonviolent activist Barbara Deming has noted, to refuse to cooperate with injustice is to exert force.[9] In a sexist society, refusing to tolerate sexual harassment is a powerful and uncompromising action in support of social justice. *Women who confront are not asking the harasser to please change and be nice.*

When women confront, they are forcing a harasser to face the real meaning of his behavior in all its stark, ugly clarity. Women are insisting on telling him—and the audience of everyone around—some hard truths that he doesn't want to hear. Women are demanding, as a matter of principle, that he stop abusing power. They are raising the costs, for him, of engaging in abusive behavior, and they are making his acts of power abuse fail. They are putting so much pressure on him that, sooner or later (and usually it is sooner), it becomes impossible for him to continue to function comfortably in his old patterns. Women are not responding in kind, trading violence for violence and ugliness for ugliness, but they are changing the context in which the harasser operates, the structure of a sexist culture, in a way that makes it increasingly difficult and increasingly painful personally for any man to continue to commit sexual harassment. Women are demanding that the harasser treat women with respect, compelling him to do so, whether he wants to or not.

Respect is the fundamental principle behind confrontation. At the deepest level of nonviolent social-change theory, confrontation works not only because it raises the costs of harassment and frees women from abuse, but because it is principled behavior: it includes respect even for the harasser himself. We do not deny his humanity with counteraggression and abuse, although he dehumanizes women. We do not excuse or dismiss his behavior; we take him seriously, show him the respect of speaking the uncensored truth to him, and hold him fully accountable for his actions. Even as we challenge his aggressive, unprincipled behavior with all the force of direct confrontation, we give him an opportunity and a motive to change. We hold out the expectation that he is capable of change, that he is capable of choices. The harasser chooses to use his power to engage in sexual harassment and limit women's freedom; he can choose not to do so. We hold out the expectation that he can and will choose justice. We demand no less of him. That is true respect.

Because of the psychology of sexism, a principled nonviolent confrontation is pure psychological judo. Every time the harasser's behavior is confronted, he trips over his own assumptions and damages his own self-esteem. As women throughout his environment repeatedly begin to confront him, he may never figure out exactly why harassment doesn't work anymore, but it *will* dawn on him that *it is not working.* Whether he engages in sexually predatory harassment, dominance harassment, strategic/territorial harassment, or some combination, he can no longer count on feeling powerful, macho, or in control when he harasses a woman; he is more likely to experience embarrassment and failure. Even for a slow learner, it may take only a few confrontations before the jarring discomfort he feels when confronted starts to outweigh the rewards he expects when he harasses women.

And the effect is not limited to the harasser himself. The men around him are watching; they may be just as shocked and baffled as he is. Because most men are so conscious of ego, status, and hierarchy, they *notice* confrontations—one of their number has just mysteriously gone down in smoke at the hands of a woman who is neither helpless nor hysterical, and they do not want to follow him. The women around will take note as well—sometimes they're taken aback (we're all products of our culture, after all), but more often they smile, occasionally they applaud, and sometimes a woman who has never heard of confrontation will even join in to help.

Women who have witnessed a confrontation will sometimes ask, afterward, "What did you just do? How did you just do that?" For women, just watching a principled confrontation can be a revelation—and a source of new strength to stand up to harassers themselves.

On a broader, societal level, confrontation systematically breaks through both sides of the sexist behavioral norms that legitimize harassment—men's long-standing "right" to harass and women's passive, victimized response patterns. Confrontation creates a new climate of risk for men who harass, as a direct result of women's unilateral action. There is no need (and no reason) to wait for harassers to stop on their own initiative. As a social practice, harassment is too widespread, too costly for women, and too damaging; we do not have the luxury of waiting for men to "get it" on their own. Women who confront not only demonstrate a new pattern of female behavior, but, like women who make a neighborhood harassment-free, shift the context in which the harassers operate. When confrontation becomes a standard response to harassment, the existing societal structure of reward and risk is reversed. The behavioral patterns that made harassment work no longer apply. The status quo is gone; harassment is no longer safe for men. We begin to replace sexism with the basic human value of respect.

Confrontation: Stopping Harassers on the Job and on the Street

> *Power concedes nothing without a demand. It never did and it never will.*
>
> *—Frederick Douglass*

Confrontation meets power with power. It is a direct-action strategy for women, based on a carefully structured combination of effective self-defense and nonviolent social change tactics. Confrontation is strong, disciplined behavior—a very successful, principled response to the unprincipled aggression of sexual harassment. But effective confrontation is not a skill that women usually learn in a sexist society.

Women who confront harassers are taking action that does not fit the stereotypes of women as (1) passive, vulnerable, and powerless, or (2) hysterical and out of control. They are responding in a way that is outside the range of typical female behavior in a sexist culture, and completely outside the harasser's own sexist expectations. Confrontation is a type of nonviolent psychological and social judo. When the harasser's behavior is despicable, he has no defense against being thrown. In judo and aikido, the defender uses the attacker's own aggressive moves and momentum to hurl him to the mat. Confrontation tactics are very similar: They skillfully use the harasser's own behavior and sexism to throw him. Women who know how to confront can leave their harassers reeling. At the same time, they are creating social change, redefining the environment in ways that make it harder and harder for harassers to function.

TYPICAL RESPONSES TO HARASSMENT

Most harassers have a definite scenario in mind. When they begin the interaction, they think they know exactly what will happen next. They've done this many times before; they've grown up watching other men do it; they may even have a certain favorite, familiar harassment routine. When they begin harassing a new target, they expect her to respond in the same predictable ways their earlier victims have responded. And they expect the same gut-level emotional pay-off they've gotten so many times before—the surge of power, the satisfaction, the firm sense of control over a woman, the feeling of success. Minor variations from one woman to the next are just part of the thrill; control is the name of the game, and the harasser has little doubt in his mind about the way the overall scenario will play out.

It's important to understand that, although harassment can create intense fear and tension for the victim, harassing a woman does not usually feel like a high-risk game to the harasser: He knows his opening moves, he's ready with his responses, and based on his past experience, he expects it to be an easy win for his side.

In simple dominance harassment on the street, his victory is brief and fleeting; he runs his game on her, she reacts, he gets his momentary psychological reward, and then he waits for the next victim to come by. The satisfaction is cumulative, and he can play the game all day. When the harasser is a boss, a coworker, a landlord, a neighbor, a teacher, a minister —someone who has repeated access to the same victim, or some position of authority in her life—the power game is more complex, more personal. It may go on for months, even years, as he manipulates the scenario he's designed and plays off her reactions. His motives may involve any or all of the three categories of harassment. But in every situation, the harasser expects to be comfortably in control. He's playing out *his* game plan, and he assumes that it will go down just about the way he envisions it.

Most of the time, the harasser's assumptions are accurate. Women *do* respond to harassers in predictable ways.

Like the harassers themselves, women follow the behavioral patterns they've learned from their community; we all respond to our social conditioning, and none of us is immune to the cultural patterns and expectations that surround us. Harassment is nothing new. It's part of the fabric of daily life, a normal, common experience for which women have learned certain standard, common responses.

Those responses fall into three broad categories: appeasement, counteraggression, and avoidance.

On the street, the classic appeasement response is silence. "Just be ladylike," many young girls learn—just ignore the harasser. "Don't stoop to his level," mothers tell their daughters, "Don't dignify that with an answer." "Hold your head up, keep walking, pretend he's not even there." Ignoring street harassment is the single most common response middle-class girls in the United States are taught, and it is the standard behavioral strategy for women in many different cultures.

But, of course, women never really ignore harassment. Their stomach and shoulder muscles tense up, they put their heads down and walk faster, they avoid whole areas of their own community or workplace, calculate the risks, and use roundabout detours to escape the presence of harassers. Women who "ignore" harassers must deal with all the emotional repercussions of victimization: fear, humiliation, feelings of powerlessness, rage. Under the surface, they are often seething with anger for hours after an incident. Maintaining silence in the face of harassment is only the superficial level of response; on every other level, women react with intense stress.

On the job, at school, and in other institutional settings, appeasement can take many forms. Many women will respond with silence, just as they do on the street, trying to ignore the harassment or pretend that it didn't really happen. Some will admit that it occurred but make excuses for the harasser, trying to convince themselves that he didn't really mean it. Some may pretend that the incident was a joke and try to laugh it off as a meaningless, one-shot episode (except that it's not at all funny and it will happen again and again). Some women will blame themselves, assuming (incorrectly) that they must have done something to invite the harasser's actions. They may start wearing unattractive or baggy cloth- ing, change their hair, or put on weight, as if they could control the harasser's behavior by simply changing their ap- pearance. That's wishful thinking. Women are harassed be- cause they are female and accessible to the harasser.

These appeasement responses are consistently unsuccess- ful in stopping harassment. They are not defense strategies. They are actually forms of psychological denial on the vic- tim's part—efforts to minimize the real power abuse in- volved and relabel the harasser's behavior to reduce the woman's own feelings of powerlessness and victimization.

Faced with blatant, undeniable harassment, some women decide to try to placate the harasser, soothe him, protect his ego, or even comply with his sexual demands to appease him. Many will just swallow their anger, try to stay calm, and simply endure the abuse, hoping that somehow the harass- ment will eventually stop. Because of their social condition- ing and their fear of retaliation, women usually seek to resolve the problem with passive, evasive behavior; they try to work around the harasser, sidestep him, and avoid angering him with a direct, head-to-head conflict.

No type of appeasement works—not silence, excuses, rela- beling, placating, complying, evading, or enduring. These are "helplessness responses," emotionally draining and al- most never effective. Appeasement does not disrupt the power dynamics of harassment or create any force to stop the behavior. In fact, it usually plays right into the power sce- nario the harasser has developed.

Even though they know it is not likely to succeed in stop- ping the harasser, women often choose appeasement be- cause it seems like the safest thing to do; that can be dangerous. In cases of sexually coercive or strategic harass- ment, appeasement is a disaster; the abuser will keep raising the pressure until the woman is in an impossible position. And in cases of rape-testing, appeasement is not only an ineffective response, but actually puts the victim in greater danger. Silence and other weak, deferential responses to verbal or physical intrusion can allow a rapist to conclude that the woman will be an easy target for attack. And because acquaintance rape is at least as common as stranger rape, it is just as risky to respond with appeasement when the harasser is someone the woman knows as it is when the harasser is a stranger.

But what's the alternative to appeasement—an equally hostile, aggressive counterattack?

On the street, the usual alternative to silence is obscenity: yelling back, "Fuck you, you asshole!" is hostile, aggressive, and most definitely unladylike. In the workplace, the parallel responses are obscenities, curses, insults, threats, name-calling, and sometimes the ultimate self-defeating action: "Fuck you, I quit!" (The use of the word "fuck" to express anger and hostility is an interesting social practice in itself; language is sometimes a very revealing mirror of the power dynamics in a culture.)

In some U.S. white ethnic and African-American working-class communities, at least a few women do teach their daughters to respond to harassment with aggressive countermeasures, to get right back up in the harasser's face, insult his masculinity, and be as crude and abusive as they can. The image of the strong, tough, working-class woman who can sling it right back at the men is not just a class-based cultural stereotype—it reflects an alternative survival strategy.

However, like appeasement, it is not a particularly safe or successful survival strategy. Responding to aggression with aggression tends to escalate the level of violence, and can do so very rapidly. On the street, because of the extent of male ego involved, slinging back obscenities and attacking the harasser's manhood are dangerous tactics. Group harassment can be an especially volatile situation, but even a lone harasser can erupt into violence. In the workplace, the classroom, or the neighborhood bar, assailing the harasser's masculinity is likely to provoke retaliation, as the harasser angrily ups the ante to put the woman in her place. The threat is real; harassers can and do use their economic power, role-based social power, and the potential for violence to inflict devastating damage. Retaliation may be instantaneous or delayed; many harassers will react immediately, but others may bide their time, planning their revenge and looking for opportunities to harm the woman or sabotage her work. This is not a game. It can get deadly serious, and very ugly.

Moreover, aggression is behavior that harassers understand. They may be momentarily surprised by an aggressive response from a woman, since appeasement is much more common, but they understand the dynamics of aggression very well. Since male power is at the core of sexual harassment, many harassers will not back down when their victims respond with counteraggression. For a sexually predatory harasser, this kind of response can be a confirmation of his own power; it may make the obscene phone call even more of a thrill or the "conquest" more of a challenge. Dominance harassers, on the other hand, may see the woman's angry, abusive response as an intolerable defiance of their manhood and their right to deference and punish the woman accordingly. And for strategic harassers, this response can be a sign that they are getting to the woman; if she reacts with counteraggression, they may use her behavior, in turn, as a justification for further harassment.

Yelling curses and obscenities can also be disempowering to the woman herself, if the harasser, the bystanders, or the woman's coworkers interpret her behavior as a sign that she is hysterical and out of control. Because control is the issue, aggression is counterproductive: a woman who is screaming obscenities and insults does not look like a person who is in control of either herself, the harasser, or the situation. The harasser may not be intimidated; he knows that she is not likely to have any real economic or social power to back up the angry threats she is yelling. Furthermore, the bystanders witnessing the interaction, who may not even know what he did to her, are likely to see *her* as the one who is out of line, an irrational woman shouting violent curses and threats.

Neither appeasement nor counteraggression works as a reliable defense against sexual harassment, and both strategies
can have substantial costs for women. Women who choose
appeasement and passively endure harassment suffer all
kinds of stress-related illnesses, from migraines to backaches
to ulcers; their job or school performance often declines
(with serious economic consequences), and both their self-
esteem and their emotional relationships with family and
friends may be seriously damaged as well. Women who use
aggression as a countermeasure, however, can find themselves in an escalating situation of physical violence on the
street, or characterized as erratic, unpredictable, and emotionally out of control in the workplace or the university.
Their colleagues begin to avoid them, they lose prime assignments and promotions, and they too can suffer both emotional and economic repercussions. All too often, managers
and supervisors will label the woman, not the harasser, as
the "problem employee."

When appeasement and counteraggression fail to deter the
harasser, women are often forced to take more drastic action:
quitting a job, withdrawing from a class, or even moving to a
different neighborhood or a new city to escape the harasser.
Such avoidance has severe costs for women (for example,
unemployment). Furthermore, it does nothing to prevent the
harasser from continuing his abusive behavior. One woman
may have escaped him—at a high cost to herself—but his
next chosen victim is likely to be the very next woman he
hires to fill the job, the next woman in his class, or the unsuspecting new female tenant who moves into that vacant apartment in his building.

Like appeasement, avoidance is a passive strategy. It
works in the limited sense of enabling the woman to flee
from her harasser, but not in any larger, meaningful sense.
Personally, she still feels victimized and defeated, and bears
all the costs of the harasser's actions; and on a societal level,
avoidance tactics in no way reduce her abuser's ability to
harass or eliminate the rewards that he receives from engaging in this behavior. In fact, in cases of strategic, territorial

harassment, avoidance is a victory for the harasser—he has succeeded in forcing his victim out.

EFFECTIVE RESPONSES TO HARASSMENT

The responses that work best are active strategies—techniques that enable women to regain control of the interaction, disrupt the harasser's agenda, minimize the possibility of escalation or retaliation, and create a social context that changes the underlying risk and reward structure for the harasser. The tactics that work are neither passive nor aggressive; they are principled, assertive, strong, and self-respecting. From the actual experiences of thousands of women, faced with thousands of harassers in all kinds of situations, it is clear that there are three strong defense strategies that do work well: (1) using straightforward, direct-action confrontation tactics, (2) building a support network to deal with a persistent harasser or a hostile environment, and when possible, (3) filing official charges with the university, the school board, the church board, the union, the corporate EEO office, or the appropriate government agency.

All three defense strategies can be used in combination, but of these three, direct confrontation is the one that is most likely to be successful in breaking off the harasser's behavior at the outset. A well-executed confrontation leaves the woman in control, reduces the risk of retaliation, and provides a powerful incentive for the harasser to rethink his behavior. A good confrontation can make legal action unnecessary by cutting off the harassment immediately; it also strengthens the woman's case if she subsequently decides to file a complaint or take the harasser to court. And a successful confrontation helps to restructure the social context in which the harasser operates; it undermines the legitimacy of harassment as a social practice and sets up a new social norm, a new cultural standard for acceptable male behavior.

Confrontation works against all types of sexual harassment. It is a new form of behavior for many women—not an angry, emotional outburst, and not part of the standard repertoire of passive and accommodating female behavior in a sexist culture. The first time a woman steps outside the predictable patterns of response to harassment, confronts a harasser with a powerful statement, and leaves her abuser staggering with astonishment can be exhilarating. It is also a new phenomenon for the harassers—this is a victim response that violates their most basic expectations about the power dynamics of sexual harassment. This is not the deference and intimidation effect they expect, nor is it angry aggression, which they would understand. Confrontation is something very different, and it leaves them in the dust. For most harassers, the only reaction to a strong, clear confrontation is stunned silence. Some harassers are so taken aback that they apologize on the spot.

LEARNING TO CONFRONT

Confrontation involves some very specific actions, using behavioral guidelines from the assertiveness and self-defense skills of the women's movement and the nonviolent social change tactics of the civil rights movement. A woman who confronts is not lashing out in anger; she is applying a very powerful, nonviolent social control technique to flip the power dynamics in the interaction. Confrontation takes self-control, preparation, forethought, and practice.

As a self-defense technique, confrontation is part of a range of well-developed responses to interpersonal aggression: *assertiveness, confrontation, self-defense,* and *martial arts.* The spectrum of effective action does *not* include passivity, aggression, or evasive, manipulative passive-aggressive behavior.

Assertiveness involves defining the problem clearly, stating one's feelings openly, and negotiating a change in behavior or some other mutually satisfactory solution to the problem at hand. For example, if Sally's roommate Ellen constantly leaves dirty dishes in the sink, there are many possible ways to address the situation. Sally could say nothing, suffer in silence, and just do the dishes herself every time (passivity—often accompanied by stress, resentment, long conspicuous sighs, and other signs of martyrdom). On the other hand, Sally could get angry and throw the dishes at Ellen when she walks in the door (aggression). Or Sally could be devious and indirect, put up with it for a while, and then pile all the dirty dishes on Ellen's bed one day, when she finally gets fed up (passive-aggressive behavior). These are *not* useful problem-solving techniques. In an assertive response, Sally would name the behavior directly ("Ellen, you keep leaving your dirty dishes in the sink"), state her feelings ("It upsets me to come home to a mess in the kitchen"), and then open the negotiations by suggesting a solution ("I want you to wash your dishes before they stack up"). The actual solution could take many forms—Ellen might start washing her dishes, Sally and Ellen might agree to take turns doing the dishes, or Sally might do all the dishes in exchange for Ellen doing all the laundry. Both Sally's and Ellen's feelings matter. The behavior has to change in one way or another, but there is a lot of room for compromise. It is not the particular solution but the format of this approach —naming the problem, stating one's feelings, and stating the change one wants—that makes this procedure work as an assertiveness technique.

Note that assertiveness does not involve any name-calling, any threats, or any rude, nasty comments about character and motives. Sally does not call Ellen a slob, or assume that she leaves all those dirty dishes on purpose just to drive her roommate nuts. The discussion centers strictly on the concrete behavior, the participants' own feelings, and the solution: when you do A, I feel B, and I want you to do C from now on. Assertiveness techniques target the behavior, not the person.

Assertiveness is a firm, clear response to a problem. It is milder than confrontation, and can sometimes be an appropriate initial response to casual, low-key male-dominance harassment when the harasser is a boss, coworker, neighbor, classmate, or other acquaintance with whom the woman has regular contact. If for some reason the woman wishes to give

the harasser the benefit of the doubt at first, she can begin
with this level of response. If the harasser truly did not realize that his behavior was offensive, an assertive approach is
often enough to take care of the problem.

However, if he fails to change his behavior, it is perfectly
fair to conclude that he now knows he is committing harassment. Assertiveness is very clear, and at that point, no
woman should be under the illusion that the harasser doesn't
really mean it. She should move up to the next step—confrontation—immediately.

Confrontation is a stronger action—a forceful response to
deliberate power abuse and unwelcome behavior of many
kinds, including sexual harassment. Like assertiveness, a
good confrontation involves naming the behavior very
clearly: targeting the harasser's specific actions, but not the
harasser personally. Like assertiveness, confrontation involves no threats, no name-calling, no insulting statements
about the harasser's character or manhood. But in a confrontation, one does not talk about one's feelings, or discuss the
harasser's feelings; the only issue is his behavior. What he
did is intolerable, and he is responsible for it. The woman
does not suggest, request, or negotiate possible solutions,
but *demands* that the offensive behavior stop. "Keep your
hands off my breasts" is not a statement that is open to negotiation. There is no other possible option here, no room for
compromise. The only acceptable solution is for the harasser
to revise his behavior immediately.

While a woman using assertiveness may take the time to
discuss the harasser's motives with him and explain her own
feelings when she is on the receiving end of his behavior, a
woman who confronts a harasser goes directly to the abusive
behavior, labels it publicly as harassment, and holds the man
accountable for it.

When the harasser is a stranger, there is no possible excuse
for his behavior. A strong, immediate confrontation is war-
ranted whether he is engaging in predatory harassment,
dominance harassment, or some form of strategic, territorial
harassment. When the harasser is an acquaintance, the

woman has a choice between the assertive and the confrontational approaches. Assertiveness works in some circumstances; confrontation works in almost every case. A man who runs his hands down a secretary's body, propositions his coworkers, or mutters, "Hey, baby, I sure would like a piece of that," to a woman on the street deserves to be confronted on the spot.

Sexual harassment includes physical actions as well as verbal abuse—unwanted touching, rubbing, leaning over or standing too close, and many other types of physical intrusion. Physical harassment requires a measured, reciprocal, physical confrontation response, in addition to a verbal confrontation. Decisively remove the harasser's hand from your body, for example, as you make your statement.

In dangerous, life-threatening situations, full-scale self-defense is justified. *Self-defense* involves not only verbal skills but the ability to block an assailant's blows, break free from choke holds and other attacks, and disable the attacker, if need be, in order to prevent him from harming his victim. If the harasser presents a threat of sexual assault or other serious physical injury, self-defense—strong, immediate verbal and physical resistance—is usually the safest strategy. There is no reason for women to be macho; it is perfectly sensible to avoid encounters with men who are physically threatening and to run from danger as soon as you can break free. A strong verbal confrontation can help to stop an assault at the outset, but no woman should stick around and deliver a lecture just to make a point, if she is in physical danger of further attack.

Martial arts training is one step beyond self-defense. All of the martial arts—judo, karate, aikido, and the many other variations now available—provide excellent training in mental discipline and physical defense techniques. Women studying martial arts focus on the athletic, artistic, and spiritual aspects, as well as the self-defense skills involved. While it is possible to learn a good basic set of physical self-defense tactics in just a few classes, martial arts proficiency usually takes several years.

With respect to sexual harassment, the circumstances of the incident determine the level of response: assertiveness, confrontation, or self-defense. All women (and girls!) should learn how to use these three basic levels of response, simply to equip themselves to handle the kinds of situations they are likely to encounter. Martial arts training can be very rewarding as well. One need not be young, slim, strong, or able-bodied to learn a basic set of skills. In fact, many women with disabilities are not only assertive, but successful at confrontation, self-defense, and martial arts.

SELF-DEFENSE GUIDELINES

Confrontation is a self-defense strategy, and learning to confront means knowing some basic self-defense guidelines. No book can replace the experience of learning and practicing in a class, but here are the fundamentals that every woman should know:

1. *Be alert.* Pay attention to your surroundings, indoors and out, notice the body language of people around you, and anticipate situations before they develop into full-blown threats. On the job or at school, notice how male supervisors, colleagues, clients, professors, and other acquaintances talk about women and how they treat the other women employees, customers, or students. Notice how you feel when different men are around. Wherever you are, talk to the women around you about the kinds of situations they have already encountered. Break the silence that protects harassers—find out who has harassed the women around you, and let those women know what you yourself have experienced. On the street, pay attention! Notice street harassers before they are right up against you. No harasser should ever again be able to abuse women anonymously in the neighborhood or work his way down the corridor at school or on the job, harassing woman after woman without being held accountable.

2. *Trust your instincts.* If a situation feels wrong in some way, get ready to confront, fight back, or get yourself out of there. Many women report feeling uneasy before an attack

occurred (particularly in cases of rape-testing, date rape, and acquaintance rape), but discounted their feelings and failed to take action because the assailant "hadn't really done anything specific" yet. Don't wait to react—your gut reaction is usually right. Trust your intuition when you don't feel safe.[1] With harassers, this means trusting your own reactions to the harasser's behavior; if a comment or action feels invasive, your discomfort is real. Take it seriously.

3. *Be prepared.* Be mentally and physically ready to take action. Know what your options are and think about what you would do *before* an incident happens. Because both harassment and sexual assault are so common in our society, being ready to act is a bit like the defensive driving skills taught in driver's education classes. A driver's ed teacher might ask her students, "What would you do if a child or a dog ran out in the road right now?" Women should practice the same kind of mental rehearsal. What would you do if you were accosted in this parking lot, or on that street corner, or on the job? Who is around at this time of day, to hear you if you yelled? In which direction would you run to get help? What escape route would you use to get out of your own house or worksite, if an intruder broke in?

One very simple preparation exercise, used in self-defense classes, is designed to ensure that women know their surroundings well: on a sunny afternoon, with a friend, take a "walking tour" of the areas where you live, work, or shop. Find out where that alley goes, what's behind the supermarket or the gas station, what's hidden behind that hedge or fence—check out any place that could be the site of an assault. Just knowing which way an alley opens out to the street, and which way is a dead end, can be critically important in an attack. That kind of knowledge has saved women's lives.

That was the case in one recent attempted rape, for a woman in Washington. She lived on a block with a T-shaped alley running through it. One corner at the top of the "T" was a dead end: nothing but some Dumpsters and the back of an office building that was deserted on evenings and weekends. The other side of the "T" connected to a side street and came out next to a convenience store that was open until midnight. Late one evening, less than two months after she had done her "walking tour" of the neighborhood, she was grabbed and dragged into the alley. She broke loose from her assailant in the middle of the alley, but could not get back out, past him. She turned and ran further up the alley. He came after her. At the top of the alley, she had to make a choice: left or right. She knew that the left side was a dead end, and took off to the right, heading for the convenience store and yelling all the way. As she burst into the store, the clerk was already on the telephone, dialing the police. The rapist ran back into the alley, and the police caught him a few minutes later, based on her identification.

4. *Rely on your own resources.* Your own intelligence and your verbal and physical skills are your first line of defense against harassment or assault. You may often be on your own. Don't assume that you will be rescued; know what you can do, yourself. Practice your confrontation skills and your basic self-defense tactics with your women friends. Know the vulnerable points on an assailant's body—eyes, nose, throat, solar plexus, elbow and finger joints, kidneys, knees, shins, arches (go after any of these while he is protecting his groin). Know your weapons—your brain, voice, hands, elbows, knees, feet, keys, umbrella, pens, and so forth. (What do you have within arm's reach right now, that could be used as a defense?) One woman, cornered in a laundry room in the basement of her apartment building, actually managed to knock out her attacker by slamming a shoulder-high dryer door into his face, and women have fought off knife attacks by using a sturdy wicker laundry basket as a shield. Take a basic self-defense class and share your skills with the women and children around you.

5. *Be loud and clear if you do need help.* If you are attacked, don't leave room for anyone to misinterpret what's happening. In a sexual assault, this means yelling "no!" at the assailant, and shouting "kiya!" or other karate yells to startle him and get your own adrenaline going. Then let ev-

eryone around know exactly what's going on. Yelling, "This is an attack, call the police," not only makes the situation clear, but is often effective in getting help—people tend to do what they are told, and they are more likely to actually call the police if you tell them to do so. Keep on shouting— it may take a minute or two for people to figure out where you are. In cases of sexual harassment, a good confrontation works much the same way: You don't usually need to shout, but your confrontation statement, loud and clear, lets everyone around know exactly what the harasser has done, and can help to generate support from potential allies—even strangers on the street.

6. *Intervene to help others who are under attack.* There are many ways to intervene from a safe distance, without endangering yourself. Armed rapists have fled when, in response to a victim's shouts, a neighbor has done something as simple as turning on the porch lights and yelling out the window, "I heard you! I've called the police!" In cases of harassment, intervening may mean standing up for another woman on the street, at school, or on the job, helping a child to confront harassment on the playground, working with a woman to plan an individual or group confrontation, talking to the harasser yourself, or asking his male friends to confront him about his behavior. Intervening can also mean standing up for men or women who are experiencing racial, anti-Semitic, or homophobic harassment—sexual harassment is not the only kind of power abuse.

Here's a success story from Maria A. describing a street harassment incident where simple intervention worked beautifully:

TEAMWORK

In June 1991, I was working in Washington, D.C. I was walking on a busy street downtown, on my way home from work. There were dozens of people on the sidewalk. Suddenly, about 100 feet in front of me, I heard a woman shout,

"Keep your hands off me!" I saw who it was—I didn't know her, but she was standing there with her hands on her hips, looking very pissed at a young man in a suit. The man stopped when she said that, and he began to argue with her, calling her a "bitch" and a few other things. This went on for almost a minute, as I walked toward them. She yelled, "I don't even know you! Who do you think you are, putting your hand on my butt as I was walking down the street!" I knew right then what was going on: harassment. I could tell that she would appreciate some reinforcement—he was a persistent and very obnoxious harasser—so I yelled, from about 40 feet away, in the middle of a crowd of people, "She's right! Stop harassing women! No woman will put up with it!" Well, that really floored him. He whirled around in shock, looked wildly up the street to see who was coming after him now, and then took off running in the opposite direction as if an entire feminist army was after him. I walked over to the woman, introduced myself, and we walked down the block together.

Intervention does make a difference. There's no need to jump in and tackle the assailant bodily, so don't let fear stop you from doing the right thing.

These elementary self-defense guidelines apply in all kinds of situations. They are part of any general community strategy for reducing the risk of sexual assault and harassment. But many women never learn any form of self-defense, either because they believe the sexist, defeating cultural myth that there is nothing they can do (movies and television programs constantly portray women as helpless victims of violence), or because they want desperately to believe that it couldn't happen to them (denial is a very common, and very risky, response to the real threat of sexist aggression). It's not that women are unable to take action; most will fight ferociously if their children are in danger, for example. But when it comes to defending themselves from harassment, verbally or physically, many women just cave in. Women need to overcome some important cultural conditioning in order to stand up for themselves: to re-examine their reluctance to make a scene in public, for example, or their paralyzing fear of male violence—or even their fear of unleashing their own anger.

There are many cultural and psychological factors that limit women's willingness and ability to stand up to harassers. The desire to avoid conflict is certainly understandable, especially when coupled with women's fear of male violence and retaliation. *Of course, the harasser has already created the conflict, with his intrusive actions. Passive behavior doesn't produce harmony; it just prevents the victim from handling the conflict successfully.*

Many women worry that expressing their anger or disapproval will lead to economic reprisals or just make the situation worse; they also dread the possibility of being labeled and dismissed as a "bitch" if they object to sexist comments and abusive actions. *The situation is very likely to get worse if the woman does nothing; a matter-of-fact, direct confrontation is often the best way to prevent men from labeling a woman as a "bitch" or inflicting other kinds of social or economic retaliation.*

Some women fear that if they say anything at all to a harasser, the entire weight of male violence will come crashing down on them. *It won't, especially if they use a confrontation technique, rather than counteraggression; there is plenty of real violence out there, but confrontation works to defuse it. Building an exaggerated fear of enormous, looming violence is one way that sexist men keep women in line.*

And some women believe—wrongly—that being submissive will reduce their risk of harassment and violence. *There is no evidence that being submissive reduces the likelihood of male aggression. On the contrary, men who have a bullying, macho personality, a taste for sexual coercion, or a need for dominance are likely to go after passive women precisely because they can torment them with little risk of consequences. Rapists look for unresisting victims; batterers will find some excuse to swing their fists, for any reason*

*or no reason, no matter how compliant the woman is; mo-
lesters have no qualms about exploiting vulnerable children; and most harassers will target any woman they think
they can intimidate.*

Some women also silence themselves for fear that their
own anger will get out of control. Handling the anger pro-
ductively seems impossible, so they keep the lid on tight
and suffer abuse with painful, self-destructive endurance,
turning their anger inward, into psychological depression.
Women's training in politeness takes a toll as well; women
are not only reluctant to be rude to harassers, but have even
been known to apologize to the men who invade their space
or verbally abuse them. One of the saddest limiting factors is
itself the result of previous victimization: some women have
grown up with no belief that what is done to them *matters*,
or have been so beaten down by sexism or male violence
that they no longer presume they have any right to defend
themselves. The most fundamental step in self-defense is
the belief that you, yourself, really are worth defending.

SIX BASIC SELF-DEFENSE GUIDELINES

1. Be alert. Notice the people around you and anticipate
   situations before they develop into full-scale threats.
2. Trust your instincts. If a situation feels wrong, don't wait
   to react—take your feelings seriously and get to a safe
   place.
3. Be prepared. Know your neighborhood, think about your
   options, and be mentally and physically ready to take
   action.
4. Rely on your own resources. Practice your skills. Know
   what you can do yourself.
5. Be loud and clear if you do need help. Yell and keep
   yelling: "No! Kiya! This is an attack! Call the cops!"
6. Intervene to help others who are under attack. Let the
   victim know you heard her or him. Yell from a safe distance; turn on lights; call the police.

No human being can passively absorb abuse without being damaged by the experience. Psychologists have documented the deep trauma inflicted by experiences of helplessness.[2] It is the feeling of helplessness, rather than the abuse itself, that often leaves the deepest scars on women who have been harassed. The stress-related illnesses produced by harassment are only the most obvious symptoms of damage; the psychological injuries can be much more profound. Repeated experiences of victimization, verbal and physical abuse, and enforced subordination can destroy any human being.

It is essential for women to learn how to stand up for themselves.

CONFRONTATION

As a self-defense technique, confrontation is extremely effective—it usually stops harassers in their tracks. Like any new technique one might learn, confrontation may seem a bit challenging at first. The basic components of confrontation are not difficult to understand and learn, but they do take some practice. Because of women's cultural conditioning, this is not behavior that comes naturally. But despite that cultural conditioning, almost any woman can learn to confront.

Like any other specific self-defense tactic, confrontation can be analyzed, step by step. It is a carefully structured technique, with nine distinct elements.

1. *Name the behavior clearly.* That means understanding what sexual harassment is and labeling it accurately when it happens. Cursing and name-calling don't work; naming the *behavior* does. The more explicitly the woman describes the harasser's behavior, the more completely she will surprise and disempower him. (Here are some examples: "Stop making comments about women's bodies." "Stop making sucking noises at women who walk by." "Stop leering." "Stop calling women 'honey' and 'babe.'" "Stop staring at my chest when you talk to me." "Get your hand off my leg." "Stop pestering women for dates when you know they're not

interested." "Stop commenting on my appearance, I'm here to do a job.") Whatever he's just done, say it, and be specific. The behavior cannot stand up to public visibility; doing the unexpected—naming it out loud and labeling it as harassment—is the first step in taking the initiative away from the harasser.

2. *Hold the harasser accountable for his actions.* Individual men decide to harass, and they need to be held publicly and personally responsible for their behavior. Don't make excuses for the harasser; don't pretend he didn't mean it; don't pretend it was a joke; don't act as if it didn't really happen—it did, and he did it. Don't laugh or smile, and don't let him off the hook. Take charge of the interaction. Let him know that his behavior is out of line, that it is harassment, and that you will not ignore it or let it slide.

Because of the fragility of their egos, harassers often crumble immediately when forced to own up to their behavior in public, in a calm, powerful confrontation. For example, one young woman, walking past a construction site, got a dose of "Legs, legs, legs—spread those legs for me, baby!" from three hardhats standing on the sidewalk. She wheeled around, marched back up to them, looked them in the eye, and demanded to know which one of them had said that. Their macho stance collapsed; each of them frantically pointed to the others and said, "He did, he did, he did." She proceeded to confront all three, and told them that each of them was responsible for the others' behavior; she was holding them *all* accountable and if it ever happened again, she'd report them all to the president of the construction company. They didn't say another word.

An individual, verbal confrontation is one way to hold a man accountable. With a persistent harasser, a woman should also keep a detailed log of the time, date, place, and exact behavior involved: what he said or did, what she said or did, witnesses, and other details. Women can also enforce accountability in many other ways: by demanding identification from the harasser (useful on the street and with delivery men who harass women); letting other women and men know exactly what he did (finding allies and using the pressure of public condemnation against the harasser); holding a group confrontation; writing the harasser a letter that details his behavior (keep a copy for yourself); reporting the harasser to his employers, his peers, his wife or parents; otherwise documenting and publicizing his behavior; or filing an official complaint or a lawsuit. A verbal confrontation, in itself, removes the protection of invisibility from the harasser, and there are many additional ways to make his behavior public.

One creative woman in Great Britain, a professional photographer, began carrying a small camera with her wherever she went. Every time she was harassed, she'd wheel around, take the harasser's picture, and jot down exactly what he'd just said. She later put together an art exhibit in a downtown gallery: large photographs of the faces of dozens of harassers, complete with captions below, quoting the men in detail. It was a powerful public statement and an ingenious accountability mechanism.

Margie Boule, a journalist in Portland, Oregon, who writes for *The Oregonian*, used her newspaper column to hold her harassers accountable. She described some of the incidents she'd experienced as a television reporter—and then, when the station threatened to sue her, she used her column again to expose their threats. The public response was enormous.

Not every woman can deal with her harassers in such a devastating public way—describing their behavior in a newspaper column for a million readers or displaying their words and faces in a public art gallery. But every woman can find some way to make the harasser's behavior visible. The possibilities are endless—the important thing is to do it. Privacy protects harassers. Visibility undermines them.

3. *Make honest, direct statements.* Don't be deferential, don't say "please" or "I'm sorry" or "excuse me," and don't surround your statement with disarming and disempowering verbal fluff and padding. Be serious, straightforward, and blunt.

It is extraordinarily difficult for many women to make a

direct, critical statement to an adult male. Without even being aware of it, women tend to use indirect language and soften their statements to men. Women may tell a child to stop misbehaving without thinking twice about it, but they get tripped up by the power dynamics of male dominance and some deep, cultural, gender-based language patterns when they need to say the same thing to a harasser.[3]

A crisp, clear message to a harasser like, "Stop leaning over me every time you come near my desk; you are two inches from me, and I want you to move back right now," tends to come out as something entirely different: "I'm sorry, Mr. Jones, excuse me, I'm sure you don't really mean anything by it, but, you know, well, I guess it makes me a little bit uncomfortable sometimes, the way you do that, you know what I mean? Do what? Oh, well, nothing really, just sometimes you kind of stand a little close, I know it doesn't really matter but—well, this is kind of embarrassing, I probably shouldn't even have mentioned it, I don't want you to be offended, I'm sure you didn't even realize, but you know, I just get a little uncomfortable, do you think maybe you could please not lean over me quite so much?" And the woman may have had to really get her nerve up, just to say that!

Even when women feel violated and angry, they tend to apply indirect, self-denigrating language in speaking to adult males. They use questions rather than statements, make excuses for the offensive behavior, and add all kinds of padding. This is "victim language"—it does not prevent the harasser from getting angry, but it certainly does disempower the woman who is speaking. These language patterns make the woman seem submissive and uncertain, and make the message she is trying to convey seem tentative, confused, and unimportant.

Practice the kind of direct statements you want to be able to make to a hypothetical harasser in the street or workplace. Practice with a friend, or use a tape recorder if you have one. Listen to how many times "um" and "well" and "please" and "excuse me" come out, how many questions and excuses the statement contains. (Most women are amazed to find out how much "victim language" creeps into their statements.) Practice until you can easily say something like, "Move back, you're standing too close," clearly and decisively, *with no modifiers whatsoever.* Try out similar direct statements, for other types of harassment. If you are currently being harassed, write down the statement you want to make to the harasser, and practice saying just that, straight out, in plain language, until you feel comfortable doing it.

Threatening to report the harasser may be believable; threatening that you or someone else will knock the tar out of him usually is not. A woman who tells a harasser that her boyfriend will beat him up or makes other empty threats of violence or retaliation loses credibility; she weakens her position.

Making honest, direct statements also means simply sticking to the truth. There is no reason to understate, overstate, or omit any part of the truth. What is the harasser doing, the actual behavior that angers or intimidates you? What kind of harassment is it? Say it out loud to him and name it as sexual harassment. The calm, blunt honesty of a confrontation is part of the forcefulness of the technique.

4. *Demand that the harassment stop.* Cultural norms and male-female power dynamics make it difficult for women to name the harasser's behavior in plain, direct language. For the same reasons, it is often hard for women to tell harassers, point-blank, to stop. The victim may get as far as saying, "You continually proposition me and the other women here, that's harassment, I don't like it"—but then fail to order the harasser to STOP IT. Confrontation involves an unequivocal demand: the behavior stops, right now—no ifs, ands, or buts. Language like, "Stop it," "Back off right now," and "Don't you ever do that to me or any woman ever again," is effective. It works precisely because it is so unusual for women to say anything of the sort to harassers (or to men in any context). Directed at an adult male, a sharp command is a shock.

5. *Make it clear that all women have the right to be free from sexual harassment.* Women who confront can

strengthen their statements considerably by speaking up on behalf of women everywhere. Objecting to sexual harassment is a matter of principle. This is not just your personal whim, and it's not just that you're a "touchy babe." Women know the difference between a compliment and harassment, and so do most harassers. Including a strong statement on behalf of *all* women—"That's harassment; I don't like it, no woman likes it!"—is not only honest, but adds to the power of the confrontation. It underscores the woman's seriousness, reinforces her message, and helps her to confront the harasser safely and effectively. This part of the confrontation statement weakens the harasser's confidence in his right to harass. The interaction is no longer isolated; the woman is explicitly holding him accountable to a broader, societal standard and emphasizing the principle at stake.

6. *Stick to your own agenda.* Most harassers, when confronted, are so surprised that they back off immediately. Some, however, are very slick—polished, well-practiced, and verbally aggressive. Such harassers are relatively rare, but be ready for men who come back at you with all kinds of bizarre diversionary tactics. Don't get caught up in his denials, his excuses, his attempts to redefine his actions, his personal attacks on you ("Whatsa matter, you on the rag? You're crazy! You're ugly. You're a bitch. Why are you getting so emotional?"), or his efforts to change the subject. No matter what kind of smokescreen he tries to use, it's what he did that counts—stick to your point. Don't answer his comments or questions, and don't let him draw you into a debate about the meaning of what he did. Harassers rarely have any genuine interest in a philosophical discussion about the nature of human behavior; they are simply using these tactics to try to regain control of the interaction. Don't fall for any of it. Interrupt the harasser in midsentence and say what *you* want to say.

A "broken record" tactic can be very effective with slick harassers. No matter what he says, firmly repeat the same statement: "You did [state the behavior]. That's harassment, I don't like it, no woman should put up with that. Stop harassing women." Repetition is powerful. It keeps you from getting tangled in the harasser's agenda, and makes you seem unshakable and decisively in control.

A few harassers also engage in face-saving behavior when confronted. It is remarkable (and very instructive) to watch the way a supposed compliment like "Hey, beautiful, nice tits!" can turn into "Hey, you ugly cunt!" when the woman does not pretend to ignore it or like it. Interrupt his face-saving remarks and continue with your confrontation statement about his intrusive, sexist behavior. He wouldn't feel the need to save face if he didn't feel he'd already lost it. If you are halfway down the hall or down the block when he makes his comment, and you have the time, it is often very satisfying to go right back and confront him all over again. It's the last thing he expects—and the second round really leaves him stunned.

7. *Reinforce your statements with strong, self-respecting body language.* Body language is powerful. Whenever there is a conflict between someone's words and her body language, the person she is addressing is very likely to believe the body language and discount the verbal message altogether.

Many women are unconscious experts in deferential body language. Women smile when they are tense or frightened, women look at the ground when they walk down the street, women avoid looking men in the eye, and women try to make themselves seem small, harmless, and invisible when they feel threatened.

No one needs a doctorate in sociology to analyze the body language of power. Watch the way people move on any public street, and you can tell who owns the turf. On K Street, in downtown Washington, D.C., the wealthy white male lawyers, stockbrokers, and high-powered lobbyists usually march down the sidewalk at a healthy clip, expecting all lesser creatures to scurry out of their way. Most women and working-class men avoid eye contact, step aside and make way without even thinking about it. Occasionally, however, a well-dressed, wealthy African-American man will challenge the assumptions of the dominant white male elite by refusing to step out of the way. It's quite a sight to see—the white males in their expensive suits will all but walk into the man, stopping only inches from him with a very surprised look on their faces. They simply presume that they will receive the physical, public deference to which they feel entitled, and they are always taken aback when someone refuses to comply.

And think about the way women usually sit in public places: with their knees close together, their shoulders hunched, their purse or packages bundled on their lap, and their arms crossed in front of their chest or tucked in close by their sides. This is clearly a defensive posture. They are taking up as little space as possible, in an environment that is often hostile to women. Now picture the way men often sit, in the park or at the bus stop, for example: legs spread, head up, shoulders back, briefcase and packages beside them, and their arms spread over the back of the bench, taking up three spaces. This is ownership body language—safe, confident, and in control.

Women do not need to play dominance games on the street or at the bus stop, just for the sake of dominance, but they do need to use their body language consciously to fortify the message they want to deliver when they confront harassers. The body language of a confronter is similar to that used by any disciplined nonviolent activist who challenges the status quo in order to stop an injustice: strong, dignified, neither passive nor aggressive, neither victimized not victimizing.

Take your action seriously and look serious when you do it. In a confrontation, stand as if you owned the street or the hallway, keep your head up and your shoulders back, and look the harasser in the eye: physically hold your ground. Take your hands out of your pockets; put them on your hips, or point at the harasser like a stern schoolteacher. You may feel tense, but don't let tension make you smile or shrink away from that strong, commanding posture. Timid, submissive body language will undermine your message, and perhaps even demolish it; the harasser will cue in on your body language, instead of your words, if your stance is inconsistent with your confrontation language. If you are sitting down, stand up to confront, if possible. If the harasser is coming toward you, don't retreat; he'll just keep coming. Take a half-step toward him, plant yourself, and look him in the eye (a full step is aggressive; a half-step forward says, "I'm here, I'm going to deal with you, and I'm not running away").

Like the verbal aspects of confrontation, this kind of body language is unusual coming from a woman. Many men find it unnerving, although they may not be conscious enough of the power dynamics of body language to know exactly what it is that is making them so uneasy. Unless there is a risk of physical assault, continue to hold your ground until *you* end the encounter. If the harasser's behavior is invasive, don't give up your space—tell *him* to move away.

Analyze your body language with a friend or in front of a mirror. Practice various stances, in combination with various facial expressions and tones of voice. What's your strongest combination?

8. *Respond at the appropriate level.* Fine-tuning takes practice, but it is not usually necessary to blast the guy in order to be successful. Verbal harassment gets a strong, clear verbal response: name the behavior, object on behalf of yourself and all women, and demand that it stop. Physical harassment requires a dual response: if the harasser is touching you, for example, physically reach over and move his hand or knee away from your body, at the same time you say, "That's harassment. Keep your hands off me. I don't like it— no woman likes it. Don't you ever do that again."

From the mildest assertive response, to the most forceful, vehement confrontation, women have a wide range of effective direct-action tactics. Your tone of voice, body language, and confrontation message can all be varied to suit the situation. You can be perfectly matter-of-fact in telling a harasser to quit it; a simple, blunt statement, delivered in a calm, normal voice, can be devastating. You can also imitate an army drill sergeant ordering a recruit to "back off" on the double. Vary the volume and tone as needed.

Women who have been putting up with harassment for ten

or twenty years may verbally dynamite the first few harassers they finally confront, just from the accumulated anger of swallowing all that abuse over the years. That's all right—the harasser will survive, and fine-tuning will come with practice.

With a common street harasser or relatively harmless drunk on a park bench, a quick, firm statement is usually adequate: "Stop harassing women! I don't like it, no woman likes it." But with a strategic harasser who is trying to force a woman out of the workplace, one who is sexually coercive, or one who may be engaging in rape-testing, it is appropriate to use a very strong level of confrontation response: naming the behavior in explicit detail, speaking in a loud, commanding voice, using very forceful body language to back up the point, pulling in bystanders as witnesses and allies, perhaps even organizing a group confrontation. Faced with severe harassment, a woman should use every tool she can, from body language to tone of voice, and every accountability method at her disposal, from maximum public visibility at the time she confronts the harasser up to and including a group confrontation and a lawsuit, to intensify the force of her opposition to his behavior.

In no case, however, does a confrontation step over the line into aggression. Counteraggression (using insults, threats, and verbal abuse, throwing a punch, spitting on a harasser) is counterproductive. Verbal violence is dangerous, and there is no need to use physical violence unless there is an actual physical attack that requires self-defense. Most harassers stop far short of sexual assault; they are engaging in male-dominance, sexual-pastime, or strategic harassment, and a principled confrontation usually leaves them baffled and defeated. The clearer the confrontation, the more completely the woman can seize control of the interaction, with no violence whatsoever.

9. *End the confrontation on your own terms.* Women do not need to stand around and have lengthy conversations with harassers. A typical confrontation on the street lasts a minute or two, at most, and many are much shorter; even

with a persistent harasser on the job or at school, it may still take no more than three minutes. Once you've confronted the harasser and delivered your statement, wrap it up. Good closing lines include any of the following: "Stop harassing women. None of us will tolerate that kind of behavior." "Don't ever do that to a woman again." "Your behavior was offensive and obnoxious. Get out of here and stop harassing women." "If you ever do that again, to any woman, I will report you."

If he tries to argue with you or engage in diversionary tactics, steamroll right over him—interrupt him and say, loudly, "You heard me. I said stop harassing women! There's nothing more for you to say. Now back off and don't do it again!" Then leave, or tell him to leave. Cut off the interaction on *your* terms. When you've finished, take pride in your successful action—tell your friends, family, classmates, and coworkers about the incident.

CONFRONTATION

1. Do the unexpected: Name the behavior. Whatever he's just done, say it, and be specific.
2. Hold the harasser accountable for his actions. Don't make excuses for him; don't pretend it didn't really happen. Take charge of the encounter and let people know what he did. Privacy protects harassers, but visibility undermines them.
3. Make honest, direct statements. Speak the truth (no threats, no insults, no obscenities, no appeasing verbal fluff and padding). Be serious, straightforward, and blunt.
4. Demand that the harassment stop.
5. Make it clear that *all* women have the right to be free from sexual harassment. Objecting to harassment is a matter of principle.
6. Stick to your own agenda. Don't respond to the harasser's excuses or diversionary tactics. *His* behavior is the issue. Say what *you* have to say, and repeat it if he persists.

7. Reinforce your statements with strong, self-respecting body language: eye contact, head up, shoulders back, a strong, serious stance. Don't smile. Timid, submissive body language will undermine your message.

8. Respond at the appropriate level. Fine-tuning takes practice, but it's not usually necessary to blast the harasser. Use a combined verbal and physical response to physical harassment.

9. End the interaction on your own terms, with a strong closing statement: "You heard me. Stop harassing women."

These nine basic steps are extraordinarily powerful when fully developed and put into action. Practice these confrontation tactics with your women friends. Pick out half a dozen actual situations in which one of you has been harassed, and role-play various kinds of assertive and confrontational responses to the harasser. See how precisely you can name what he did. How would you hold him accountable, if the same incident happened today? Can you strip away the appeasing verbal padding in your statements? What can you do to make your body language stronger? Practice!

Here are a few sample scenarios:

- You are waiting at the bus stop at 5:00 P.M., with two other women, when a man walks up, looks you up and down, and says, "Hey, baby, I sure would like a piece of that ass—how much?"

- You walk into your high-school math class a little early and find that someone has scrawled "Maryanne sucks cock," along with her phone number, on the blackboard. There are four young men in the room, all of them classmates. They are snickering, waiting to see your reaction. (A) You are Maryanne's best friend. (B) You are Maryanne.

- You are alone in the photocopy room at work, running off ten copies of a large report. The room is the size of a closet. Tom, the office sexist, sees you and steps into the room. He has no papers to photocopy. He begins to pressure you for a date, although you've told him twice before that you are not interested. He puts his hand first on your shoulder, then on the small of your back. You tell him no, but Tom continues to talk and move into your space. Your friends, Alice and Kathy, work just down the hall, within earshot.

- You are walking down a busy street at lunchtime, heading for a job interview. A well-dressed, older white man mutters under his breath as he passes you, "Oooh, baby, sure would like to suck those tits."

- You are a young Hispanic woman, with a brand new law degree, working in your first job in a large law firm. You are doing quite well in the firm, but Casey, one of the young male lawyers hired at the same time you were, is not; the senior partners are not impressed with his work. One day, as you are trying to finish an important assignment on a tight deadline, Casey strolls over to your desk and says, "Hey, Sylvia, is it true that Hispanic women are really hot in bed?"

- As you are coming home from work, you notice a man standing on your front porch. He is holding a clipboard and wearing a gray uniform with a patch that says "Metro Gas Company" but there is no gas company truck in sight. There is no one home in the house. Your neighbor, Mrs. Jones, is out in her yard next door, watering her petunias. You stop at the foot of your front steps and ask the man what he's doing there. He says there's a report of a gas leak, and you must let him in to check it immediately. You ask him who reported the leak; he says he doesn't know, the gas company doesn't tell its inspectors that information. He insists that you let him in at once. He is very persuasive. (Hint: Do not go up on the porch, within reach of him. Make him come down off the porch and leave the area.)

- You are in the library stacks, in the back section of the university library, trying to find some information you need to finish your term paper. There is no one else nearby. You pull out one book, then another. Five minutes later, you look up to find a man standing at the end of the row, grinning at you and masturbating.

- You are standing in the back of a crowded elevator. There is a middle-aged man immediately behind you, a woman on your right, almost pressed against you because the elevator is so full, and three teenage girls in front of you. You suddenly feel a hand running up your rib cage, cupping your left breast, then dropping away.

- You are the new electrician, and the only woman, on a building maintenance crew. The men on your crew are okay; some of them even seem fairly helpful. You were unemployed for several months and you really need this job. You tell the foreman you'd like to work all the overtime you can, to make some extra money and pay off the bills that have piled up. Several of the men on your crew would like to work some overtime, too, and have also asked for it, but the foreman always gives the overtime assignments to the same two guys, his buddies. After two weeks on the job, the foreman calls you aside and says, "Honey, if you really want that overtime, there's one way you can get it."

- Anne is a young African-American woman, working in a bookstore near the university. She takes pride in knowing the store's stock and being helpful to the students and professors who come in. She notices that one professor never speaks to her when he comes in; he always makes a point of asking the other (white) clerk to check on his book orders and ring up his purchases. Anne realizes that she is going to take one of his classes next semester, so the next time he comes in, asking for an obscure philosophy book, she jumps right in and says, "I'll be glad to get that for you—I know just where it is." He turns to her and says, "What would a nigger bitch know about philosophy? When I want cheap sex and babies, I'll ask you." (A) You are Anne. (B) You are the white clerk, female. (C) You are the white clerk, male.

- Susan is fourteen years old, out on a picnic with the church youth group. There are thirty kids playing softball and racing around, two church women, and several of Susan's friends. In the middle of the afternoon, the new minister asks Susan to take a walk with him. He says that he wants to talk with her privately about the "difficulties of adolescence." A quarter of a mile into the woods, he pins her against a tree and tells her that ministers have special needs, and God sometimes brings very special people into our lives, and she is one of them. He quotes scripture as he unbuttons her blouse. (A) You are Susan. (B) You are Susan's best friend, Maggie, back at the picnic; you realize that she and the minister have been gone for a while.

- You are a young attorney with a promising future in a downtown government office. There are several other male and female attorneys in the division, as well as two female administrative assistants. Your boss is a conservative, sexist male who seems threatened by competent, professional women. One day he calls you into his office and begins describing a pornographic film he saw the night before. You are embarrassed and find an excuse to leave the room quickly. A week later, in the midst of another one-on-one meeting in his office, he interrupts a work-related conversation to say that there is a pubic hair on his Coke can.

What would you do in each case? How would you name the harasser's behavior and confront him? Who are your potential allies? When and where would you confront?

After you've practiced a variety of scenarios, then, with a friend by your side, try it for real. Make it easy on yourself —plan a simple confrontation statement like, "Stop making comments about women's bodies. That's harassment—I don't like it, no woman likes it. Stop harassing women!" Confront a lone harasser first, in daylight, in some location where you feel relatively safe (a shopping mall, perhaps, or a busy downtown street corner). Work your way up to confronting multiple harassers, in less secure settings, as you develop confidence and skill. If you need to confront an employer, landlord, minister, neighbor, or coworker, ask your friends to help your script out what you want to say, to practice the confrontation with you, and perhaps even to accompany you when you confront the harasser.

In addition to individual confrontations, women should consider using the confrontation survey approach with common dominance harassers, and group confrontations in cases of severe or sustained harassment. Both are described below.

THE CONFRONTATION SURVEY

One of the most remarkable—and effective—forms of confrontation is the survey technique. This ingenious tactic, originated by Cheryl Benard and Edit Schlaffer in Germany, has two advantages: it often works exceptionally well, and it can produce some useful information for women who are conducting research on sexual harassment. As Benard and Schlaffer note, "If you want to transform a lewdly smirking man into a politely confused one within a matter of seconds, you need only pull a mimeographed questionnaire out of your bag and inform him that he is part of a research project."[4]

Use the confrontation survey from Appendix A of this book and carry a couple of copies with you. The next time you're harassed, whip out the survey and begin asking the harasser the questions: What's his name? What exactly did he say or do? (Tell him you want to get it right and want to get his exact words down—he will be mortified.) Don't smile. Look very serious and purposeful. Then continue: How old was he the first time he said or did this to a woman? How many times a day or week does he do this? What does he get out of this behavior? Does he harass in groups, or by himself, or both? Does he say or do other things to harass women, and if so, what? Why does he do it? How does it make him feel? How does he think it makes women and girls feel?

As you continue down the list, you are in full control of the interaction. His invasive, aggressive macho posturing will deflate like a pricked balloon. Ask the survey questions in a rapid-fire manner. This is a confrontation, after all, and you do not want to give the harasser any opportunity to regain the upper hand in the encounter. Most harassers will be dumbfounded and meekly answer the questions, but if a harasser starts to give you a wise-ass answer or begins to go off on a long, rambling dissertation, cut him off with a curt "yes, I see" and break in immediately with the next question. If he stalls or refuses to answer a question, don't worry about it; just jump right to the next one. (If you want to, you can always go back to the ones you skipped after you've run through the list.) Keep your tone crisp and decisive; you're the one in charge here, and you're not about to put up with any nonsense from him. Harassers' answers can be truthful and insightful or incredibly stupid and self-serving—in both cases, they are very revealing. Don't get drawn into an argument about anything he says; just jot down even his stupidest answer. When you're finished, wrap up the confrontation with the firm, businesslike statement noted at the end of the survey and go on your way, leaving a very disconcerted harasser behind you.

The survey technique is a powerful way to name the behavior and hold a harasser accountable. Women who have used it report that a large percentage of men will actually give their names and answer most of the questions—the survey flips the power dynamics beautifully. It is slightly more time-consuming than a standard confrontation, but should not take more than three to five minutes.

GROUP CONFRONTATIONS

It can be very easy for a pair of women to confront harassers. The fact that there are two of you, both condemning the harasser's behavior as a matter of principle, makes your confrontation exceptionally effective. Be sure that your friends know how to confront and know that you expect them to back you up; there's nothing more undermining than to have one woman trying to confront with a strong, decisive statement, while the other acts intimidated and tries to pull her away. If your friend is the one the harasser is targeting, step right in, stand right beside her, and reinforce her statements with your own.

With persistent or high-ranking harassers, it may take an organized group confrontation to stop the behavior. This is particularly true in dealing with predatory harassers (for example, a minister or landlord who is extorting sexual services) and in cases of strategic harassment, where male workers are systematically trying to force women off the shop floor or out of the office. Group confrontations are very powerful, but they take careful planning and teamwork.

To organize a group confrontation, gather five to ten supportive women at a safe site and hold some brainstorming sessions. An all-female confrontation team is most effective. The harasser's victims should decide what they want to say to him and script it out. Other women may also want to say a few well-chosen words. The team should research the harasser's schedule and investigate possible sites for the confrontation. Where is he likely to be at any given time of day? Which of those places would be a good site to confront him?

Working together, the harassment victims and their support team then develop the scenario for the action and choose a time and place for the confrontation that gives the confronters at least some control over the physical site. A public setting can be useful, to hold the harasser accountable in a highly visible way, but a private office where the confronters have complete control of the room can also work well. For maximum effect, a group of women might confront a minister in front of his deacons or his congregation, a corporate vice-president at his country club, or a factory foreman in the company lunchroom. For a less public action, the group might confront the harasser in his own office, home, or shop. Do not forewarn the harasser; the element of surprise is key.

The action plan should include a gathering place for the group on the day, plans for transportation, entry and exit from the confrontation site, the order in which the victims will speak, and a debriefing site where the confronters can meet to celebrate and evaluate the action afterward. Depending on the complexity of the plan, the women who will carry out the confrontation may want to hold some practice sessions or rehearsals in private before going ahead with the action. The speakers should practice their body language and memorize what they want to say. If a victim does not want to speak for herself, she can designate someone to speak in her place.

On the day of the confrontation, at least one woman should have a camera to record the confrontation, one should carry a tape recorder, and one should bring a notebook to describe what is said and done. As the victims and other speakers file into the confrontation site and face the harasser, the support team stands beside them in a strong, silent phalanx. (The support team may also surround the harasser or block his exit for the few minutes the confrontation lasts.)

The powerful visual impact of a group of stern, unsmiling women standing shoulder to shoulder underscores the impact of the speakers' verbal confrontations. The message is clear and simple: women know what the harasser is doing, they will not tolerate it, and they will be watching him. Do not let the harasser speak (except to apologize). If he tries to regain control, interrupt him and tell him that he's said and done more than enough; it's his turn to listen now. If he persists, tell him there are no excuses for his behavior; there is nothing more for him to say. If he tries to get up, order him to sit down. A well-organized, disciplined group confrontation takes the power of direct action to a higher level; it is an extraordinarily forceful, frightening experience for a habitual or coercive harasser, and an excellent way to change his behavior.

Presenting the harasser with a written list of his actions, describing incident after incident with the time, date, place, and details of what he did, can add to the impact. The group can also provide him with a specific list of the alternative, replacement behaviors the women expect from him in the future (for example: do not call any woman in this office "honey," use our names; do not touch any of us at any time, keep your hands to yourself; stop displaying pornography, keep it out of the office entirely; keep your sex life to yourself, never proposition any woman in this office again). That list gives the women considerable control over his future actions; there is no ambiguity at all, no room for him to maneuver around it.

MINIMIZING THE RISK OF RETALIATION

No single technique can guarantee a woman's safety in every situation. Male power is real, and harassers, by definition, are men who have already demonstrated that they are willing to abuse their power over women. There is always some element of risk involved when women challenge male power in any way. Confronting harassment can feel especially frightening because it goes against everything women have been taught about deferring to power.

But consider the alternatives. Tolerating harassment carries a high risk in itself. Doing nothing virtually guarantees that the harassment will continue; the harasser's actions often get increasingly ugly if he is allowed to proceed unchallenged, and he will continue harassing women as long as he can get away with it. Appeasement is ineffective (and dangerous with predatory harassers); avoidance does not solve the problem; and counteraggression can escalate the situation. In most circumstances, the risks of relying on the usual responses to harassment are far more serious than the risks of confronting.

The surest way to prevent retaliation is a group confrontation. It is so powerful and so public that it leaves the harasser almost no room to turn; too many women know what he has done and are ready to stand up to him. But even an individual confrontation usually makes retaliation unlikely. A strong, direct confrontation comes as a shock to the harasser; it upsets his most fundamental expectations about how his victims will behave. Confrontation turns the force of effective self-defense and principled nonviolent action against the harasser's power. Just being compelled to face up to his behavior is demoralizing; the shock of being confronted by a woman, the principled nature of the confrontation, and the loss of power and control he experiences all serve to heighten the impact. At the same time, confrontation does not produce the kind of angry, retaliatory reaction that counteraggression can provoke. Naming the behavior and seizing control of the interaction reduce the harasser's ability to exercise his power. The use of allies, documentation, publicity, and other forms of public accountability will further undercut his ability to retaliate.

Instead of anger, a harasser who has been confronted usually feels deflated and unsure of himself. He doesn't know quite what went wrong, but something certainly did. The woman used no insults, no attacks on his manhood; everything she said was perfectly clear and straightforward, and suddenly he finds himself way out on a very uncomfortable limb. Being confronted is an emotionally upsetting experience of failure for the harasser. Predictably enough, sexist males do not feel powerful when they fail. They feel lousy. Instead of retaliating, they tend to withdraw, lick their wounds, and reconsider their behavior.

USING THE TOOLS FOR CHANGE

Women have no choice but to deal with sexual harassment, in all its many forms. *Predatory harassers* use women sexually against their will. Sexual-pastime harassment is a unilateral invasion of women's lives that bears no resemblance to mutual, freely chosen sexual activity. Sexually coercive harassment is sexual assault—rape by abuse of economic power, rape by abuse of authority, rape by intimidation and the threat of violence—the illegitimate use of power to force an unwilling partner to comply. And rape-testing is the calculated behavior of a predator stalking his prey. *Strategic, territorial harassment* is not a matter of offending women or hurting their delicate feelings; it's a cold-blooded intimidation strategy to defend male power, disable women in male environments, and maintain male control of public and private institutions and resources. And on a broader scale, routine *male-dominance harassment* turns public and private space of all kinds into hostile male territory. Women's taxes may pay for the streets, the parks, the schools, and other community facilities, but men still effectively own them, as long as harassers feel free to invade women's daily lives with daily acts of intimidation.

The question is not *whether* women will deal with sexual harassment, but *how* they will do so. It's time for women to step past the traditional, unsuccessful strategies of appeasement, counteraggression, and avoidance. Confrontation may seem scary at first, but it works on many levels, from individual self-defense to societal change, raising the costs of sexual harassment and making harassers fail. It does not provoke the kind of escalating, angry reactions that result from counteraggression; it actually limits the harasser's ability to retaliate. Women who know how to confront have a new behavioral skill, a powerful, ethical form of nonviolent action that undercuts the harasser's abusive behavior with great force and clarity. Although it is men who are responsible for ending sexual harassment—it is a male social practice—there is no reason for women to stand by passively waiting for that to happen. Women's direct-action tactics have changed the world before, and can do it again.

PART
two

THE SUCCESS STORIES:
CONFRONTATION IN ACTION

When Children Are the Target: Kids Who Defend Themselves

There are few threats more frightening—to parents and children alike—than the possibility of a child being accosted by a molester. The statistics are horrifying: in the United States, researchers estimate that one in four girls and one in every five to seven boys are sexually abused before the age of eighteen. We tell our children to beware of strangers but we rarely prepare them to defend themselves against the risk of violation by a neighbor, grandfather, uncle, older brother, or family friend. The abuser is most often a friend or acquaintance of the family, fairly often a family member, and least often, a stranger. Sexual abuse often starts when children are as young as two or three years old, and can continue until they are teenagers, finally old enough to escape. Many runaways on the street are in fact running from sexual abuse at home. All sexual abuse is damaging, but incest is especially destructive, since it involves a profound violation of the child's trust in an adult or older sibling that she or he loves and needs.[1]

All children need to be taught some basic principles of self-defense and self-esteem. Even very young children understand the difference between a "good touch" and a "secret touch." Here are the basics that every child, male or female, should know:

1. Her body belongs to her, and anything covered by a bathing suit is her own special property. No one has the right to touch her in public or in private in any way that she does not like. If doctors or nurses need to touch her special parts, they should only do so in

front of her mom, and they have to explain to both her and her mom what they are doing.

2. She has the right to say no to *any* adult or older child, including a family member or friend, who tells her to do something that doesn't feel right; she does *not* always have to obey older people (when we teach kids to obey no matter what, without asking questions, we make them more vulnerable to abuse). If someone tells her to touch his or her special parts or do something else that seems wrong, she is right not to obey that person.

3. Yell and tell: If someone tries to make her do something that seems wrong, she should yell "NO!" as loud as possible, run to the nearest adult she knows, and tell that person what happened right away.

4. If someone touched her or made her touch him or her in a "secret" way, *it's not her fault;* adults sometimes do bad things, and she is not to blame.

5. She should always tell you or the person in charge where she is going and with whom, before she leaves the yard, school, store, church, or playground with *anyone*.

6. She should never keep a secret about something that seems wrong; you want to know, you love her, and you will help to make it right. (Some abusers will threaten to kill the child's pet or hurt a younger sibling, if she tells anyone—it is essential for you to reassure the child that telling you is safe and is exactly what you want her to do.)

There is no need to scare children with this kind of information; parents can handle this lesson in the same calm, matter-of-fact way they teach their children about the danger of crossing a busy street or the need to stay away from a hot stove. Repetition is important, and playing the "what would you do if . . ." game is a good approach. Children feel much safer if they know about a danger and know exactly what to do. Many rape crisis centers have special self-defense programs for young children; see what is available in your community.[2]

It is essential for adults to respect children's boundaries—not only to believe a child and take immediate action if she tells you about an incident, but to pay attention if she starts to fret every time Uncle George is around, suddenly doesn't want to be hugged by Grandpa, or doesn't want to go to her favorite playground anymore. Never force a child to hug, kiss, or stay with someone she is uneasy with—ask her, privately, calmly, and gently, whether something happened that made her uncomfortable.

Verbal confrontation is part of elementary self-defense. Yelling NO and running are the first step; telling people is the second. The child needs to know that she can and should tell you, even if the abuser is someone in the family. But self-defense skills alone are not enough; understanding that she has rights, that her body is her own, is just as important as knowing what to do.

One of the best ways to help children to protect themselves is to teach them to stand up for themselves in all sorts of situations, including casual harassment at home, at school, or in the neighborhood. Girls, in particular, get a lot of gender-based harassment from boys, but kids may target any child who is different. All children need to know how to confront a harasser, whether the harassment is based on gender, race, appearance, ability, or any other factor. And because sexual abuse is so common, learning how to stand up to sexist harassment is important training for self-defense, as well as self-esteem.

Here's a good example of an eight-year-old girl who successfully confronted territorial harassment by boys on the playground:

GIRLS HAVE RIGHTS, TOO

My name is Anna Marie. I am eight years old and I live in Maryland. I think girls have rights, too. This summer, I was playing on the big slide at my school. Two boys came over. They said get off the slide!

Then they said, "You're a dumb girl, get off, we want to play." I didn't say anything. I stayed on the slide. Then they called me a dumb girl again. I didn't like it.

Then they started singing a stupid yucky song, I see London, I see France, I see Annie's underpants. That made me so mad!

I called my grandmother to come over here please. She was sitting on the bench by the sandbox. She goes to marches for women's rights. She took me to a big march once in Baltimore, it was neat. She was busy and didn't hear me so I went to get her. I told her what the boys did. She said you go right back and tell those boys to stop harassing girls.

I went back and they were on the slide. My grandmother was watching me. I said real loud, "YOU STOP HARASSING GIRLS! THERE'S NOTHING FUNNY ABOUT BOYS' UNDERPANTS! THERE'S NOTHING FUNNY ABOUT GIRLS' UNDERPANTS! THAT IS A STUPID SONG! GIRLS HAVE RIGHTS, TOO!"

They looked so surprised! They got off the big slide and ran away. I was proud of myself. My grandmother was proud of me, too!

With her grandmother's backing, Anna Marie was able to name the boys' behavior—loud and clear—and reclaim her right to play on the slide. It's never too early to start teaching girls to be assertive. Surrounded by cultural messages that portray females as helpless, passive, and unimportant, girls need to be commended and rewarded regularly for speaking up to defend themselves.

Note the specifically gender-related nature of the harassment—the comments about "dumb girls" and the targeting of the girl's underwear were both intended to humiliate her *as a female.* When this kind of language is used, the interaction is not simply a matter of routine playground sparring among kids; this is an incident of gender-specific, sexist harassment. It is as inexcusable and unacceptable as a racial or an ethnic slur, and requires the same kind of strong, clear response—either from the child herself, or from the adults around.

Here's another example of sexist harassment among young children—this time, a story from a nine-year-old, about an incident when she was five:

STICKING UP FOR MYSELF

My name is Claire Sandberg-Bernard. I am nine years old now but when I was five something happened where I stuck up for myself.

One day I was crossing the monkey bars on my swing set in the back yard. (And I was wearing a dress.) Below me was a neighbor and his friend. Both boys at the moment were staring up, laughing and pointing at my underwear. I was so embarrassed that I simply let my hands go from the bars, then ran to my mother. Then my mother asked me what had happened and how I felt. I said I felt very embarrassed and mad.

My mother suggested that I should ask them, "What's so funny about underwear? Is your underwear funny?" So I went back down and did that. The boys looked at each other. They were very quiet for a long time. I think they felt embarrassed.

Like Anna Marie, Claire confronted the boys' behavior directly and simply. The boys reacted the way most adult harassers do. They loved it when she got flustered, but they were embarrassed and abashed when she confronted them. Confrontation works. Even a five-year-old can do it.

It is also interesting that Claire remembered this incident so clearly several years later. It was not trivial; although she handled the situation very well, the humiliation she felt was painful and the incident stayed with her. As noted in Chapter

2, the sexual harassment girls experience can be a formative influence in terms of their self-esteem and their sense of freedom in the world. Harassment in childhood and adolescence teaches girls about their subordinate status in a sexist society. Resisting and confronting harassment teaches girls self-respect.

When adult males are the harassers, the situation is even more dangerous, and the ability to confront it is even more important. The power imbalance between adult males and young girls is so lopsided that strong, immediate resistance is essential. Here's Catherine Ann Gilbert's story:

SEVENTH GRADE

When I was twelve years old I learned the value of street confrontation in dealing with verbal harassment, although at the time I did not understand its significance.

I was in the seventh grade. During the fall, I returned to school after a one-day absence due to illness. I was informed by one of my teachers that I had missed a quiz the previous day and that I would have to stay after school that afternoon to make it up. I asked if I could take the test during class time the following day, since staying after school meant missing the bus and waiting at least two hours for my mother to pick me up after work. Not a chance—the teacher was adamant about my taking the test after school.

When classes ended at 2:15, I went to the teacher's room to find her, but she was not there. After some searching through the halls, I located her in a home economics lab, making gingerbread houses with some other teachers. She laughingly explained that she was having such a good time that she did not want to stop to give me my exam and that I would be allowed to take it in class the next day.

Needless to say, I was furious, but unable to express my anger.

I was hesitant to walk home, since there was a new construction site on my route. Recently, when I'd walked past

*it, some of the workers had called out embarrassing things to
me. Bear in mind, I was only twelve years old—although
their comments were not obscene (more the "hey, baby!"
variety), I was humiliated by them.*

*After some deliberation, I decided to walk home after all,
since the idea of waiting around the school with nothing to
do for two hours was even worse than the comments I would
have to face.*

*As I walked on, I grew angrier and angrier at both my
teacher's inconsideration and the expected harassment
ahead. By the time I reached the construction site, I was
furious. When I heard some comments and a wolf whistle
directed at me, I stopped, turned to face them, and screamed
the most obscene thing I could think of, which was "Fuck
off, you goddamn bastards!" These were obscenities I had
heard, but had never dared to say. I was greeted with a satis-
fyingly stunned silence. Then, as I turned and resumed
walking, I heard, "Ah, leave the kid alone."*

*Although I never yelled back at another construction crew,
I was never again as frightened or embarrassed by their comments. I think that ever since that incident, I've felt that they
couldn't hurt me with their words, and anyway, I can dish it
out as well as they can.*

Verbal harassment on the street is humiliating and deeply
damaging to young girls who are just beginning to deal with
their own sexuality. At this age, many girls are excruciatingly
self-conscious about their changing status and appearance,
feel terribly constrained by the need for male approval, and
are trying to sort out all kinds of issues involving sexuality,
power, and identity. The deluge of street harassment from
older males that starts for girls in late childhood has important psychological effects. It affects girls' confidence and
sense of self, as well as their decisions about where they can
and cannot walk in public places. It is both acutely embarrassing and threatening; it conveys a hostile message about
male power and the very meaning of being female. Most

preadolescent girls try to shrink into invisibility when harassed—but Catherine used her anger to challenge her harassers. She did the unexpected by yelling the worst obscenities a twelve-year-old could imagine. It was not a standard confrontation, but it did the job. She silenced an entire group of adult men and came away with a sense of herself and her power that has stayed with her to this day.

In addition to street harassment, young girls also have to contend with direct propositions from adult males. In some cases, the harassers may be engaging in sexual-pastime harassment, getting a sexual thrill from the victim's response to the proposition. Others are very serious about sexual access, and will manipulate their young targets until they comply. The sexually coercive harasser is more likely to be an acquaintance or a family member than a stranger, which makes it even more difficult for young girls and teenagers to be assertive in standing up to this abuse.

At the same time that teenagers are trying desperately to be "more adult," they are extremely vulnerable. Most have no training in assertiveness or self-defense, are too self-conscious to resist, and dread the idea of making a scene—panicking in the face of a sexual threat is definitely not cool.

So far, unfortunately, very few teenage girls have the sort of verbal self-defense skills or the presence of mind that Debra Riggin Waugh demonstrated in the following success story:

WHEN I WAS SIXTEEN I WAS COOL

When I was sixteen I was cool. I didn't take no shit off nobody.

Before I turned sixteen, I'm in G. C. Murphy's one day—that's the five-and-dime—and I'm looking at something (all right, it's mascara). And this white man who's old enough to be my father (and maybe then some) comes up to me and says, "I've got the money if you've got the time." Well, I'm only fifteen, so I walk away real quick, kind of scared.

A few months later, I'm turning the rack of birthday cards in Drug Mart, and the same man comes up to me and says the same thing. But now I'm sixteen, so I look the man straight in the eye and I say real loud, "Look, buddy, if you don't leave me alone, I'm going to call the manager." Well, this guy practically gets down on his knees and begs me to please stop yelling. He promises he'll never bother me again. That might have been my first real taste of power and I really liked the way it made me feel.

At fifteen, the best Debra could manage was fear and avoidance; at sixteen, she was able to confront. By standing her ground and threatening to report the man, she flipped the power dynamics instantly. Her strong body language, direct statement, and loud tone of voice emphasized her seriousness and her control of the situation. Instead of acting fearful and intimidated, she took charge of the incident and put *him* at risk.

Like many harassers, this man had an established pattern of behavior, in this case soliciting teenage girls for sex. Debra was certainly not his only victim. Reporting predators like this one is always a good idea; they tend to be repeat offenders and will keep exploiting children and teenagers until they are caught.

Reporting a harasser is exactly what Debra did later that same year:

HITCHHIKING AT SIXTEEN

Another time, when I was sixteen, I was hitchhiking to my boyfriend's house—I used to do that all the time back then —and this white man in a suit and tie picks me up in a brown station wagon. I'm fooling around with my seat belt because it won't stop buzzing, and he says, "How do you like that?" I look over to see what he's talking about, and he's whipped out his lizard—you know, he's got his dick in his hand. I don't even flinch—I'm cool, remember—I just look at him like I'm so bored, and I say, "You can let me out here," like I've seen bigger. He looks embarrassed and says, "Just thought I'd ask," and lets me out.

I keep repeating his license plate and walk up the street to the Iverson Mall. I go into the record store that sometimes gives me free posters, and I borrow a pen and write down "MF 1707, Maryland" on the back of my hand. Then I go back out into the mall and find a rent-a-cop, which is what we call the security guards. I ask him, hypothetically, if I'm hitchhiking and someone picks me up and exposes himself, can I get him in trouble or will I get in trouble for hitchhiking. The cop says, sure, I can report him and I won't get in trouble.

He takes me to the security office, which is the size of a closet, next to the mall entrance by the barbershop. Sergeant Doyle's in there. He's the head rent-a-cop, who always throws me and my friends out of the mall for loitering and bumming spare change. My best friend Rose and I always call him "Ossifer Obie," after the pig in "Alice's Restaurant."

So Doyle calls the real pigs. One comes, and he's actually pretty nice, but back then pigs were pigs—we didn't distinguish between nice ones and mean ones. The real cop says I should press charges because this guy's done this before, which I later find out may not be true, but just something he says to get me to do it. Ossifer Obie says to me, "That'll teach you to hitchhike," and the real cop says to him, "Oh, you know you did it, too, when you were her age," and Doyle can't say anything about that because he knows the real cop's right, but it's hard to imagine Ossifer Obie ever being sixteen and not wearing a blue uniform.

A couple days later, I get a call from the Bureau of Criminal Investigation. My sister takes me over there to give a written statement and pick the man out of six Polaroid photos, and I do.

Meanwhile, my sister's sitting out in the little lobby, and some other woman sitting there asks my sister if she works there, just making conversation, I guess. My sister answers *no, that she drove her sister down to report an "indecent exposure." The woman says that it was her husband—which means that this guy is down there at the same time I am, but in another room. My sister feels bad for her and asks, "Why did he do it?" The woman says she doesn't know, she had no idea that he had this problem.*

Anyway, I take the man to court, and he gets two years' probation and loses his job, because he was in a company car at the time he decided to pull out his wiener. He moved to another state to find a new job.

Debra held this man accountable on many levels: in front of the law, his employer, and his wife. Despite her mistrust of "Ossifer Obie" and the cops, she took action. By reporting the harasser, she raised the costs of his behavior to the point where real penalties applied. The social penalties were probably the strongest—while a court hearing and probation are awkward and embarrassing for the harasser, the real deterrent that Debra's action created was the loss of his job and the fact that his wife now knew what he had done.

Some adult males go beyond street harassment, beyond a proposition, beyond indecent exposure. Here's a success story from a young girl who used confrontation to stop an attempted rape:

THE MAN IN THE BLUE CAR

My name is Stephanie, and this happened when I was walking home from church one Sunday, two years ago, when I was ten years old. My brothers had run ahead, but I was in a dress and my Sunday shoes, so I couldn't run and keep up with them. That was okay with me. It was a nice sunny day and I didn't mind being by myself.

I was about halfway home, just walking along on the grass near the school, about three blocks from home, when I noticed a car go by real slow. The man turned the corner and then a minute later came up the block again. He was an old white man and the car was blue. There was nobody else around.

He slowed way down and said, "Hi there, honey, you sure look pretty." I said thank you. Then he said, "Want a ride?" I said no and kept on walking. Then he said, "Hey, come on, I won't hurt you, let's go for a ride." I said no thank you. He said, "It's okay, I know your mom, it'll be okay with her." I started to think that he was really creepy. I'd never seen him before. I didn't want to make him mad. I kept walking and he kept driving real slow beside me.

Then he said, "Hey, honey, I bet you've got a real pretty little pussy. I sure would like to play with your pussy. Come on, get in the car."

I knew what that meant. I started to get scared. He said, "Ever had anybody play with your pussy? It feels real good, I bet you'll like it. Come on, get in."

I looked at him real good and then I backed up to look at the license plate on his car. He stopped the car just ahead of me and started to get out. Then I started to run. I slipped and fell down, because of my shoes. I was really scared. He was only ten feet away from me.

I started yelling. I yelled as loud as I could, "Get away from me, you creep! I know what you want! Leave me alone! I'm going to tell everybody about you! You are a creepy old man and I know the license plate on your car!" I got up, put my fists up, and kept screaming at him, "You leave girls alone! You get away from me!"

He stopped right where he was, got back in the car, and drove away.

When I got home, my mom gave me a hard time about the grass stains on my good dress. I told her I'd fallen down but I didn't say why. I never told her what happened until this year, when I decided to tell my success story for this book. My mom got very upset when I finally told her what happened. But I think I did a good job of taking care of myself. And I always wear shoes I can run in now. So does my mom!

Stephanie's response was a superb example of the power of verbal confrontation. She yelled strong, direct accusations that were specific enough—and loud enough—to let anyone around know exactly what this man was doing. She backed that up with physical action, scrambling to her feet as fast as she could and getting her fists up, but it was her verbal self-defense, not her physical size or strength, that convinced this rapist to take off and succeeded in stopping the assault.

Her actions were nothing short of heroic. But like many children who are threatened or molested, Stephanie did not want her mother to know. Just like adults, children are often reluctant to tell other people about frightening experiences; being a near-victim, even one who successfully fought off an attack, is not something most children will talk about easily. All too often, children blame themselves for whatever happened, feel confused, and confide in no one. Even though Stephanie knew that she had done the right thing and was proud of herself, she kept silent because she didn't want to upset her mother.

All adults—not just mothers—need to encourage children to talk about anything that frightens or confuses them. Praising children when they show courage and intelligence in dealing with tough situations is one way to do that. Sharing one's own problem-solving skills in difficult situations is another, teaching by example that scary things can be discussed and handled. Your own everyday reactions to problems are important: when adults panic or get angry, children stop telling them anything that might upset them; when adults stay calm, listen, and talk about what to do, children develop confidence and coping skills.

In this case, Stephanie learned that she could defend herself by actually doing it in a crisis. She has since taken a self-defense class, where she was publicly applauded for her quick thinking in the incident and her courage in confronting the man. She learned some additional physical self-defense techniques to match her verbal defenses—and everyone in the class, including Stephanie's mother, learned to wear shoes that they can run in.

Confrontation is a survival skill. Start talking to your daughter *now* about how to confront. Whether she is five or fifteen, she is likely to be harassed, simply because she lives in a sexist society in which harassment of all kinds is still common. She is vulnerable not only to humiliating male-dominance and territorial harassment from the boys at school and in the neighborhood, but also to sexually predatory harassment from the adult males around her—acquaintances, family members, and strangers. She is at risk, but she does not have to be helpless or passive. Teach her to confront— and then practice these techniques with her.

When the Job Becomes a Misery: Confronting Harassers at Work

Women in almost every occupation report at least some harassment on the job, even in professions like nursing, teaching, or library science, where the workforce is predominantly female. The likelihood of harassment depends not just on the percentage of women in the profession, but on the context in which they work. According to the U.S. Department of Labor, 98.8 percent of secretaries are female, for example, but they are among the employees most often harassed.

Women in some traditionally female fields may be shocked when harassment happens. For any woman, however, a good understanding of harassment and confrontation can be useful in sizing up the situation and reacting quickly and accurately. As noted in Chapter 4, ignoring the harasser's behavior or making excuses for him, in an effort to make the situation seem less threatening, are common reactions, but useless as defense tactics. Harassment is abuse of power— it's important for women to evaluate what's really going on and respond with appropriate *action*. The context, type, and level of harassment determine the level of response that women will need to use, from basic assertiveness, through various degrees of confrontation, to self-defense or formal administrative procedures and lawsuits.

Sometimes, the harassers themselves are not even adults. Here's a success story from Mrs. G., a teacher who used a very basic form of low-key confrontation:

HARASSERS BEGIN YOUNG

I'm a schoolteacher. In the middle 1970s, I transferred to a primary school where it was very much the fashion for the young boys to mutter, growl, and sometimes even yell "bitch!" at the teachers. I tried dealing with this behavior as my fellow teachers did—with punishment, painful ignoring, and trips to the principal's office for the offenders. None of these actions made a dent at all in the frequency of this obnoxious behavior.

I decided another approach was necessary.

I took to getting down to eye level with my seven-year-old students whenever they did this and asking them very seriously if they knew what a bitch was. They, of course, did not. I then explained to them very carefully that a bitch was a female dog, and that since I didn't walk on four feet or bark they needed to use my name, or call me just "teacher" if they liked.

It took a couple of months for the word to get around the school that calling Mrs. G. a bitch just got you a quiet little talk about "lady dogs." It certainly was effective—took all the starch right out of that little power game they were playing.

This was a case of young boys enjoying an early taste of dominance harassment, testing their newly emerging male power, and relishing the ability to upset adult women. It was gender-specific behavior, in terms of both the language used ("bitch") and the targets for abuse (adult women, not men). Mrs. G. recognized the dynamics of the behavior. Her confrontation style was honest, direct, and appropriate—naming the behavior clearly, taking it seriously, using her body language and tone of voice to emphasize her control of the interaction, and holding the boys accountable for what they said. She cut right through the power-testing and neatly removed the psychological rewards of the behavior.

Some adult male harassers specifically go after young women on their first job. They will work respectfully with a thirty-five-year-old secretary, for example, but repeatedly manipulate the eighteen-year-old summer interns or the youngest workers on the assembly line. For predatory harassers, young women workers are all too often easy victims. They are trying so hard to be adult in a workplace context—to not overreact with what feels like childish, unsophisticated embarrassment and discomfort—that a sexually coercive harasser often has little trouble maneuvering them into situations in which they have no control or recourse. Feelings of helplessness and shame are a very common psychological reaction to victimization of all kinds (sexual or otherwise), and those feelings keep many young women from reporting abuse. Instead of recognizing that they were conned by a slick pro, they blame themselves. That reaction is so common that harassers have come to count on it. And the more outrageous the harasser's behavior is, the more certain many young women are that they will not be believed if they do come forward. For some men, the sexual exploitation of young women workers is a lifelong practice, one of the benefits they take for granted as a prerogative of their maleness and their status as senior employees.

But some young women, despite the harasser's status at work and his skill in manipulating the situation, are able to analyze the situation clearly. And sometimes, despite their own acute embarrassment, they figure out what to do about it. Here's one woman who did:

THE TEXTILE FACTORY

My name is Judith and I'm Native American. I was raised in the mountains of Pennsylvania. After graduating from high school in 1962, I went to work at the local sportswear factory. My mother, sister, and two aunts also worked there.

Anyone who has ever worked in one of these shops can

attest to their mind-numbing, back-breaking nature. The noise, fiber dust, stale air, and nonstop pressure to work faster on the assembly line are intense.

During the two years I worked there, I saw more than one woman suffer a breakdown. Their screams would make the hair on the back of your neck stand up. Other women would carry them out, and barely a minute of work would be lost. I guess we felt if we slowed down, the spirits would catch us next. It was a hellish place for a naive teenager.

For the most part, positions of authority were held by men. As a teenager, I was ill-equipped to deal with adult men. Back then there was no term for sexual harassment. Somehow, the word "fresh" was meant to cover all forms of it.

When one of the line supervisors started hitting on me, I was shocked. He was old enough to be my father. I worried that even with all the noise of the sewing machines, the other women would hear what he said, and they would think that I had done something to deserve his disrespect.

Among many things, he told me that "virgins are a pain in the ass, and I would be doing you a favor by busting your cherry." I thought if I worked even harder he would see that I was someone worthy of respect. Needless to say, he just grew bolder.

There was a union at our workplace, and I decided to file a grievance. I had always heard wonderful things about unions, and it didn't hurt that my aunts were both officers in this one.

When I told them what had been going on, they were outraged. I was too embarrassed to tell them everything, but they knew and trusted me as a person who would not lie to elders.

They went to management with what I had told them, and all hell broke loose! They would not back down.

An earlier sit-down strike in the factory, over another issue, had been very successful, so I'm sure the shop knew that my aunts would not hesitate calling a strike over so just a cause.

The man who harassed me tried to say I was lying. When that didn't work, he tried to convince me that I had misun-

*derstood him. With my aunts' strength backing me, I refused
to let him intimidate me. It was very scary.*

*The memory of that incident has always stayed with me. It
taught me to be on the lookout to help other women. Young
or old, we all need others to believe us and stand with us.*

*Years later I ran into the harasser. He was parking cars. No
lie. His mouth cost him a good-paying career.*

Judith had the courage to speak up, and her aunts were
magnificent allies. The harasser's response was a typical, dis-
honest counterattack: first accusing his victim of lying, then
trying to redefine his actions and blame Judith for "misun-
derstanding." Sarah Burns of the Clinical Law Program at
New York University, an expert on harassment cases, has
commented, "People will go to extremes to discredit their
accusers. . . . I have not handled a single case of sexual harassment where someone has not alleged that the woman
was deluded, was having sexual fantasies, [or] was a lesbian."[1] As Judith discovered, visibility and allies are the
keys to overcoming the harasser's counterattack.

Making the abuser's behavior *visible*—by confronting it
directly, finding witnesses who saw or overheard him, telling allies, documenting or tape-recording the incidents, or
finding other victims who have had similar experiences—
is critically important. Judith's aunts did everything but
stand up on the shop floor and read a list of the harasser's
words and actions out loud, in public—and they clearly
would have done that, if that was what it took to hold him
accountable. They were the kind of allies every victim
wishes she had—the kind of allies all women should be, for
one another.

Some women are much more isolated. Especially in the
years before sex discrimination was illegal, before sexual harassment was even defined, it was very difficult for women
to talk about what they were experiencing, even with their
friends and family. But at least a few gutsy women were
finding ways to take some public action. Evelyn was one of
them—here's her success story:

THE MALE CLUB

I'm a tall, slim, African-American woman. I take pride in both my professional appearance and my professional competence. In 1967, I was working in the downtown office of a large technical firm. Occasionally, my supervisor would meet with an officer of the company, Mr. B. Whenever their meetings were in our office suite, Mr. B. would invariably compliment me on some piece of clothing I was wearing on that particular day.

I simply viewed him as someone who liked giving compliments and never gave it a second thought until one day he stopped me in the hallway.

Mr. B. proceeded to tell me about a "male club" in which he was a member, and said that they were always looking for attractive females to "attend" the meetings. As he continued, it became very obvious that to "attend" really meant to parade in front of the male club members with no other clothing on except boots.

I wondered if I had in some manner given him the impression that he could take such a liberty, and decided that I had not. I was stunned and greatly insulted that he would even suggest something like that, and I told him so in no uncertain terms. In response, Mr. B. just asked me if I had any friends who might be interested. I said that I did not and turned and walked away in a huff.

I really thought that this would be the end of it, but to my surprise he approached me again the next day. I told him never to mention it to me again.

To my dismay, he approached me again the following day. Again, I said the answer was no and told him never to bring it up again. At that point, I wondered whether I should report it (and if so, to whom?), or simply drop the issue. In 1967, there was nothing even remotely similar to a Board of Appeals for Harassment. Behavior like this was considered a normal part of the workplace—behavior that women just had to accept, hoping it would go away.

But then I thought, "No, why should I just dismiss it?" I told the director of personnel what had happened and asked what type of action I should pursue. She suggested that I write a memo to the file, to be inserted in his personnel folder, but added that there was not much else I could do.

Well, I wrote the memo, and also told my supervisor what Mr. B. had done. My supervisor was sympathetic but said, "Those things happen." No disciplinary action was ever taken against Mr. B., but I have always felt good about the fact that I didn't just accept his behavior. And the exposure worked. He never mentioned the "male club" again.

Women like Evelyn, who insisted on reporting sexual harassment even before there was anyone to officially report it to, laid the groundwork for the entire range of administrative and legal remedies women have today. Many of these "founding mothers," like Evelyn herself and Judith's aunts, were women of color.

Some harassers have both racist and sexist motives when they harass women of color today. While it is not clear whether that combination was operating in the case of Judith's harasser or Mr. B. and his "club," there is no question about the racial aspects of the harassment Naima Washington faced in the next story. The man she was up against considered it his right, as a white male, to demand the attention of a woman of color at any time he chose. Her determined refusal to give him that attention on command was a direct challenge to his power on both counts. Here is Naima's story:

THE WHITE ATTORNEY'S POWER GAME

I was born in Harlem, and have lived everywhere from San Francisco to Atlanta to a small rural town with a population of only a few hundred people.

Even though I realize that employers have the power to make decisions based on whether or not they feel that a potential employee "fits in," I have chosen to reject Euro-centric standards of beauty, at least for myself, and recognize that the African race has a wide range of standards of beauty. I do not find it amusing when white males begin to act in ways that indicate that they are attracted to me. I am not interested.

I have encountered many sexual harassment incidents. When I was less experienced, I was more easily victimized because I felt that I had no alternative but to obey the messages coming from a society that said that a woman should learn to be flexible, learn to take a "joke," ignore sexual remarks, not act uncomfortable if someone touches her, and ultimately adjust HER behavior in such a way that she spares the OFFENDER any embarrassment.

The "work ethic" dictates that workers do as they are told, refrain from having any opinions which are not in the best interests of their bosses, and accept subordination as part of the price one pays for the "privilege" of earning a living. Likewise, people of color are expected to believe in the un-questionable superiority of whites, women are expected to believe in the superiority of men, and poor people are expected to believe in the superiority of wealthy people.

Not long ago, I was working at a large law firm, and sometimes worked in the same area as a white attorney who often stepped out of line. I'm convinced that some harassers only want attention; they need to believe that their victims find them sexually attractive. They want to know that they have the power to get their victims to smile, blush, react, etc., whenever given the signal to do so. Going out on a date or going to bed with their victims may be the last thing on their minds; however, they need to know that they have the power to get their victims to do these things. This attorney was one of those harassers, and he felt both the need and the right to command black women's attention at any time.

I noticed that he was very chummy with his black secretary, often chatting with her about personal matters. I did not participate in these discussions and refrained from even listening to them whenever possible. The attorney could not tolerate the fact that I refused to give him my attention. He would make it a point to call out my name in the middle of these personal discussions, direct a comment or question to me, or sometimes come and stand near my desk. Many times I would look up and find him staring at me, even though he was talking to his secretary.

During one of these conversations, he told his secretary that he was expecting his brother to show up at the office for lunch. He then said that he should introduce ME to his brother. I asked him if his brother could be mistaken for someone in my family. He thought about that for a while, and finally realized that I was asking if his brother was black. It was obvious I was not interested in meeting a white male, especially one that I'd have no business dealings with.

Many other attention-getting incidents happened. I got to the point where I'd made up my mind that if he said another word to me I was going to bypass Personnel and Administration and go directly to the managing partner to file a very loud, angry complaint against him.

The showdown came one day when he told his secretary that he was going to a meeting outside of the office. He then said, intrusively, "Maybe I should take Naima out with me." There was no reason for me to attend the meeting; he was just throwing his weight around, demanding my attention one more time. I told him that he was not "man enough" to "take" me anywhere. I was ready to file a complaint, but fortunately, HE bit the bullet and left without another word.

After that, he spoke only when necessary—which was the way I wanted it, since his "conversations" were nothing more than attempts to make himself feel good at my expense.

Both men and women fail to make official complaints because they fear that they will not be believed, or worse, fear that they will be labeled as a troublemaker, be subjected to reprisals, etc. As a result, many victims feel compelled to remain victims, quit the job, or relocate, even if that is very burdensome. Those who are empowered to address grievances in the workplace are often passive, particularly if a woman complains about the behavior of a male, a person of color complains about a white person, or a "subordinate" *complains about a "superior." While a passive, listening role may be suitable for a priest or therapist, when officials respond that way to power abuse in the workplace, they only compound the problem.*

Sometimes victims have to take matters into their own hands. A woman who refuses to "go along to get along" is seen as one who challenges the authority and power of the harasser—someone who refuses to see the harasser as the superior human being he thinks he is!

Naima's analysis of the harasser's motives was right on target. However, her final tactic—insulting the harasser's manhood—could have resulted in retaliation. In this case it didn't; it worked to stop the harassment. Her decision to use counteraggression left him angry, but Naima was perfectly willing to live with the attorney's silent hostility. It was much easier to take than his constant intrusions.

As Naima points out, officials in the workplace usually have the same gender, race, and class biases one finds in the culture at large, and women often need to take matters into their own hands. Women who use confrontation tactics almost always succeed in ending the harasser's behavior. It may take some women a while to work up to a confrontation, but when they finally stand up to their abusers, they often do it exceptionally well. Here's Camille's story about a harasser with an ego the size of Mount Everest:

A LADY AND HER RESTRAINING ORDER

I'm an African-American woman, a senior office manager, a mother, and nobody's fool. I was raised in Pittsburgh, and I've been an independent, strong-willed woman all my life.

This experience of prolonged harassment happened during my tenure at my first "real job." I was working for two attorneys and very excited about the prospect of doing a good job. There was an attorney who worked in the office next to mine who made a point of stopping by on my first day and welcoming me on board. I thought nothing of this—just a friendly gesture.

However, the number of visits increased over the next few weeks and began to be accompanied by invitations to lunch and dinner. I declined in the ladylike fashion which I had been brought up to exhibit. I felt that if I just kept saying "no," eventually the invitations would stop, but they didn't. My firm, polite refusals fell on deaf ears. Eventually, whenever I saw him, I would make all sorts of detours just to avoid running into him. In the three years I worked there, his harassment never stopped.

Finally, I was offered a position with another company. I was very relieved that I would no longer have to deal with him. I never told him where I was going, or even that I was leaving the office.

To my complete disbelief, the very first week on my new job, I looked up and there he was, standing in front of my desk. He asked me why I didn't tell him that I was leaving and said that he was "very disappointed in me." This statement took me by surprise, since I had been so careful not to ever encourage him or lead him on. I had consistently said, "No, I have no interest," to every one of his overtures.

This was the last straw. I asked him to step outside the office into the corridor and I let him have it. I left my ladylike disposition "on the doorstep" and told him that if I ever saw him again I would call the police and have a restraining order sworn out against him.

I never saw or heard from him again.

The arrogance of this harasser was astounding. This was not friendly "courtship" behavior; he did not care about Camille's feelings. He assumed the right to disregard her wishes and intrude into her life for *three years*. As women today would say, "Just what part of the word *no* don't you understand?" Camille was absolutely explicit and consistent in refusing his requests for dates, went through elaborate gyrations to avoid him, and even left for another job—but only direct confrontation finally stopped him. The strong tone and content of her confrontation (including the threat of a restraining order, prohibiting him from entering her new workplace) finally made it clear to him that she was dead serious.

In fact, restraining orders are becoming a more useful option for women who are being stalked by harassers, on or off the job. A restraining order itself is only a piece of paper, issued by a court, making the man subject to arrest if he comes within a specified area (usually, the victim's home). The threat alone can sometimes be effective, as it was in Camille's case, but for many years, such orders provided only a minimal deterrent. Most states had laws limiting their application (for example, to ex-husbands, but not to harassers or unrelated men). Even when courts issued such orders (usually in cases in which there was a history of assault), police were rarely on hand to enforce them. However, as more and more women are insisting that harassment be taken seriously, some states are now beginning to use technology to give women more meaningful protection. New electronic monitoring devices, attached to the stalker, can set off an alarm at the woman's home or office and at the police station if the harasser comes within her vicinity. Check with your state legislators and your local police force; make sure that your state laws cover all kinds of serious harassers, and that local authorities understand the importance of using this technology.

Sometimes women succeed in stopping harassers on the job only by going through formal channels; they may not need a restraining order, but they do need to persevere through the official process. That process can be very difficult, especially if a woman's friends and colleagues do not understand the real meaning and severity of sexual harassment as a social problem. Support from allies is important, and lack of support can be very painful. Even in professions like teaching, where much of the workforce is female, the victim may not be able to count on support from some of her peers. But as Kathleen Wood realized in the following success story, many harassers will continue with victim after victim until someone finally stands up to them and forces them to face some real consequences.

THE ASSISTANT PRINCIPAL

"Why did you do it? It wasn't that bad, really." That's what my friend, who taught down the hall from me, said the day she found out that I'd pressed a sexual harassment charge against our assistant principal. Her words left me feeling exposed, challenged, lonely. How could I explain to someone who had to ask, why I chose to do what I had done? So maybe this story, written five years later, is the answer I wished that I could have given her then.

I'll never forget the day I met him. He was the new assistant principal we'd all been waiting for. We'd heard that he was very liberal, open-minded, fair, and extremely supportive of teachers. I was working on a committee that planned to shake up the school with a new, innovative curriculum. We knew that he'd be supportive of our work.

It was a humid, hot July day. I was sitting on the floor in my classroom with two fans on and my jam box blaring Ferron's music. When he appeared in the doorway, I knew it was him: a teddy-bear-like man, looking like the kind of guy who would give a workshop on hugging or something. I jumped up and shook his hand as I introduced myself.

He said he'd "heard about me," which threw me off balance a bit because I wasn't sure, from his tone, what he'd heard. Did he know that I was a good teacher and that the students trusted me and succeeded in my classroom? Or had he heard that I was "unconventional," known to turn cartwheels in the hall and come dressed in period costume to teach history? As he left, I felt insecure but I was hopeful that what all my friends had told me was true: "He's the strongest feminist man you'll ever meet."

By October, with the school year under way, I was beginning to notice that many of my encounters with him were awkward. I couldn't put a finger on it, so I never mentioned it to anyone. I thought that any discomfort I felt was just an adjustment period, getting to know a new authority figure.

Then one night, at dinner with a friend, I mentioned a few of the recent encounters. I told her about the time I was walking down the hall discussing my exercise workout with another friend, when he came up behind us and looked me up and down and said that he thought I looked good. It made me feel off balance again—his looking me up and down didn't match with the situation. I felt like I was in a singles' bar instead of the hallway in front of my classroom. I told my friend about how I reddened, giggled, and then got angry and ashamed, all at the same time.

That was the turning point in my awareness of what exactly was going on. She did not have to say the word she did, because I knew it too, in that moment: Icky! From that moment on, when I chose to break the silence with my closest friend and share something that was wrought with anger, shame, and confusion, there was no turning back. There was no room for rationalizing or hoping things would change. I mobilized.

The next week I was reading every book I could find on harassment and sexual abuse. I started talking with my teacher friends at school. Many of them had had similar experiences with him. All of us were getting angry. By the beginning of the spring semester, things were clear to me. I was not to blame. And I had to put an end to it.

Then he did it again.

After running across the school's soccer field from the cafeteria, trying to beat the kids back from lunch, I encountered the harasser in the hall chatting with a large group of teachers. I approached the group, slowed to a walk to catch my breath, and commented on how I was hot and out of breath. In front of everyone, he looked at me and said that if I was ready then so was he. At that very moment, not days later, I registered the comment as sexual harassment and did not giggle or respond.

By the next morning, I had decided that it was time for me to let him know that he could not do or say these things to me anymore. I had role-played a dozen times what my response would be. I wanted to expose him and let him know that it needed to stop.

The next time it happened, we were coming back from a break at a faculty and administrators' curriculum meeting. As we were all filing back into the room, the harasser poked me in the lower hip.

When I swung around to see who it was, he was there. In a very loud voice I asked him why he poked me in the hip like that. Everyone turned and looked at him. Stage one of my plan had worked. By making it public, I had transformed his action into something that embarrassed him, not me.

After the meeting I walked over to him to engage in step two of my plan: be direct and confront him. With two of my friends listening, I told him that I did not like what he did and that if he did it again I would kick him. He put his right hand up to his face in a ridiculing "tsk-tsk" gesture and in a mocking, venomous voice he said, "Oh, I just don't know what made me do it . . . you have all your witnesses, why don't you press a sexual harassment charge."

So I did.

I submitted the sexual harassment papers to my principal's office. Within hours, the principal located me, pulled me out of my night class, and whisked me off to the local McDonald's so that he could hear my story. He'd been responsible for hiring the harasser and he told me that he took this sort of complaint "very seriously."

The next months were a blur of meetings in which I had to reconstruct the history of the harassment to various school administrators. Finally the day came when I, along with two representatives from the teachers' union, had a hearing in the presence of my principal and a lawyer for the school district. I told my story for what seemed like the hundredth time.

Then the two representatives from the union started in. They reiterated how serious my claims were, how harassment created an intolerable work environment, and then added that he was inadequate as an administrator in several other areas. I was not prepared for the way they began turning my harassment experience into a lever they could use to oust this man from his job. I wanted to get this harassment into the light of day, get it substantiated, and get it into his permanent personnel file, but the representatives from the union had a separate agenda. As I listened to their complaints, which had nothing to do with sexual harassment, I stood up and announced that this meeting was not going the way I expected. I said it was canceled and would be rescheduled when I secured a lawyer. I walked out shaking, but sure it was the right thing to do.

By the next week, I had one of the best sex-crimes lawyers in the city. With her support and direction, I went back to the other teachers who had told me their stories of harassment. There were seven in all. Although none of them was willing to go through the hearings, two women did write their stories, which we used as further evidence. After some investigation, we also learned that he had been "let go" from his previous assistant principalship for sexual harassment. No one there had filed any formal charges against him; there was nothing in his permanent file.

The hearing was rescheduled for the summer, when only the secretaries and principals remained at the school. But this time I was ready. My lawyer and I went into the meeting, and I told about the repeated harassment and how it had changed my work environment. I described how I was uncomfortable in meetings with him. I explained how dealing with the whole sexual harassment procedure had taken time away from my work with the students.

The lawyer for the school district asked what I wanted done with the harasser. I said that I wanted my claim substantiated and that I wanted this information put in his permanent employment record. The meeting was over and before I knew it I was on my way home.

That should have been the end to my sleepless nights and frantic days. But it wasn't. In fact, as I look back on those days, it was the backlash that hurt more than anything. A few mornings after the hearing, when I was leaving for work, I found a note taped to my front door. It was written by a close friend whose support I had never questioned. I realized with a shock that she was not supportive at all, as I read her haunting question: *Did I know what I had done to this man's career?* And later, from another friend: *Did I not realize that I had some unresolved anger with men and was taking it out on this assistant principal?* And from a relative: *Why was I such a man-hater?*

My claim was substantiated a month later when I received a letter from the head of the district school board: "After a thorough investigation of your complaint, it has been determined that Mr. ——'s actions were inappropriate. Therefore, I can assure you that appropriate action has been taken with Mr. —— in hopes that this type of activity does not occur in the future." He was suspended for a week without pay, in July.

I received the news with relief and celebrated the long-awaited end to the chaos his behavior had created in my life. After another year of working in a school where the man who harassed me and probably several others was still conducting our faculty meetings and was rumored to be still harassing women, I decided the time was right to leave. I am now teaching at a new school, with a principal who does not harass me.

That should be the end of the story. But last summer, four years after I filed my complaint, the harasser resigned and the man who hired him, the principal, was fired. When I called my friends to get the details, they told me that he had harassed a new secretary one too many times and she had gone to her immediate supervisor about it. The supervisor asked her if she had ever heard of me and my complaint four years before. The secretary was not aware of his history of harassment, but when she heard about my success in documenting his behavior and the record in his file, she filed a charge too. Minutes into his next meeting with the school district administrators, he turned in his letter of resignation.

The next day, on the front page of the local paper, was a

story about his resignation. They mentioned that he had poked someone in the hip and made some inappropriate comments, and quoted him as saying that "some of the statements he'd made and how he interacts with women have continued to be misunderstood, although he's worked to be more sensitive to their concerns." The paper also interviewed a former staff member who didn't want her name used. She said that the charges of sexual harassment came from disgruntled staff members who were looking for ways to force him out of office. The truth is that I was not disgruntled until after I had been harassed, and I wanted to stop his behavior, not force him out of a job.

So, yes, it was that bad. My life is changed because this harasser chose to harass me. I live with the memories of that angry, lonely time.

But I survive with serenity and strength.

As Kathy found, sometimes the hardest part of dealing with harassers is overcoming women's own tendency to excuse and accept abusive conduct. Absorbing hostility and aggression for months or years takes a real toll on women's psychological and physical health, but both the victims themselves and their friends may bend over backward to try to pretend the harasser's behavior is something other than what it really is: an invasive, illegitimate use of power. It is disconcertingly easy for women to get locked into a downward spiral of denial, excusing harassment from a supervisor or coworker, month after month, as the behavior just continues to get worse. But that is finally beginning to change. Ever since Anita Hill testified before the Senate, women have had new courage and clarity when it comes to taking action, and a whole new level of support. Here's Nora Fraser's story:

THANKS, ANITA!

I have been a secretary since I was in high school. Upon graduation, I became a full-time professional secretary, and for the past two years I have worked as a division secretary at a university in Brooklyn, New York.

When I first began working for my current boss, I was handling the workload for two people, him and another male professor. By the end of the first year, two female professors were hired and added to the division. They increased the workload, but that didn't bother me at all.

As time went on, my boss's attitude about his work got a bit lax. He was paying more attention to his private affairs than to the division and university business. Since the work kept piling up, I was left to pick up the slack. Because I was familiar with official procedures as well as internal office matters, it was simple for me to pick up the pieces that needed to be taken care of. As summer rolled around and classes were finished for the semester, things got a lot lighter and I was able to relax a little.

When the summer passed and classes were back in session again, my boss returned to a smooth-running office with no complaints and everything taken care of. However, this did not sit well with him.

He started becoming agitated, constantly complaining about one thing or another. He was never satisfied with the work. It always had to be done over to meet his standards. As time went on, he also got very loud and verbally abusive. He didn't care who was around or who heard.

I gradually became immune to most of his yelling. The disorder he created totally destroyed my office system, but I never focused on how abusive his comments were until I happened to mention it to a friend. Without a second thought, she said that what my boss was doing was a form of sexual harassment. But at the time I just brushed it off and continued to take the abuse.

When the Anita Hill hearings began, I remembered what my friend had said and for the first time really took notice that what my boss was doing was in fact sexual harassment. After watching most of the hearings, all weekend, I returned to work confused and in total amazement of myself, that I had let this kind of behavior continue for more than a year and not done anything about it.

The final blow came that Monday after the Senate hearings. During the day, a professor stopped by. He made casual conversation with me while waiting for my boss to finish a phone call. Just as we were in the midst of discussing the Anita Hill hearings, my boss appeared from his office. Without any consideration, he broke into the conversation. He said, "From now on, if I say anything that you think is rude or refers to sex, write it down, document it!" And he threw a pad of paper down on my desk.

To me, this was the breaking point. As he went to lunch, I decided to call my union representative and talk with her about what had just happened, as well as previous incidents.

After I spoke with the union rep and described the incidents that had been going on for more than a year, we both decided that it was time to send in the shop steward that handled my area. As it turned out, after asking other secretaries in my area, it was not necessary to call in the steward. Several secretaries confirmed my story, and together we gathered enough information to file a complaint against him.

Once we filed the complaint, I was very scared for my position. What if I got fired because I filed a complaint against him? Would I be able to get another job? Should I continue, or just drop it and continue to take the abuse? I went with these questions to friends as well as coworkers. They were very supportive of me.

I didn't get fired. My boss got a warning from his boss, and he has been transferred to another department in the university.

As for me, I still work in the same division, and I'm happy that I decided to file a sexual harassment complaint. Even though he still works at the university, I am glad to this day that I filed charges. It has made a great difference in my life.

Nora's success story is a good example of the way women are not only changing the workplace, but breaking out of their own assumptions about what they should be expected to tolerate. Before Nora could take action to ensure that her employer would apply some real penalties for abusive behavior, she herself had to stop excusing the harasser's behavior. Anita Hill's testimony was the turning point for this young Brooklyn woman, as for so many women across the country. Nora's decision to reclaim her right to decent treatment and press charges against her boss took real bravery, but thanks to the changing cultural climate, she had immediate support from many sources—her friends, her coworkers, and her union representative. The university took prompt, positive action to reprimand and transfer the harasser, and Nora suffered no retaliation.

The support Nora received was quite a contrast to the dismaying personal criticism Kathy had experienced, only five years earlier, when she filed similar charges against her assistant principal. Not only were Nora's friends and colleagues much more supportive than Kathy's had been, but the union representatives played very different roles in these two very similar cases. While Kathy's union reps had used her complaint to further their own agenda, Nora's union rep was right there for her.

Both Nora and Kathy had to deal with harassment from their supervisors. In fact, harassment from coworkers is even more common. A "typical" workplace harasser is older than his victim and often outranks her in terms of seniority or job title, but he is more often a colleague than a direct-line supervisor.

Coworkers, like bosses, should be held accountable for their abusive treatment of women. In any work-related setting in which networking and respect are important factors in job performance, put-downs of women, sexual innuendos, or direct verbal abuse can severely damage both a woman's reputation and her ability to get the job done. Coworkers who engage in this kind of disparaging behavior need to be handled decisively. That's just what Anne did, in this success story:

A HOT TIME

I'm an attorney, and I work in government affairs. Last spring, I was in a meeting with a group of about a dozen bureaucrats, all men except for me. I was scheduled to go on an out-of-town business trip with one of the men, Jack, later that week. At the end of the meeting, just as we were wrapping up the discussion, George B. said to Jack, looking at me with a leer, "Guess you're going to have a hot time with Anne in San Francisco this weekend!" Jack started to smile, as if he agreed. A couple of the other men chuckled.

I was furious. I decided to confront, but low-key. I stood up, kept my voice level, looked George in the eye, and said in a dead-serious tone, "What did you just say?" He actually started to repeat it, and the rest of the men in the room froze. George took one look at my face—I wasn't smiling—and stopped in midsentence. I just let him hang there for about fifteen to twenty seconds; I'm sure it seemed like an hour to him. None of the other men said a word—they looked at me for the next cue. I didn't need to add, "Don't you ever make a remark like that about a woman colleague again." It was very clear. I just let the stark silence continue for a few seconds more. I finally broke the tension by turning to one of the other guys and saying, casually, "So, you're going to get that report to me next week, right?" He said yes, and the meeting broke up. George couldn't get out the door fast enough.

On the way back to the office, I talked to Jack about it— just a sentence or two about why the remark made me angry, and why it was important for him not to smile and go along with a "joke" like that. I asked him how he might respond to an equally ugly racist or anti-Semitic comment. I was assertive and straightforward about it, but I didn't need to confront him like I'd confronted George; he was embarrassed by his own behavior, and I knew he got the point.

It really worked—it stunned them. I work with these guys all the time, and not one of them has made a stupid sexist comment around me since.

Anne's body language, eye contact, and tone of voice were critical in making this confrontation work. She had to gauge her behavior carefully to walk the fine line between being too soft (ineffective) and too harsh ("strident," as self-respecting women are often labeled). She chose to use a combination of fairly strong body language—standing up, cold voice, no smile—and a low-key verbal format. Her message was clear, but rather than making a full confrontation statement, she used a softer form—a question—to challenge George's behavior in front of his peers. Then she simply held the silence to raise his discomfort level and underscore her point. It worked very well.

As noted in Chapter 4, this kind of fine-tuning takes some practice. Try out various scenarios for yourself, with combinations of stronger or softer verbal and body language. The specific technique Anne used—strong body language and a simple, chilly what-did-you-just-say question, followed by a long silence—is effective in confronting many kinds of racist, anti-Semitic, homophobic, and other bigoted remarks in an office setting.

In addition to the many possible variations on a confrontation statement per se, some women can restrain a harasser's behavior, right at the outset, just by their own wit. Kim had a real verbal knack for defending her right to do her job in peace:

THE SECURITY GUARD

I figured out a long time ago that men don't have any corner on the verbal intelligence market. And I—well, let's just say that I've learned how to create a "suboptimum environment" for male harassers.

I was working in a hospital emergency room, as the psychological evaluation intake counselor. Psychotic breaks, drug reactions, suicide attempts—I dealt with one crisis after another, on every shift. I had no time or patience for harassers who wanted my attention.

One night a security guard sauntered up to me. "Hey, Baaaaby," he said, "I don't know whaaaat you did tooooonight, but you look reeeeeeal sharp!"

I looked at him. "I am delighted to hear that," I answered in my most polite tone, "because it is really important for me to be properly ornamental for you. Why, just today, when I was getting dressed I was thinking to myself, 'What will that security guard like to see, why don't I put on this dress or this blouse, that might work.' Well, I'm glad to hear it. I want you to tell me whenever you think I look good, because, like I say, the only reason that I bother to dress nicely is so that I can be properly ornamental for your sake."

He looked confused.

Several days later, I ran into him again in the hall. "How did I do tonight?" I asked, pulling on my cheek. "Am I ornamental enough, is the makeup okay by your standards?"

I repeated this several times with him. He backed off, stopped inflicting his greetings on me, and let me get on with my job.

Kim's technique worked like a charm with this harasser. Unfortunately, many men are oblivious to sarcasm—they just don't get it. And most people are not as witty as Kim when it comes to responding on the spot. Sarcasm can come across as hostility. With serious harassment, don't try to be witty; script out a serious and straightforward confrontation statement.

Confrontation works, in part, because it surprises the harasser. And sometimes an unexpected response can turn out to be very funny, after the fact. Mrs. Johnson, an older black churchwoman, is a powerhouse in her congregation and a person with deep religious values. Now retired, she continues to convey a commanding, almost regal, sense of personal dignity and presence. Long before the current women's movement began, she developed a technique for confronting sexual harassment that left her harassers shocked. Here's Mrs. J.'s tactic:

THE ROCKET TECHNIQUE

I worked for the federal government for thirty-seven years, first as a young secretary, then as an administrative assistant and office manager. Harassment was a frequent problem, both for myself and for the younger women I supervised.

Even as a youngster, I made no secret of my religious principles. The men I worked with knew that I did not approve of cursing or crude language, and I always maintained a dignified tone and proper language myself in the office.

I refused to tolerate any abuse at any point during those thirty-seven years.

Every time I or one of my girls was harassed on the job, I would smile and motion the harasser to come over to my desk. They always came. I would remain seated and motion the man to bend down, as if I were going to whisper something sexy in his ear. They always bent down. When his face was about six inches from mine, I would turn, look him in the eye very seriously, without smiling, and say in a very direct, matter-of-fact voice—as if I had a straight razor just waiting in my desk drawer, ready to do the job—"Do you value your balls? Do you want to keep them?"

Well, they always whipped right straight up like a rocket, turned six shades of red (whether they were black or white), and marched double-time right on out of the office.

No one bothered me or my girls twice.

Bravo! The "rocket technique" worked because it was such a stunning contrast to Mrs. J.'s usual dignified and proper demeanor. Coming from her, that blunt message had a resounding impact. Mrs. J. also added, "Tell those young girls out there now that they do *not* need to put up with insulting behavior. They have a right to maintain their dignity in any situation, and no man has as much power as he thinks he has."

Deep in Hostile Territory: Confronting Harassers in Male-Dominated Jobs

More and more women are beginning to enter historically male occupations, but they are often isolated when they get there. According to the U.S. Department of Labor, in 1990 it was still true that women accounted for only 15.7 percent of all physicians, 9.7 percent of lawyers, and 7.1 percent of salespeople for big-ticket items like cars and boats, for example. Women make up almost 50 percent of the total U.S. workforce, but are grossly under-represented in many high-wage occupations—in technical fields and in the traditional blue-collar trades, as well as at the top levels of corporate management and government.

Women who do go into predominantly male occupations run an above-average risk of harassment.[1] Often, as we saw in Chapter 2, strategic harassment is used deliberately to drive women out of such professions. To some extent, however, the higher risk of harassment is simply a function of numbers. Even if there is no territorial harassment going on, the fact that there are more men around on a daily basis means that a woman in a male-dominated worksite is more likely to be harassed. An auto assembly-line worker surrounded by one hundred men is more likely to run into some dominance harassers, some sexual-pastime harassers, possibly even some rape-testing harassers on the job, than a woman who works with five men in an insurance office.

Harassment is also a function of the gender ratio in the workplace; the proportion of males and females at the worksite does affect the overall work culture. In a shop with ninety-eight men and two women, the men control the work environment and can harass at liberty if senior management condones the practice, tacitly or explicitly. In a shop with sixty men and forty women, on the other hand, the women can usually exert sufficient presence to curtail some of the machismo, even without any overt assistance from management. Like women who create harassment-free neighborhoods, women in an organization with a 40 percent female workforce often have enough social power on the job to redefine some of the norms of acceptable behavior and apply at least some social penalties for abusive behavior.

In many cases, even an eighty-twenty split seems to be sufficient to begin to shift the balance and curb the worst abuses. Based on anecdotal reports, the minimum threshold seems to be around 15 to 20 percent. If only 10 percent of the workers on a jobsite are women, they will probably have to stick together and support each other strongly in order to put a dent in the patterns of male-dominance behavior in the workplace. They may need to recruit some male allies as well, in order to protect their rights.

That basic sociological arithmetic of harassment seems to apply in any field historically dominated by men, blue-collar or white-collar, from steamfitters to stockbrokers. There is no clear evidence, for example, that working-class men in the blue-collar trades harass their women colleagues significantly more often than middle- or upper-class men employed in comparably male occupations. Remember Dr. Conley, the neurosurgeon mentioned in Chapter 1? Her harassers were wealthy, well-educated fellow surgeons, asserting their customary sexist prerogatives in an upper-class occupation that is overwhelmingly male. Men of all class backgrounds harass the women who venture into their territory.

And women in every occupation resist sexual harassment whenever possible. Women in manufacturing and blue-collar trade jobs are just as self-respecting, just as angry, and just as determined to stop sexual harassment as women who work in offices, retail stores, universities, or any other setting. Some studies indicate that blue-collar women may get slightly more physical harassment, and white-collar women more verbal harassment, but the reality is that women in any male-dominated occupation or worksite can and frequently do experience all forms of harassment.[2]

In short, stereotypes that portray working-class women as passive in the face of harassment are as misleading as stereotypes that brand working-class men as inevitable harassers. If blue-collar women face more harassment than white-collar women, it is because they are more likely to be working in jobsites that are dominated by men, not because the women are more willing to tolerate abuse.

However, because so many well-paying occupations continue to be overwhelmingly male, women who go into the trades, manufacturing jobs, technical fields, or other largely male professions need to know how to deal with harassers.

Here's a bittersweet success story from World War II, before the days of confrontation or sexual harassment laws, from Suzanne R., who just kept on trying to make her harassers treat her like a human being, and succeeded, in part, through sheer grit:

PERSISTENCE

During World War II, women went into the factories to replace men who had gone to fight. Men generally were threatened by the employment of women—threatened that women would permanently replace them and there would be no jobs for returning veterans.

I was hired as an inspector at an airplane plant in Detroit, Michigan. My job was to inspect the work of a group of eight men, each at his own individual machine.

As I went from machine to machine, the men would explain to me the use of their micrometers, their gauges, to determine if their machine was meeting the precise specifications for the airplane parts they were turning out. Since no one had trained me, I was beholden to their help.

That help came with constant sexual innuendos. For exam-

ple, many of the aircraft parts were cylinders, and the measuring gauges fit inside them like a penetrating penis. I had to stand there and check—insert, measure—one after another.

The comments felt hostile and demeaning, but this was before the women's movement—without my understanding myself as a woman, without understanding the role of women in our society, without understanding any effective way of confronting sexual harassment.

I saw my only option as not to play their game, and I tried to ignore their behavior. I talked to them about the real issues of the job—the exhaustion of standing on a concrete floor, in one place, for eight hours, the daily monotony of the work, the feel of the cold, dark, damp mornings when we met at 5:30 A.M.

The innuendos never did stop entirely, but our relationship got better—friendlier—over time. I kept trying to talk to them like human beings. We were all waiting for a new day, for better understanding and for better relationships—the day that came with the women's liberation movement.

Suzanne's determination was impressive, and poignant. Women today have a far wider range of tactics. Group confrontation is an excellent strategy for women in male environments; it is the single most powerful form of direct action. If, like Suzanne, she is the only woman in the worksite, it is perfectly appropriate to recruit women friends, off the job, to help plan and carry out the confrontation. Individual confrontations can be effective if the confronter has at last a few allies, male or female, among her coworkers. In any male-dominated environment, intervention on behalf of other women is essential and should be a routine practice by all of the women and their male allies. The turning point often comes once a few men begin to speak up and criticize the harassers' behavior. As in any case of workplace harassment, in addition to confronting their harassers, women should also keep a written log of incidents and follow up with union grievances, complaints through the company personnel office, complaints to state or local human rights agencies, and other legal remedies, as appropriate.

Jo Massey, an African-American woman in a blue-collar job in Texas, used her harassment-incident log itself as a tool for confrontation:

HELL IN TEXAS

In the summer of 1980, I quit school, packed my bags, and left Detroit for Houston, Texas, and a job. It took a while, but I eventually found the best-paying job I ever had. Until then, the summer had been most memorable for a killer heat wave. Now I remember it as the summer I really learned what growing up meant. And sexual harassment was my tutor.

"Harding Tool and Die" was one of the area's biggest oil tool manufacturers and well known among Houston's working people as the place to be. I knew I was lucky, and having limited experience with machines, I was a little scared. My fear soon became confusion, and then anger at the daily ordeal of sexual pressure. I was twenty-one, but I guess I looked younger because the men in the shop were constantly asking if I was sixteen or seventeen.

I hired in with one other woman, and there were two union sisters already there when we arrived. The production shop we were assigned to was as dangerous as the work was hard and boring. Almost immediately, the men in the shop— regardless of age or marital status—began to entertain themselves by constantly pursuing my friend and me for "dates." After dealing with the minor but recurrent irritation of wolf whistles and "hey, babys" on our way through the open plant to start our shift, we were not in the mood to "flirt" with our coworkers when we got to the shop.

At one point, after I emphatically refused to go out with him, the tool bin operator spread a rumor that the reason my friend and I were not dating our coworkers was that we were dating each other.

We said we were not looking for a man, but for a decent wage, good benefits, and a chance to learn a marketable skill. Just like they were. Had it occurred to them that we had applied to a jobsite, not a dating service?

In reality, although their actions ranged from mildly irritating to downright unpleasant, these men really weren't the threat, because they had as little power as we did. They were amateurs. The bosses had sexual harassment down to a fine art. They had the power, and in every way they set the tone on the shop floor for the "journeyman harassers," our co-workers.

The dayshift boss was "Vernon." No lie, he really did look like Boss Hog. Not the comic version—but the kind your black self don't want to meet on the highway, alone, at night. Deputy Sheriff in Charge of Disappearin' Folks.

The dirty games he played were notorious, pitting workers against each other by race and gender daily. In fact, we later discovered, all the women in the shop had affectionately been dubbed "Vernon's Harem." Thanks, Vernon. My friend was white and, although we were both started together on the dirtiest job there, he soon separated us and assigned her to a machine in another part of the shop, where I couldn't see her. That started the workers abuzz and some of the black guys came over to me to express their outrage. Although I was confused and hurt, I didn't want to participate in this criticism of her.

Later, when I transferred to the night shift and met Good Cop, Bad Cop, and Ugly Inbetween, I realized that Vernon's tactics were small potatoes. I was about to learn that you can't outrun this stuff. Apparently, night shift is the refuge for the refuse of bosses everywhere.

"Ziggy," the Bad Cop, was a strange bird. Glassy-eyed, he rode around in a cart all night, trying to catch workers asleep or "goofing off." His most predominant personality trait? Absolute hatred of women. To him, we were born incompetent and out of place. Bad girls who talked back were sent to the shop with the worst reputation in the plant: the Forge. It was purposefully (thanks to the company) the dirtiest, darkest,

most dangerous shop in the plant. Trips to the Forge often lasted a shift or so—just long enough to teach all the bad girls and boys a lesson.

Somehow (unbelievable, huh?) I got on Ziggy's bad side and earned a trip to the Forge. It was indeed scary, but I just folded my arms and refused to work. Just lazy, I guess. Proving useless there, I got sent back to my shop in a few hours.

"Rollo," a token black boss-type, played Good Cop. His shtick was to promise to make things better and get Ziggy off my back, if I'd just go out with him ("Just a movie and popcorn? Pleeezzzze!"). He'd come by two or three times a night. Even if his behavior had been appropriate, which of course it wasn't, he didn't look like he could even deliver.

"Alan" was the Ugly Inbetween. He was another black boss-type whose main goal in life was to stay out of the line of fire and ire. He would suggest that I make it easy on myself and go out with Rollo. This was his helpful contribution to this criminal behavior.

My stubborn will did not stop this crap. Loose-fitting, ugly clothes did not stop this crap (and who wants to wear those anyway?). My subsequent marriage did not stop this crap. Because this is not a "sex" thang, it's a "power" thang.

The few long-time women workers had already retreated into emotional shells, thanks to previous disrespect from those dogs. But by now, I had gained the respect of most of my male coworkers.

How did it stop? I'll tell you the beginning of the end. I was so pissed at Rollo that I was ready to smash his nose in with a hammer. Ziggy, too, was on a roll. (He had recently gained ghastly fame when a shop coworker lost his finger in a machine; the worker got to the hospital long before his finger did, because, upon finding the extremity, Ziggy put it in a little box and displayed it to every worker in sight.)

Totally frustrated, I finally did what I should have done from the git-go. I approached some union sisters and asked their collective opinions.

Thanks to those tough ladies, I began a "Harassment Journal," in which I made conspicuous entries, complete with time and date, after—and sometimes during—each occurrence. Sometimes, if I was particularly pissed, I'd whip out the notebook and the pen if I even saw Good Cop or Bad Cop come 'round the corner at me. Preventive medicine.

Once Ugly Inbetween came up to me as I was replacing the book in my toolbox. He warned me—in a nice way—that something might happen to that little book (insidiously threatening that my box and tools might be destroyed in the attempt). As I spun the dial on my little Master Lock, I said, "Oh, that's okay, I always make a carbon," and patted my back pocket.

The harassment stopped.

I believe that national and regional economics and politics clearly play a role in setting an atmosphere (which kinds of people are identified as scapegoats, are considered worthless, "deserve" lower pay, etc.)—it's not just individual bosses. The specific history of the workplace can come into play as well. At Harding, there had been two major waves of hiring women: during World War II, and during a hard-won strike, as strikebreakers. Needless to say, there were very bad feelings aimed at this latter wave. It also didn't help that some women did marry bosses—I had that thrown at me from time to time. But long after I won my battle, I began to realize that there are ways for women to organize, anywhere —any "little girls' room" plantwide is a haven for rebellious and beaten-down women alike.

In retrospect, although bosses and national politics set the tone, we can still maintain our dignity. We have a right to be anywhere we choose. You can win cross-gender allies. You can stand your ground. But not alone. My mistake was not approaching the union first and making the entire local face up to this madness. I know now that I used collective knowledge to win an individual victory—and yet harassment there continued, for other women. We only outwit them together!

Jo's tactic of recording the harassers' behavior in her log involved the classic elements of confrontation—naming the behavior and holding the harassers accountable. Every time she picked up that pen, they knew that she considered their behavior harassment and was about to begin documenting every word they said. It put her in control of the interactions, intimidated the hell out of them, and—as is often the case when women confront successfully—made it all but impossible for her bosses to retaliate against her.

As Jo later realized, having the support of allies in this kind of situation is also important. Her confrontation technique was excellent in solving her individual situation, but it would take a united effort—consistent intervention by male and female workers, black and white, on behalf of all the women who were harassed—to change the overall workplace culture at "Harding Tool and Die." Talking to other women was the first step in her own solution, and talking to other women—and men—is the first step in the larger, long-term solution. Many managers, like "Vernon," play race and gender games to keep workers divided and off-balance. Recognize *that* behavior as the control tactic that it is and don't fall for it.

Here's another impressive success story from a woman who was on her own in a very male environment—the only woman on a painting maintenance crew. Kathleen A. Hopwood used a powerful, carefully controlled physical confrontation to stop an incident of physical harassment by a group of men and succeeded decisively.

THE PAINTING CREW

In 1974 I was working as a painter in the maintenance department of a major university in North Carolina. I was the first (and to this day, the only) woman the physical plant director hired to work as a full-time painter. I was paid the same wages as the men, but in the early 1970s feminism and women painters were not warmly embraced.

The men I worked alongside of were southern, white, and uneducated; most were in their late fifties and early sixties.

Many of them could not read the work orders given out each day. (There was, and still is, a great class disparity between the students at the university, seeking an education, and the maintenance workers, seeking a weekly paycheck.)

You can imagine the reaction the crew had when informed that a "girl" would be joining the painting department—and at their pay scale, too. Now, I grew up poor-to-working-class in Washington, D.C. My father had been a housepainter and I had worked for two paint crews before moving to North Carolina. In my naivete, I didn't think there would be a problem since I knew how to paint.

During the three years that I held this job, I met much resentment, harassment, and hatred from the men in the maintenance department, including the men I worked with. Their attitude made my job dangerous. I had to rely on my coworkers to steady the sixty-foot ladder when I was at the top of it, trust them to hold the tie-line as I was lowered off roofs, and hope that the buck board they'd clipped onto the window ledge wasn't rigged to fall.

I did not trust these guys, and with good reason. I spent three years ducking paint cans that would suddenly drop on me, constantly dodging the paint pole when another painter was rolling walls, and watching my back to make sure that none of them could get close enough to "accidentally" rub up against me. And that was only the physical aspect of the harassment.

There were also endless verbal jabs. Even the compliments I got were always double-edged swords: "I'll say one thing for Kathy, she sure tries!" I didn't try to paint or try to hang off buildings or try to carry five-gallon buckets of paint. I actually did all these things—but the men couldn't accept that fact.

Why did I stay in such an unhappy and dangerous environment? The answers are simple: I needed a job; the pay was good (men's wages); and, being "formally uneducated" (not a college graduate), I didn't have many other choices. Most important, the job gave me time to devote to my first love, martial arts training.

I started training in the martial arts in 1972 and pursued it with a passion. This gave me an edge in some of the harassment I faced. The guys were never sure whether little five-foot-one me could take them on physically.

One morning when I entered the paint shop, all the guys were hanging around waiting for a shipment of paint to arrive. Waiting was extremely boring, so they had already begun to pick at each other. When I entered the shop, it became open season on me. The head supervisor walked up to me and began to touch the strings on the front of the hood attached to my sweatjacket. He was smiling. He moved very quickly and touched so lightly that I barely felt it at first.

Another painter took this as a signal to continue. He sidled over to me, grabbed each of the strings, and stroked them back and forth around my neck, laughing at me. He was very close to touching my breasts. I told him to stop. He held on for a few seconds longer, then let go. This entire scene was watched by sixteen men. They were holding their breath, waiting to see what would happen.

I was just turning to leave the area when a third painter reached out and grabbed my hood strings, to see what he could get away with. I'd had enough of this. Without any hesitation, I did a beautiful circular kick to his head. I judged my distance perfectly. I never touched his head, just his hair. My foot got just close enough to graze his slicked-back hair and pull a clump up away from his head. He went entirely pale. The other men were frozen in shock and couldn't make a move. I told them never to touch me again, and walked away.

Every one of them knew that I, like the other maintenance workers, wore steel-toed boots. If I had wanted to, I could have done him serious damage. I knew that I had the control in my kick to scare him without hurting him. I didn't like being pushed to this level of physical response, but I knew the men would respect a physical action if they disrespected my verbal statements.

Word got around campus that I had "knocked out" a guy with my martial arts. The men began to give me a little bit *more room—no one tried to stand too close to me, and not one of the guys ever said anything to me or even tried to make a joke about it.*

Kathleen used one of the main elements of confrontation —body language—to convey a powerful message in no uncertain terms. Because she could control her kick so precisely that she just flicked the harasser's hair, her response was perfect for the situation. That precision was essential to make the response work—a wild, flailing kick would have only made her look powerless, and a kick to cause injury would have been an unnecessary escalation. (She did not need to knock him out, and, given her skill level, it would have been unethical to do so.) In terms of the psychological impact on her harassers, the discipline she showed was as important as the shock value of her martial arts skill.

Because this was physical harassment by a group of men, Kathleen needed to seize control of the situation quickly. Like Jo, here Kathleen was up against multiple harassers, and they were following the lead of a supervisor who initiated the harassment himself. It is especially important to confront supervisors who set the tone this way. In this case, the crew chief was responsible for beginning the incident, and he knew it. Kathleen's calm, blunt statement, demanding that they never touch her again, was addressed to him as well as to her coworkers. Because of the power of her body language, a simple statement was all she needed.

And like Jo, Kathleen faced no retaliation. The clarity and justice of her carefully controlled physical and verbal action, in front of the supervisor and the entire crew, made retaliation virtually impossible. She left the men not angry and out for revenge, but stunned and apprehensive.

(Do not try this particular tactic unless you have studied martial arts and are very confident about judging your kick. The alternative is to use a less forceful physical action, combined with a more forceful verbal statement. For example, grab both of the harasser's wrists, hold them up in the air for a few seconds, then throw his hands down against his own body as you tell him to keep his hands off you. Label the behavior as sexual harassment, look each of the men in the eye, and address the rest of your confrontation statement to the supervisor and the entire group. Any attempt at face-saving on their part gets the broken-record tactic, in a steely tone of voice: "You heard me. There's nothing more for you to say.")

Rebecca Edelson is not a martial arts expert, but she found another way to confront an entire group of harassers in a hostile workplace—a creative and productive approach that also had real, long-term consequences.

THE AMBULANCE COMPANY

I hate pornography. Always have. Always will. So, I wasn't really thinking, just sort of acting on impulse, when I threw out the porn magazine that was sitting on the table in the common room of the Boston area ambulance company I was working for. I certainly didn't think about the chain of events it could, or would, begin.

It was the summer of 1983 and I was twenty years old. I was a new EMT (emergency medical technician) who had graduated at the top of my EMT certification class only half a year earlier. I had gotten a job on one of Boston's many private ambulance services. Not unlike most police forces, the Emergency Medical Services (EMS) field—which includes EMTs, paramedics, and firefighters—was (and still is) overwhelmingly male. I could tell almost immediately from the comments and jokes told by my instructors and fellow students in the EMT training course that the field allowed a climate where sexism and racism could flourish. Of course not all the white men in the field were, or are, contributors to this climate. But there was a rather large and vocal group who certainly did seem to have issues around women, race, and power. They would make their presence well known with continual talk, put-downs, and jokes regarding "infe-

rior" racial groups, "welfare-dependent" minorities, and of course sex, sexy women, breasts, bras, and pornography.

I was fast discovering that, contrary to popular belief, the EMT field was not made up solely of those who wanted to be caregivers, supporters and saviors of human life. Instead there were a healthy number of folks in the field who were drawn to the drama of messy accidents and blood as well as the attention and fun that come with the brightly colored rotating lights, wailing sirens, noisy radios, and the loud PA systems of the fast-driving ambulances. We called the EMTs who were into these types of things "Hockeypucks" or "Frustrated Firefighters." They tended to walk wide, long steps like urban cowboys, liked to be associated with firefighters and police, and kept unneeded handcuffs conspicuously dangling on their EMT belts.

More often than not these were the men who acted the most disrespectful toward women and racial or ethnic minorities.

In between calls we would either wait on the streets in the "truck" (ambulance) for our next call or go back to the station and sit in the common room. Waiting in the common room with the other ambulance teams on a slow day was hell. Often I'd be the only woman in the room and the men would begin to talk about some female patient they had picked up on a call. In one instance they joked about the idea of twisting the nipples of unconscious women they picked up, just to test if they really were unconscious, and of raping them if they really were out cold.

In another instance, the manager and one of the nicer (or at least nicer-looking) EMTs and I were sitting around the common room table. Then, as if I were not even there, they suddenly began discussing in great detail the porn movie they had shown the night before in the coed bunkroom during the overnight shift.

These "jokes" and discussions succeeded in doing what I think they were intended to do. They offended me, made me uncomfortable, and intimidated me. I would often leave the room and go wait in the truck. Even when another woman

was present in the common room with me, it made no difference. There was no solidarity among the few women in the
company. They just sat there and ignored the men's talk. If I
silently made a face or rolled my eyes to let the other women
know I was disgusted by the topic of conversation, they usually ignored me as well. I was constantly fed up with, and
angry at, my male and female coworkers, though I rarely
actually said anything to them.

The racism I saw and heard about from my best buddy in
the company, a black man, was even worse. When he was
interviewing for the job, two EMTs ran around behind him
with sheets over themselves to look like the Ku Klux Klan.
And then after he got the job, a group of coworkers physically
attacked him one night during an overnight shift. They
pinned him down and shaved off his chest hair. On another
occasion they handcuffed him to a stretcher and then handcuffed the stretcher to a parking meter and left him there on
the busy street. My friend laughed it off as a mild form of
hazing. He was unwilling to tell the manager, who we both
knew probably condoned the acts anyway.

In the five months I had been with the ambulance company I had already gone through two male partners (the company refused to partner up two women) and had been
unhappy with both due to too many comments about women
and blacks. I was now with my third partner. He did not talk
to me much, and this was an improvement. I was slowly
beginning to gain his trust by making stupid jokes (something I'm rather good at).

One day, in between calls, my new partner and I went
back to the station. We walked into the empty common room
only to be immediately sent back out to do a final call for the
day. Only enough time had passed for me to walk into the
room, see a porn magazine on the table, pick it up, be told
we had a call, throw the thing into the trash can, and leave. I
didn't really think about my action. I just did it.

We had only gotten about two blocks down the street when
the dispatcher put out a general call over the radio to all the
ambulances on the road. "OK, who threw out Timmy's
book?" he angrily asked.

Oops, I had thrown out the supervisor's porn.

I called back and said that I had. The dispatcher called our ambulance back to the station. I was ready to be reprimanded. But by the time I got back the dispatcher and manager had realized that the "book" Timmy was complaining someone had dumped was actually only a porn "book." They laughed and sent me back out on the road. I thought the incident was over, finished my last trip for the day, and went home.

Of course the incident wasn't over. Everyone had heard the general call on the radio about Timmy's "book" and by the time I got in the next morning the whole company knew the story. Rebecca had thrown out the supervisor's porn. Rebecca has a thing against pornography. As soon as I walked in, some of the guys jokingly called me "the porn queen." Ha, ha, I responded with little patience and little humor. Luckily, I was sent out on a call.

When I came back to the common room and saw the porn centerfolds prominently hung on the walls, it became quickly obvious to me that I was now to be the target of a new group intimidation campaign: the porn-reading men in the company versus me. Unfortunately, that meant almost all the men in the company, including the day and night supervisors, the manager, and the dispatcher. It was the dispatcher who scared me the most. He was physically big as well as outspoken and unafraid to say what was on his mind in a rather threatening tone.

The next few days were sheer hell. I was constantly joked about and taunted, and my already near-silent partner stopped talking to me altogether (not a good thing when you need to work as a team to care for the sick or wounded, especially in an emergency). A full-page note written by the dispatcher was posted on the common room wall next to more porn pictures. This time the porn pictures were meant to be more appropriate for our medical work. One was of two elderly men dressed in diapers simultaneously sucking on the nipples of a large breasted "porn-nurse." The note from the dispatcher was some fabricated story about my sexual activities and about how I should be chained to a bed with a chain only long enough to reach the kitchen. I left the porn up, but I tore the note down.

In another instance, the manager of the company came up behind me and rubbed my back for about three seconds in a seemingly friendly manner, only to then declare to the dispatcher, who was in the room with us, "Nice tits for a girl with no bra." I jumped up and told him to keep his f——ing hands off me.

In perhaps the most upsetting instance of the lot, the dispatcher called me into the common room and, with the two of us standing in front of a number of seated male employees, he presented me with a large, erect, chocolate penis and a scroll which he proceeded to unroll and read aloud. It said something or other about me and sex, and my "really liking it." Without saying anything I took the penis he gave me and dumped it in the trash on my way out the door.

In each case I was acting on impulse. None of my actions were well thought out. I was nervous and could not think very clearly.

Needless to say, I went home a wreck almost every night. Often I would cry myself to sleep. I dreaded going to work the next day. I had no confidence or self-esteem when I was at work. And I actually feared going into the common room or being called into the dispatcher's office.

Not surprisingly, none of the few women in the company supported me. They all sided with the men in support of pornography, or remained silent. I did have three male friends on the company. They all saw the harassment as wrong, but thought I should simply shut up and just let the whole thing die down.

Contrary to their advice, I knew I had to take action, though I didn't know exactly what to do. I met with a long-time supporter of women's causes and my all-time best male ally, my father. After a long meeting we decided on a two-track approach. One track would be a letter that he would write to the manager, clearly laying out the harassment he heard me describe (including the "back rub" and "tits" remark that came from the manager himself). He would state that as my father he found the acts horrendous and would not hesitate to support me in a suit against the company.

I must admit that I felt somewhat reluctant to use my father's help in this way. It made me feel like a little girl who could not fend for herself and needed her father, or any man, to protect her. I also felt that the manager should be able to listen to me, take my concerns seriously, and take the necessary actions to remedy the situation, not wait to hear it from a man before it was a matter worthy of his attention. I decided to ignore these "I-can-do-it-alone" feelings and to solicit all the help I could get from my father.

The second part of our two-track approach would be my going to the Massachusetts Commission Against Discrimination (MCAD), a state agency, to see if I had any grounds for filing a formal complaint or for suing the company. I did go to the MCAD. They said I could very well have grounds for a legitimate complaint of sexual harassment. They said that they would have to investigate the company themselves and would do so upon my request, though it could take some time.

I left unsure as to what to do. I was scared that if I registered a formal complaint with the state of Massachusetts, my name would become known in the field and I would never again get hired at any other ambulance company in the state. My career as an EMT passed before my eyes. I decided to wait to see the manager's reaction to my father's letter first and use the formal complaint with MCAD as a threat if he did not respond.

After he got my father's letter, the manager suddenly became a new man. Not wanting to be sued, he pulled me aside and spoke to me for the first time as if I was an adult with some power. I also think that he saw me for the first time as someone's daughter, in other words, a real person and not just a "broad." We sat alone in an ambulance to discuss the matter. He asked me what I wanted to see happen. I told him that I planned to quit but that before I did I wanted a new rule to be passed in the company: no pornography in the common spaces. He agreed, and soon afterward a letter stating that fact was posted on the wall in the common room and the new policy stated at a staff meeting.

I left the company with mixed feelings. I felt successful, even vindicated, by the passing of the new rule. But I also felt defeated; the jerks in the company had succeeded in pushing me out.

In my eyes the real success came months later. I knew that the sexism I had experienced (and the racism I had seen) at that one particular ambulance company was a statewide problem. I decided that someone should address the issue on a statewide level. I knew that all EMS personnel must take a number of continuing education courses each year to stay certified. I decided that was the route to take.

I called the EMS state office and asked to speak with the person in charge of Continuing Education Training. I suggested to him that a course be offered in "Dismantling Discrimination" in the EMS field. The gentleman in charge was African-American. He obviously knew what I was talking about, as any nonwhite or nonmale in the business would. We met. He took my idea completely seriously and he agreed to give me almost complete control over organizing and leading a one-evening accredited course on "Dismantling Discrimination" for Emergency Service personnel. Throughout the months it took to organize the training he never once wavered in his support or belief in me.

I organized outside experts in affirmative action and the law to come speak. I also got minorities and women from high-up positions within the field to come and tell their stories. And I planned a talk I would give to introduce and close the one-night training. I was so scared that I would be verbally attacked (or worse), or that the event would flop and I would be ostracized from the field, that I couldn't eat for four days before the training.

The training session got a good deal of publicity. Over sixty people showed up—ambulance technicians, firefighters, emergency room personnel, administrative directors of emergency rooms from some of Boston's most noted hospitals, and much to my surprise, the firefighters who had originally trained me to be an EMT.

I would guess that over two-thirds of the audience came out of defensive curiosity. There were far more men with condescending looks on their faces standing (hiding?) toward the back of the room behind the waist-high partition than there were attendees sitting in the front actively participating. To me they looked as if they were watching a show —and one they did not like.

But the evening ended up being a huge success. Each of the speakers did a great job in front of a tough audience. They presented important legal information on how to address discrimination (including how to file a formal complaint with the state). And the participants got to share stories of their personal experiences with discrimination. The skeptical people who stood in the back of the room all evening, the people most similar to the perpetrators of the sexism I had experienced, did not leave offended or angry and were thus able to hear all the important information given. That was important to me.

It was the first time the state of Massachusetts had ever held any type of training dealing with sexism or racism for EMS personnel.

A final success was that I did live through it all. Actually, I felt more of a sense of relief than anything else. But looking back now, I see that it was a real personal success for me. I had experienced harassment that left me with little confidence and almost no self-esteem, and yet I did not let that stop me. By doing something constructive, such as the training, I turned the situation around so that I helped both myself, by rebuilding my confidence and sense of power, and others who might someday find themselves in a similar situation.

Rebecca's response was, in the end, a means of naming the behavior on a large scale. She chose to confront harassment as an institutional, not just a personal, problem. In taking action on this systemwide level, she put the state EMS office on public record as opposing harassment, paved the way for women after her to come forward, and began to set up some new behavioral expectations for the EMS workforce as a whole—quite a turnaround from her initial feelings of helplessness and victimization.

And finally, here's a success story from another woman in a traditionally male job—not a blue-collar or community-service worker, but a professional public health engineer. Mary A.'s story is an excellent example of what happens when organizations handle sexual harassment responsibly. In this case, it was a senior officer at the Army Corps of Engineers, rather than Mary individually, who took definitive action to hold the harasser accountable for his behavior.

HAZARDOUS WASTE

In the mid-1980s I was a public health engineer with the Colorado Health Department and was assigned to perform a hazardous waste facility compliance inspection at the Rocky Mountain Arsenal near Denver. I was accompanied on the four-day inspection by three men: an enforcement officer from the regional office of the U.S. Environmental Protection Agency (EPA), an environmental officer from the Arsenal, and an industrial hygienist (IH) from the Army Corps of Engineers.

During the inspection, I was subjected to obscene remarks and suggestions from the IH at every opportunity. I was in the position of authority as the compliance officer, but that did not deter him. We inspected a jet fuel tank farm and wore protective equipment (coveralls, boots, and breathing apparatus); after the inspection I was washing my face and hands amid crude remarks about showers together. Later, I was inspecting buildings stacked full of drums, amid remarks such as, "She can't come out yet, she doesn't have her clothes on—ha, ha!" I did my best to ignore these comments, not even acknowledging them. This same man also dropped in a few bathroom-type jokes toward the male EPA inspector. I kept my own responses controlled and mature, not becoming defensive or encouraging the behavior in any way.

Back at my office, I did not complain to anyone about the

harassment, because I felt that I had handled it as well as I could have, it did not affect the quality or rigor of my inspection, and it was in the past. I dismissed the industrial hygienist as a jerk and let it go at that. However, a few weeks after the inspection, my supervisor called me into his office to find out what happened during the inspection. I told him of the two specific comments and the general behavior of this individual during the entire inspection.

He told me the environmental officer for the Arsenal had complained to the IH's supervisor at the Corps of Engineers. The environmental officer said that he did not confront the IH during the inspection because he was unsure of the hygienist's position and authority (i.e., rank) until after the inspection was completed.

I met the hygienist's supervisor at a meeting at the Arsenal several weeks later. He apologized for the behavior of the IH, assured me that this was not the first incident of its kind involving this individual, and told me that the hygienist had been dismissed.

In retrospect, I was fortunate to be accompanied by witnesses who were as offended as I was. I did not complain directly to the harasser or promptly to my supervisor, as I should have, but the incident turned out to be a success nevertheless, because the behavior was outrageous to others who were willing to speak out with me.

This time it was the harasser, not the victim, who ended up out of a job. Instead of enjoying the ability to harass risk-free, he found out that sexual harassment carried a steep penalty.

Mary's story underscores the importance of individual action and witnesses who are willing to be allies. A male ally, the environmental officer from the Rocky Mountain Arsenal, took the initiative in reporting the IH's abusive behavior. Once he spoke up, Mary faced no risk of being disbelieved. His decision to act allowed Mary to come forward in much greater safety.

Even then, reporting the behavior might not have been

enough. As might be predicted in a technical field like this one, both the harasser's supervisor and the victim's were men. Either or both might have dismissed the hygienist's behavior with the usual sexist rationalizations, despite the fact he clearly had a history of engaging in sexual harassment. But in a rare display of organizational responsibility, both supervisors took action—one to confirm the incident by talking with Mary, and the other to fire the harasser.

This is exactly the kind of prompt, principled action that women should be able to expect from their male colleagues and from the corporations and government agencies they deal with. If the Army Corps of Engineers can do it, so can your company.

Not All Men Harass: Men as Allies for Women

Men who say that they care about women have a responsibility to take action when it comes to sexual harassment. It's not enough to sympathize with women who are being harassed, or make sure one never does it oneself, or agree philosophically that women should have the fundamental human right to do their jobs or take a class or walk down the street unmolested. It is time for men to deal with their coworkers, buddies, fathers, sons, and brothers. Every harasser is surrounded by men in his life—men he respects and relies on —men who know injustice when they see it and can take steps to end it.

If you are male, stopping sexual harassment begins with actions as simple as not laughing at sexist jokes, not smiling at comments that put women down, and not letting harassers interpret your silence as approval for what they do. Speak up! It may feel awkward or embarrassing to let a friend or coworker know that you don't like his comments or behavior toward women, but you can do it, and do it successfully. (Think how much more uncomfortable and difficult it is for the woman who is on the receiving end of those remarks or actions.) It's a disservice to every woman around when men who know better take the easy way out by remaining silent in the face of sexism.

In fact, because most harassers are extremely sexist, they are actually more likely to respect men's opinions than women's. For that reason, it's important for men who object to sexual harassment to make it clear that they themselves do not admire or condone this behavior. If your friend Joe makes a crack about Shirley's breasts, your disapproval may carry far more weight with him than the fact that Shirley is offended by what he said. Joe doesn't care about Shirley's feelings and rights, but he does care about being respected by other men. And that means that *you* have real leverage in changing his obnoxious behavior. So when you speak up, speak on your own account—say that *you* think Joe is out of line (not just that Shirley doesn't like it). Instead of casting yourself in the traditional and somewhat sexist role of Shirley's "protector" by speaking for her, communicate the message that *you* no longer consider harassment acceptable behavior.

Here's a good example in which one man did exactly that:

THE RAPE JOKE

I'll never forget the first time I heard a man confront another man. It was 1985. I was thirty-five years old, one of two senior women in the division, and known as the office feminist. I walked into the front office of my section one afternoon and heard Doug, one of the senior analysts and the office lech, telling a rape joke to a group of the guys just around the corner in the office. It was a really stupid and insulting joke about an older woman who was so desperate for sex that when she was raped, she asked the rapist to come back. Not very funny, to say the least. I don't think rape jokes are amusing anyway, but I found that particular joke really inexcusable (one of my aunts was raped, in her own kitchen, when she was in her sixties, by a man who broke into her house).

None of the guys saw me come into the office. The women who worked in the front office, Sally and Mary Lou, looked embarrassed and very uncomfortable, but they were just sitting at their desks, not saying anything. I decided I had to confront Doug and put a stop to this.

But then, just as I was about to step around the corner and break it up, I heard Sam, one of my coworkers, cut Doug off at the knees. He said, "That's not funny. I don't like it, and I don't want to hear that kind of crap again." He didn't say that Sally wouldn't like it, or Mary Lou would be offended (Doug knew that—he liked to make the women uncomfortable). Sam spoke up for himself: he said that he didn't like it. Doug shut up in a hurry.

The women almost cheered—talked about it for days. I realized that it was the first time in my life that I'd ever seen a man confront sexism on the job. Sam and I have been friends ever since.

Sam's confrontation was effective: simple, direct, and strong. It embarrassed Doug, and made Sam a local hero to the women Doug had been harassing. Because even decent men have been silent around this kind of behavior for so long, Sam's response came as a surprise to everyone involved—to the women, to the men in the group, and most of all to Doug himself. Sam very neatly overturned Doug's sexist assumptions about his male listeners. Instead of going along with the good-ol'-boy camaraderie Doug expected, Sam raised the psychological ego-risks involved for Doug in this kind of sexist behavior and made it clear on the spot that Doug could not count on his approval for rape jokes. By challenging the joke so clearly, Sam not only turned the tables on Doug but showed the other guys how it could be done.

When men like Sam speak up, they can make a profound difference in the daily level of workplace sexism women face. That is true even in male-dominated environments like the U.S. military. Here's Nita M.'s story:

AN ALLY IN THE MILITARY

In 1977 I completed military tech school and was transferred to my first duty station. Before I left the school, I received a very nice letter from a higher-ranking man, wel-

coming me to the unit and offering to assist with the transition.

Upon arrival, I was assigned to do some paperwork at my supervisor's desk. Needing a pencil, I opened the top desk drawer. To my horror, I found another "welcome" letter, addressing me as the first female to be assigned to the unit and graphically detailing the extra "duties" I would be expected to perform for the men in my unit.

I was only twenty-one and not accustomed to dealing with older males. Not knowing what to do, I spoke to a younger male I'd gone to tech school with, assigned to the same unit. I explained to "Bill," whom I trusted, that I did not want to get started off on the wrong foot—but neither did I want to ignore this behavior. He offered to be a witness for me, and read the letter. He was very supportive.

Together we wrote a note on the letter, explaining the circumstances under which it was found and our feelings about it. We then put the letter back in its place.

Two weeks later, my supervisor apologized for his conduct and told me that he really appreciated the way I handled the situation. I let him know I was sure he did appreciate it because it would have cost him his job. It felt great!

I never experienced any other sexual harassment from anyone at the unit. Nor did I experience any retaliation.

In one simple, decent act, this young man helped Nita to resolve a serious incident of harassment that easily could have developed into a very nasty long-term situation. He did so despite the fact that the harasser outranked him and despite any fears he may have had about his own status in the unit. Nita was the only woman on the crew, but once Bill wrote the note with her, both Nita and the supervisor knew that she was not going to be left to deal with this kind of behavior on her own. The note was a low-key but assertive way of putting the harasser on notice. By joining her as an ally right at the outset, Bill immediately accomplished three things: He made Nita much less isolated and vulnerable, cut the chances of retaliation against her, and significantly raised the risks of continued harassment for his supervisor. Any plans the officer may have had along those lines suddenly began to look much more problematic. Bill also demonstrated some real leadership, the kind that put his superior officer to shame. The short-term result was an apology to Nita, and the long-term result was an officer who did the right thing and a military tech unit that treated Nita with respect instead of abuse. One man, in one key incident, can accomplish a great deal.

Sometimes, getting a harasser to change his ways can be much tougher. Here's David's story, about a die-hard male-dominance harasser whose pattern of abuse and disrespect is aggravating even to the men around him:

THE PROBLEM WITH AL

I am a white male who works with a guy who does not realize that he has the annoying habit of making himself a nuisance to the women in our office. He's in his late thirties and treats most of the women who are younger than he is (he likes them ten to fifteen years younger) as objects of flirtation or potential dates, instead of colleagues. I will refer to him as Al, with no offense intended to any real Als who may be reading this.

His constant pestering and unwanted attention have annoyed many of my friends and made him an object of ridicule and scorn within the office, but he still doesn't get it.

Al insists that he is just being "friendly." We have all noticed that this "friendliness" is not a feature of his interactions with any of the men and older women in the office.

Al's history of harassment preceded my arrival at the company, but very early on I heard both first- and secondhand accounts of it, one of them from the perpetrator himself. Al has as much as admitted the acts of which he was accused, his defense being that those harassment charges were the result of "misunderstandings" by women who "overreacted" to certain congenial, "ribald" conversations. He got off the hook with mere reprimands from the personnel office for all of those earlier offenses. Now, rather than learn from experience and alter his behavior, he has chosen to play the part of the persecuted victim, condemned for a past in which he was wrongfully accused.

During the time in which I have had the dubious pleasure of working next to him, Al has continued to display the same kind of behavior. I would classify it as obnoxious rather than threatening, but that does not make it any less intrusive or reprehensible. As a friend who has experienced this told me, the first time Al meets a woman his eyes scan up and down her body. If a woman "passes" his initial test, she is "rewarded" by having Al approach her whenever possible in the hallway or the cafeteria and attempt to engage her in conversation. The typical politeness of a new employee allows Al to leap to the self-serving conclusion that he and the new woman are hitting it off.

This initial stage then progresses into a period when Al can make women feel that they are prisoners to his attention; they can't escape him no matter where they are in the office. Al is seemingly unable to figure out that women know what his real intentions are. He is repeatedly taken aback and becomes defensive when they finally make it clear that his attention is not appreciated. He then refers to them as "stuck up" or "snobby."

Compounding Al's problem is his belief that certain co-workers must be telling new employees about his reputation and past behavior, leading some women to have negative perceptions of him before they even meet him. I have frequently been the recipient of harangues from Al, mostly along the lines of "If you'd just keep your mouth shut and stop spreading these lies to women (who you secretly lust after anyway), I wouldn't be having any problems." When I tell him that he should take responsibility for his actions and stop harassing women, Al usually goes on to call me a radical feminist and question why I do not make advances on them myself.

When Al starts blaming others for his predicament, I usually try to explain to him just how intrusive and insulting his behavior is. Sometimes I lose my cool and get nowhere. Sometimes I am able to very clearly and calmly state my case —and still get nowhere. Oh, well, one can't expect much from a guy like Al; but I hope that my continued efforts will eventually increase his awareness and make life easier for the next woman who joins our company.

One of my more restrained efforts to confront Al about his harassment occurred a few months ago when he made a flippant sexual remark. For once, Al was not attempting to harass any women with the comment, there being none in the room at the time. But it was offensive enough, and I was bored enough with my work, that I decided to challenge Al for making it. He sarcastically asked if I thought he was harassing me. I replied that given his past, he more than anyone should know harassment when he saw it. That triggered the usual denial from Al, which set off a twenty-minute discussion about harassment, with each of us more or less getting a chance to explain our views.

During this discussion, I suggested to Al that he consider his encounters with his female coworkers, and any woman for that matter, from their perspective. I explained that I believed he truly thought he was just being friendly and doing nothing wrong, but that by now he must realize the effect his actions have. I went on to say that making a woman uncomfortable by constantly annoying and pestering her when she is trying to eat lunch or just walk through the office constitutes a form of sexual harassment. Al continued to deny that most women were annoyed by his "friendly" overtures; he said the "few" who had taken exception were "snobs" who had been unduly influenced by me. This was on the verge of turning into another exercise in futility, but remarkably we were able to keep it going for another fifteen minutes. I repeatedly tried to make Al accept the fact that his invasive actions are a type of harassment, while he refused to budge from his very narrow definition: Anything short of overt sexual advances is perfectly OK.

I don't know whether this exchange can be classified as a success story, but it was one of our first long conversations on the subject, and we've continued to have discussions that focus on his interactions with women in our office. Al still has his persecution complex, and I, of course, am still the main reason for all his dismal failures with the women around us, as far as he's concerned. Al still gives no indication that there is even the slightest chance of any light at the end of the tunnel. But I refuse to sit back and watch him continue to inflict the same behavior that he's committed in the past. Thankfully, many other men and women in my office feel the same way. Maybe there is hope after all.

David's story is a portrait of a sexist under siege. Clinging desperately to old patterns of male-dominance behavior that no longer work, Al has made himself into a pathetic caricature of the dominant male he idealizes. Neither the men nor the women he works with see him as a commanding, macho figure; he's just a ridiculous pest. David is not particularly threatened by Al's insults because at this point Al is not a man whose opinions matter to the men around him. And the women in the office barely tolerate him.

Because the culture has changed, Al's sexist behavior is now costing him the two things he wants most: women's attention and men's respect. With every discussion, every challenge to a sexist comment, and every negative reaction to Al's invasive behavior, David and his coworkers are raising the costs of harassing for Al and eliminating the rewards. With or without a formal group confrontation, at some point they will force Al to face up to the fact that his self-pitying justifications are no longer fooling anyone—not even himself.

Confronting harassers is not easy for either men or women. It takes courage and skill—and sometimes, as David found, it takes a lot of dogged persistence. That men like David and Al are now having lengthy conversations about sexual harassment is a measure of how much the culture has changed and a success story in itself.

Gay men are also confronting harassment these days, and sometimes they can do it with considerable humor. Tom is a midlevel executive in a major corporation. Every morning, to get to his office, he walks through the large, open, central room where fifteen members of the engineering staff work. Every morning, with sneering contempt, one of the engineers would conspicuously lean away, tilting his chair back as Tom came past, as if even momentary proximity to a gay male was more than he could stand. The man's blatant homophobia was too insulting to ignore.

Tom was angry; he had to do something. Everyone in the area was now watching this minidrama every morning. Then Tom had an idea. Every day, he walked slightly closer to the harasser. Over the next two weeks, Tom moved in closer and closer as he came by. The harasser responded by tilting his chair back farther and farther, until the day he fell over backward, chair and all. The room erupted in laughter. The harasser looked preposterous, and that was the end of that.

In Tom's case, both the harassment and the confrontation were entirely nonverbal, but the message came through loud and clear. In general, men who confront any form of harassment—sexist, racist, or homophobic—should avoid name-calling, obscenities, and attacks on the harasser's manhood. It is useful to follow the basic confrontation guidelines: naming the behavior, holding the harasser accountable as a matter of principle, and demanding that the harassment stop. Strong body language—head up, shoulders back, eye contact with the harasser, and use of a firm, serious tone of voice—is just as important for men as for women, to reinforce the seriousness of the confronter's statements. Like women in this tense situation, men who are dealing with harassers need to be careful to not undermine what they say out of nervousness; smiling or offering excuses for the harasser may seem to defuse the tension but it can demolish the effectiveness of the confrontation. Responding as if the harasser just did something bizarre or incredibly gross is often a good tone to take—make *him* feel acutely ignorant and uncomfortable, by acting as if any clod would know that no one does that kind of thing anymore.

Here's a story from Michael in Washington, D.C., dealing with a colleague who certainly should know better:

MICHAEL'S STORY

I'm a young African-American man, well-educated and working in a very demanding, high-skilled technical profession. I see sexual harassment as a pervasive problem in our society today. It is common in the workplace, whether it is intentional or unintentional.

My office has twelve staff members. Jane, the only woman employed here, has been with the company for approximately four years. Jane is very knowledgeable and always helpful. She has maintained an excellent rapport with her male coworkers.

However, in an office with one woman and eleven men, discussions about women are a common topic. Sexually related comments are frequently made but they are not usually directed toward any one individual. Jane maintains a degree of poise and tolerance when the general office banter is going on.

Jane recently announced that she was expecting a child. This announcement was accepted cheerfully by the majority of her colleagues. However, there were a few negative comments. One coworker decided to express his views about the economic difficulties of a single woman giving birth to a child. Of course, this is an everyday occurrence, and his comments were ridiculed and ignored.

The other negative comment was mean-spirited, sexist, and totally inappropriate. Seizing on the topic of single women becoming pregnant, another coworker, Roger, grasped this as an opportunity to express his own sexual desires toward Jane. His exact comment was, "Can I be next?" The implication was obvious and very insulting: that a single woman who decides to have a child is an easy lady, open to sexual advances from any man around. Jane did not respond, but her cold silence said volumes.

At this point I decided to intervene. I spoke with the abuser, explained that I knew the gentleman Jane was seeing, and defined in no uncertain terms the repercussions Roger might face in the event that his comments were revealed to the prospective father. I did notice a change in Roger's behavior, but it was short-lived.

A week ago Jane received a pair of tiny-tot shoes and showed them to her coworkers. Roger again saw this as an opportunity for a sexually explicit remark. He asked to see "her booties" with an accompanying snicker. Again her reaction was a stark silence, full of concern, frustration, and anger.

Recognizing her reaction, I felt that inaction on my part would have been a sign of compliance that no man should convey. I sensed that a variety of discriminations were on display in this verbal behavior, racial as well as sexual (Jane is African-American, Roger is white). I told Roger that if he didn't stop, I was going to kick his ass. He didn't have too much to say, after that.

But I think that this may be an ongoing situation. Jane's silence has done nothing to stop him. She could sue management for not taking action; some of the senior people have been there when Roger has made these kinds of comments. Furthermore, our contract is up for renewal; if Roger is doing this type of thing with our clients, we could lose the contract.

I know that Jane does not want to make a federal case over this, but Roger's behavior is affecting all of us—he's not only targeting Jane but damaging the cooperative, professional environment in the office. He may even be putting our contract at risk. I hope that we can develop a strategy that won't embarrass Jane but will let Roger know, once and for all, that none of us will tolerate these kinds of remarks. Together, I think we can take care of it.

Roger is a persistent male-dominance harasser. He does not really expect Jane to agree to have sex with him, but he enjoys his power and her discomfort when he makes suggestive remarks. And, like many white men who harass women of color, Roger expects to get away with it; he does not believe that Jane will feel free to call him on his behavior, and indeed so far she has not.

Michael's use of not-so-subtle threats was less effective than a confrontation would have been, but his thoughtful, perceptive analysis of the situation and his willingness to speak up make him a valuable ally for Jane. He is right to be concerned about the effects of Roger's behavior on the entire office; Jane is not the only one affected here. Michael is also right that the firm itself could now be subject to legal liability because the supervisors who witnessed Roger's actions did nothing to stop the harassment. While Jane initially chose to respond to Roger only with icy silence, she could very well file a lawsuit if Roger keeps this up. Before it gets to that point, Michael and Jane—or Michael and the other men— might want to consider a group confrontation. Michael's individual actions slowed the harasser down, but the possibility that Roger's sexist behavior could jeopardize their contract should be enough to persuade several of the other men in the office to step forward and lend their support in a carefully planned group confrontation. Reminding the supervisors of their legal obligations might be an excellent idea as well.

Like Michael and David, Jim decided to intervene after a woman in his office was harassed. This incident involved Jim's supervisor, not just a coworker. It happened in Baltimore in 1992.

LOOK AT HER FACE, NOT HER BREASTS

I was talking to a colleague about this book, because I knew she'd enjoy the success stories. After chuckling at some of the stories, she said, "Do you know the most obnoxious person in this office?" I was surprised when she named the lead programmer on my project because he is a self-avowed committed husband and family man. She was annoyed by his general arrogance, but especially bothered when he talked to her for half an hour one day staring almost exclusively at her breasts. I hadn't known about that, but I decided to act on her comment.

This was kind of tricky, because the guy is essentially my boss. I met with him privately. I told him that I was not asked to talk to him and that I was not going to pursue it further, but that I would certainly want to know if negative feedback was getting around about me, so I wanted him to know what a friend had told me. I quietly described the incident and mentioned that she was offended. I suggested that his eye-contact was on the undisciplined side and that he might want to be aware of how he looked at people.

His response was defensive. He had some demeaning comments to make about the woman, too. I listened patiently, then pointed out that, just like his wife, women did notice how they were being treated, and he might want to consider being more aware.

Today the woman came and thanked me for talking to him. He had gone up to her and apologized.

He told her that he was afraid she would initiate a formal complaint against him and he wanted to remain in this job. She raised the issue of his overall arrogance and mentioned that this viewpoint was not only her own. He has started going to lunch with people, and I think he seems more friendly, which supports my suspicion that when someone improves in one area things get better all over.

Jim used an assertiveness approach, rather than a formal confrontation, to make this harasser aware of how his behavior was perceived. It was gutsy, since the harasser was his own boss. Jim was not at all sure that the message would be well received, and he was careful in choosing both his words and his tone of voice. He took a chance, thought about how to say it, did the right thing—and it worked. An apology from a harasser is a true victory.

Interestingly, the apology came despite the fact that the harasser's initial response was hostile and defensive. That kind of delayed reaction is not uncommon when men confront other men. To save face in front of another male, the harasser may refuse to admit he did anything wrong; nevertheless, knowing that another man thinks his behavior was a problem has an undeniable impact. When men do speak up, they often find that a negative response at the outset is followed by a positive change in the harasser's behavior. The message does get through.

Jim felt willing to tackle this difficult situation partly because he'd thought about sexual harassment ahead of time. He makes a habit of speaking up against sexism. He says, "When I think about confronting harassment, I think of dozens of small things I've done that add up. I respond to stupidity often. It really is my commitment against hurtful behavior. I think I've made a difference with many of my friends. Listening and having in-depth conversations about their relationships with women, I stand up for appropriate human (that is, nonsexist) behavior every time." Jim adds, "When I worked at a cabling company, I got them to change the radio station they played. They listened to the 'Greaseman,' a rock radio personality who excels at portraying women as bimbos, willing victims, and whores. I argued it was a quality-of-life issue and won. I also put up a 'This insults women' sticker on a travel agency window in front of a sexist poster of a woman. The next day, the poster was gone. And when I was in high school, I challenged a buddy who was mistreating his girlfriend. I said to him, 'Gosh, I'm glad I'm a male. I certainly am glad you don't treat me that way. I'm your best friend, and I wouldn't put up with that for ten minutes. Do you really have to behave like that?' Today he is a fine father and husband, and still one of my best friends."

While Jim's approach is principled and serious, some men can also successfully use their sense of humor to challenge sexual harassment. Adam, a big, good-looking guy who's not afraid to speak his mind, was walking into a shopping mall one afternoon when two men standing outside the doorway whistled at a woman walking just in front of him. He stopped, looked at the men, and gestured at himself, as if to say, "What, are you guys whistling at me?" They immediately backed off in confused embarrassment, saying, "Oh no, sir, we weren't whistling at you, we didn't mean you, no sir!" In telling his story, Adam said, "I thought the way they were whistling at that woman was ridiculous. Who would do that anymore? I wanted them to feel ridiculous for doing it."

Some men step forward on their own to confront harassers, and some men come through with flying colors when women ask them to be allies. Here's a success story from Andrea, who worked in an office that was almost all male, but found that she could count on at least a few of the men around her:

SNEAK ATTACK

This incident happened in broad daylight in a public building, a few years ago, when I was a federal employee. It was only my second real job, and I was very serious and dedicated to my work. There weren't many women in the agency; it was a technical department, with a very masculine environment. But I liked the men I worked with; most of them were ten or twenty years older than I was, and they really knew their stuff, so I worked hard to learn fast and make a good professional impression. My job involved checking and cross-checking various kinds of international data and writing technical reports, and I went over to the reference section a lot.

The reference division included about fifteen senior specialists, mostly men in their late forties and fifties. They sat in one large room, with the reference volumes in big gray government-issue binders on tall library shelves all around the walls. Off to the left side of the room was a small annex, with a door that opened into the main room and a second door out to the hallway. I worked just down the hall.

By the time I'd been there six months, I was feeling pretty comfortable. I knew my way around the technical material pretty well and felt like I'd established good working rela-

tionships with the men, both the analysts in my own division and the specialists in the reference section. I was dumbfounded when the harasser struck.

The sneak attack happened one afternoon, as I was standing at the small table in the annex room, looking up some information. I was alone and my back was to the room. Bradley D., one of the specialists, a large man in his fifties, quietly came in from the hall, heading through the annex into the big room. I thought he was just going to walk past, but he suddenly stopped right behind me. He ran his hands up my body—he started at the back of my knees, ran both hands up my thighs and buttocks, then up to my waist and ribs, around to the front and over my breasts. Then without a word he walked quickly through the door on the right, into the main room. It was over in a matter of seconds.

I was in shock. For a moment I just stood there, trembling with rage and violation. A lot of things went through my mind—I thought I knew this man, how could I have been so wrong about him, what happened to my good professional relationship? I wanted to race into the main room after him, yelling, but I was sure no one would believe me if I did. I took a step toward the door and saw him calmly sitting there, at his desk, in that room full of men. I felt completely powerless. He would deny it; they would all think I was hysterical, crazy, if I ran in there, accusing him. All the professional credibility I'd built up in six months would be destroyed. After a minute or two, still in shock, I turned and went out the other way, out the hall door and down to my office. I sat down at my desk in a daze.

I got no work done the rest of the day. I felt as if I couldn't trust anyone around me—was I just as wrong about the rest of them, too? I'd been deluding myself, thinking that I'd established myself as a colleague here, among these men—all I really was, in their eyes, was a chick, a broad, a pussy. I should have somehow seen it coming—but how? I didn't have a clue about Bradley—if he thought of me this way, who was going to do it next? In an instant, he managed to demolish my sense of being safe and respected and competent on the job. I felt like the ground had turned to quicksand right under me.

That evening I pulled myself together. I decided that I had to deal with this or go crazy.

I started with my boss, the next morning. I described exactly what had happened and told him who had done it. He believed me, but he got very nervous. I could tell that he was desperately hoping that I wasn't going to ask him to do anything about Bradley's behavior. I let him off the hook for the time being—I told him that I had a couple of strategies and would get back to him if they didn't work. He said good luck.

Then I went to the other women up and down the corridor, the office secretaries. They were sympathetic—some of them said that Bradley had made off-color comments to them on occasion, although he hadn't actually touched them. But they didn't feel that they could do much about it, since he outranked them. I got a lot of moral support, but they weren't willing to confront him with me.

That evening I drew up a list of the men I thought might be supportive. I did this partly to reassure myself that not every man around me was a jerk, and partly as a matter of principle: I decided that since a man had done this, it was fair to ask the other men to help me deal with him. Two days after the incident, I went to the handful of men I thought I might be able to count on, and told each of them, one by one, what had happened.

I was very tentative in approaching them. I described the attack, without any names, and asked them what they thought of a man who would do something like that. If they laughed or joked or minimized it, I shut up and left. Only if they responded seriously did I tell them that it was Bradley and he had done it to me, two days earlier.

Four of the men I approached agreed to be allies for me. I made my expectations clear. I told each of these men that I was coming to him because I thought he was the kind of man who would not tolerate this kind of behavior. Two were in Bradley's section itself; the other two worked down the hall *from him and knew him. I told the four about each other, and asked them to get together and deal with Bradley in a way that would make him understand that he could never do this again to anyone. I didn't ask them to protect me, like some poor, pitiful victim—I said,* "I want you to do whatever it takes to make it absolutely clear to him that you know what he did, you *think it is despicable, and* you will not put up with him *treating women this way."*

Within a week, they dealt with him. To this day, I don't know exactly what they did. My four allies would never tell me the details, but whatever it was, it scared the hell out of Bradley. I don't think they hit him (he had no obvious bruises) but they certainly got through to him. He never touched me again. He didn't retaliate in any way; in fact, from then on, he seemed intimidated and subdued whenever I was around. As a tactic, it was very effective.

My allies felt exceedingly virtuous about their role in all this. Several told me afterward that they were glad I'd asked them to do it—it made them feel like they were men who acted responsibly, who stood up for women's rights. My boss, of course, was immensely relieved and grateful that he didn't have to do anything. And when I told the other women how I'd handled it, they were amazed—they did not think of any of the men around them as potential allies when it came to sexual harassment and were pleasantly surprised to find out that some men, sometimes, were actually willing to hold other men accountable for the way they treat women.

At the time, I didn't know what else to do—these men were the only allies available, in that environment, and I'm glad that they came through for me. But now that I know that some men can do it, I think that this is the least we should expect from any man who says that he cares about women, or about moral justice.

Andrea reacted quickly to her harasser's attack, using the men around her as resources. Legally, she could have filed assault charges against Bradley as well as a harassment complaint, but like many women, she wanted to find a remedy that would stop him without bringing the law into it. She examined her options—individual confrontation, action by her supervisor, a group confrontation with the few other women around, and finally, action by some of her male colleagues. While many women would prefer not to depend on male assistance, it is important to consider the possibility of men as allies—especially if that is the only kind of assistance available.

In effect, Andrea asked these four men to plan and carry out a form of group confrontation. She made it clear that she didn't want them to speak for her or "protect" her, but to let the harasser know that they themselves, as men he had to work with, knew and disliked what he had done. They, not Andrea, were the ones who held him accountable for his sexist behavior. And Andrea is entirely correct when she says that this is the kind of support women should be able to expect from the men around them.

Gerry Sütter, a member of the National Organization for Changing Men, has thought about men's responsibility for ending sexual harassment. He has this story to tell:

A MATTER OF RESPECT

It was Paris in the spring. I was enjoying an unexpected day off with a North African coworker, my friend Marcel. As we were heading down the road, he yelled at a woman, "Hey you, babe, you with the beautiful blue eyes!" He continued with jokes, sneers, and excited observations about the anatomy of the women we passed.

At first I tried to ignore it. And as is often the case when you ignore oppressive behavior, it increased. This was my first lesson. I didn't want to complain. However, I wanted even less to listen to Marcel ogle at women and watch the pained responses of the women he hassled. So I asked him: "Why?"

"Why what?"

"Why do you say that to women?"

"Oh, they love it," he said.

"Really?" I said, but before I could get him to look at his behavior, he proceeded to tell me about his girlfriend in Lebanon. He talked about his true love for her; he even showed me her picture.

My second lesson for the day was that when you call someone on stupid behavior, they don't pretend to justify it. More often they change the subject.

My third lesson was to work out the paradox: the deprecating way Marcel looked at women on the street, and the way he talked about those close to him (mother, girlfriend), putting them on a pedestal. It seemed contradictory, until I realized that in both cases he was not thinking of the women as full human beings in their own right. Women on the street were objects to be ogled, and women he cared about were objects to be doted on, pampered, guided, and controlled.

Marcel and I had some time to kill, so we went over to his house for lunch. I was warmly greeted by his father and ushered into the dining room. My fourth lesson came from the way both men actually treated the women in the family. What stunned me was that there was no eye contact with the women; they were not even introduced, but merely pointed out: "That's my sister, and that's my mother." A young girl who was gazing at us was quickly scooted out of the room.

I am not really competent to make a statement about North African sexism, except to observe that it is qualitatively different from sexism in the United States. My fifth lesson of the day was that sexism takes many forms, depending on the culture and the family.

So I want to talk about the culture I would like to change: our own. This is about the male pattern of checking out women and hassling them with both verbal and nonverbal behavior. There is no cookbook approach to gender-appropriate behavior, except the principle of respect. A comment that would be welcome from a husband to his spouse is frightening between strangers on the street, and criminal between a boss and his employee. Out of attraction, fear of rejection, machismo, and old adolescent patterns of behavior, many men behave like caricatures of ourselves. We need to understand that being obnoxious is a way of distancing, not endearing.

We have a problem here. And it is precisely a problem of perception. We have half the population looking over their shoulders, staring at the ground, staying in at night, and scurrying away from demeaning slurs, while the rest of us respond to sexual harassment with something between a grunt and a guffaw. It's a woman's problem, right? Wrong.

Disrespect detracts from all human beings. Women do not enjoy being "looked over" any more than men in prison enjoy being "looked over" by other men in prison. Let us cease the euphemisms: In either case, the process of "looking over" expresses domination and subjugation (along with an implicit threat of violence). We men who want satisfying intimate relationships with women will not benefit by behaving in ways that make women look for escape routes every time a man is in the same hallway or street. This is what it is like for many women who are hassled by men.

For those who want to eliminate the gross indignity, distress, and emotional damage produced by sexual harassment in our environment, here are some suggestions about contradicting sexist behavior:

Don't laugh. No matter how unsafe you feel, you can refuse to laugh at a sexist joke. You don't have to say, "Yeah, I know what you mean," or whatever verbal stroking you usually give people when you want them to know you are following them. Don't validate stupidity.

The Socratic approach. The most powerful technique for getting people to change their ways of doing things is to really listen. Take seriously their most frivolous comment: "Oh, that's interesting. What do you mean by that?" "Really? Do you think so?" Just listen very attentively. Often people will talk themselves out of their own tasteless or derogatory statements, under the spotlight of that kind of serious attention.

Interrupt lightly. Men, as men, are able to be powerful allies with women. Where women may be discounted or put on the defensive, we are in a very powerful position to interrupt sexism in action. A subtle "Lighten up, Harry" will do wonders without wounding male egos. Especially in work environments, I'm often able to do more by staying light: "Well, that sounds real intelligent. I don't know how I've missed the experience."

Interrupt anyway. Where violence is happening or about to happen to women or children, I make a habit of intervening. Sometimes, barking "Stop it!" in your loudest, deepest voice is what it takes to get some people's attention. Using the bark of the drill sergeant works in the world.

Talk about what's at issue. Learn how to lobby for what matters. It is appropriate to want to live and work in an environment unpolluted by distress. Use your network of friends and coworkers to discuss issues of ethics and policy, including situations involving interpersonal behavior. A discussion with a couple of people can get the idea passed around the office and change the environment. You sometimes need to be explicit and insist on it.

Don't let fear control you. I suppose there are dangers that come with being too visible. It stands to reason that the more you succeed, the more you may be targeted by the diehards. Meet slander with righteous indignation on your part and that of every friend and supporter you have. If physical threats come from someone you know, you might respond with a visit from a couple of your most muscular friends.

I choose my battlefields carefully, and this area of men's harassment of women is one of mine. If we want a just society, we need to begin somewhere, and what better place to start than in our relationships with women?[1]

Gerry's suggestions are good ones—a basic, personal blueprint for building a workplace that is free of sexual harassment. His first suggestion—don't promote stupidity by laughing at sexist jokes or comments—will in itself go a long way toward withdrawing male approval from sexist behavior. That simple, virtually risk-free action deprives harassers of the negative male bonding they so often seek at women's expense. And his suggestions for active intervention include a range of practical, effective options that can be tailored to the specific type of harassment being challenged.

Stopping flagrant harassment is the first, essential step. But there are also all kinds of dominance games that involve abuse of power in more subtle forms. These power moves are a standard part of many harassers' repertoires, because they work. And harassers are not the only ones who use them. Consciously or unconsciously, men who do not commit overt harassment can silence and disempower women by engaging in the routine male-dominance games embedded in language patterns, speaking styles, and a great deal of interpersonal behavior. Condescension, constant interruptions when women are speaking, and many other types of common sexist behavior can be identified, named, and confronted.

For men who want to move beyond a harassment-free environment to create truly nonsexist social and working relationships, here is a list of twenty standard dominance behaviors to recognize and challenge—power moves that drive women up the wall whenever they are applied as part of a consistent, sexist pattern:

- *Hogging the show:* dominating every discussion, talking too much, too loud, too long.
- *Condescension and paternalism:* "Now, do any women have something to add?"
- *Restating:* saying in another way what someone else, particularly a woman, has just said perfectly clearly.
- *Speaking for others:* "What Susan really meant was . . ." "What black/Asian/Hispanic women really want is . . ."
- *Interrupting:* bulldozing right through the speaker, on the assumption that one's own contributions are of paramount importance, overriding anything the present speaker may be in the midst of saying.
- *Self-listening:* formulating a response after the first few seconds, not listening to anything from that point on, and leaping in at the first pause.

- *Nitpicking:* pointing out every minor flaw in others' statements; emphasizing the exception to every generality.
- *Put-downs and one-upmanship:* "That's stupid, how could you say that?" "I *used* to believe that, of course . . ."
- *Fleeing from emotion:* ignoring, trivializing, or ridiculing emotional content; taking refuge in jokes, withdrawal, or intellectual abstractions to avoid dealing with statements about feelings.
- *Attention seeking:* using all kinds of verbal and nonverbal dramatics to gain and hold the spotlight.
- *Arrogant problem solving:* continually jumping in with The Answer before others have had a chance to contribute.
- *Overexplaining:* assuming women have no technical skills or mechanical knowledge and need to have everything explained in words of one syllable.
- *Speaking in capital letters:* pronouncing one's own opinion as the final word on the subject, accentuated by aggressive body language and tone of voice.
- *Inflexibility:* going to the mat for one's position on even the most minor items.
- *Selective attention and body language:* leaning forward when men speak; shifting restlessly and staring at the floor, the wall, or the clock when women speak.
- *Treating women like audiences, not equals:* competing with males and taking men's ideas seriously, while expecting only polite attention and support from women.
- *Dominating the terrain:* insisting on discussion of one's own topics, while ignoring issues raised by women.
- *Running the show:* always taking charge of meetings and tasks; arrogantly assuming that no one else (female) can step in and take care of business.
- *The invisibility trick:* introducing every person present at the meeting except the one woman in the room.

- *The inferior/superior trick:* automatically assuming, when any given male/female business team walks into the room, that the male is the female's boss.[2]

No one, male or female, enjoys being on the receiving end of these power moves. When men repeatedly use these moves against women in a workplace or social setting, they can create, on a much more subtle level, the same atmosphere of exclusion and powerlessness that sexual harassment produces. From the most blatant sexual harassment to the most routine daily expressions of gender-based power, men who care about women's lives need to recognize and understand the dynamics of power and gender. Men who want to be allies for women will have no lack of opportunities for action.

onstruction Workers, Subway Creeps, and Other Daily Hazards: Confronting Harassers in the Community

Harassment on the job is frequent enough, but most women face an even greater probability of being harassed out in the community, everywhere from bus stops and bars to cafés and art museums. All three categories of harassment (sexual predation, dominance, and territorial harassment) happen regularly in public areas.

Community harassment of all kinds appears to be committed more often by strangers than acquaintances, although both occur. Casual, male-dominance harassment is the most common form of harassment on the street and in public facilities; it seems to be most prevalent in downtown areas where the population is highly mobile and the protection of anonymity is readily available for the harassers. All harassers take advantage of opportunity to some extent, but one type of anonymous community assailant—the groper, a sexual-pastime harasser who gets his thrills from fondling women in public—is highly opportunistic, specifically striking in crowded buses, subways, and elevators full of strangers.

Harassment in the community has real economic repercussions, both for women and for merchants. Women lose the right to use large areas of the public space that their own taxes support; they pay for many public facilities that they cannot freely enjoy. The risk of harassment strongly influences women's decisions about where and when their own towns are safe: which parks are a pleasant place for lunch and which are battle zones; which public streets offer an uninterrupted walk and which are hostile male territory; which stores, restaurants, and shopping centers to patronize or to avoid. Merchants who are oblivious to harassment can lose a large share of potential business. Allowing even a few harassers to operate in the shopping center, in the parking lot, or on the street out front (never mind in the store itself) drives women away even more efficiently than having a pornography/sex-paraphernalia shop next door. Sexual harassment (including the use of crude sexist advertising, the public equivalent of pornography in the workplace) very efficiently defines which parts of the public environment are accessible and which are off limits to women.

As the writer Katha Pollitt has noted, "Many women act—and are treated—as if the urban outdoors were alien ground. . . . A city in which women claimed their share of public space would look rather different and feel even more so." Pollitt cites the "constant low-level aggravation" of harassment, the fact that a bus stop is a "stage for female vulnerability," not just a place to wait for a bus, and half a dozen other examples. She describes the simple experience of walking through a small New York City park on an autumn afternoon: Within moments, two men harassed her; one "invited me to take my clothes off and [the other] wanted to know why I wasn't smiling." The park was unacknowledged but undeniable male territory: "[There] were perhaps 50 men, strolling, ambling, striding along eating hot dogs, sitting on benches and reading the paper or trading illegal substances as though they had all the time in the world—and 3 women, all walking quickly and grimly, as I was now doing, as though late for an appointment with the dentist." When a male friend later objected that the problem wasn't the men but the petty criminals in the park, Pollitt noted how interesting it was that he still felt comfortable enough to eat his lunch there, but the women he worked with did not. Pollitt concluded, "A great deal of what we call public space is, in fact, male turf."[1]

Sexual harassment transforms the urban landscape into a very different kind of terrain for women. Activities that seem perfectly unremarkable to men turn into steep, uphill battles for women. For example, when a national health and environmental magazine suggested a few years ago that running in the city was a delight and hikers should jog through downtown parks and streets to stay in shape, many women in Washington hooted with scorn. The article was, of course, written by a man, who assumed that *his* pleasant experience of running in the city was universal. The author never bothered to ask women what their runs were like, and had no idea of the barrage of interruptions, sexual comments, and verbal threats women receive every time they put on their running shorts.

Here's Sharon Roger's story about her month-long effort to establish the right to walk unmolested (in work suits, not jogging shorts) in downtown Washington:

THE HARASSERS IN THE PARK

I am: angry, tired, feminist, biracial, African-American, woman-oriented, the first child of upper-middle-class parents, a rape and incest survivor, a woman.

I live in the nation's capital, a city of extreme wealth, poverty, violence, oppression, power, and arrogance, and I have been confronting men's public acts of sexism and aggression since 1989, when I was twenty.

My most memorable confrontation happened last summer. Every day, on my way to work, I walked from my bus stop through a park to my office. Every day, two groups of men, one at the beginning and one at the end of the park, harassed me. Without fail, they greeted me with, "Good morning, pretty. . . . Hey, baby. . . . Good mooooooorning, yeeessss!"—leering, grinning, staring, rolling their eyes, and rolling their hips—all this, every day, before I'd even had my first cup of tea.

Each time they harassed me, I confronted them and held them accountable for their behavior. For every leer and "baby" they hurled at me, I responded, "Don't harass women! I don't like it, no woman likes it!"

Our power struggle continued for more than a month. The men continued to interrupt and harass me (and any other woman walking past) as though we were public property; I continued to assert my humanity and women's right to live without men abusing us just so they can feel powerful at our expense. Although I often felt that it would never end and that confronting them was useless, I refused to let them wear me down.

Finally, one morning, after having confronted the first group of men, I reached the second, already prepared to confront their daily ritual of leering and shouting. Just as one of the group opened his mouth to yell, and I took a breath to respond, another man threw his arm across the first's stomach and said, "Don't say anything—she won't like it."

I was ecstatic; those few words, from a man who, the day before, had treated me like a nonhuman plaything, made my day.

The men never bothered me again. My constant, daily message, demanding that they stop harassing me and notifying them that no women enjoy harassment, had finally taken root.

Women can end verbal violence against us; indeed, we are the only ones who can.

Sharon succeeded through sheer persistence: a clear, simple, principled message, delivered over and over again. Imagine how much faster the behavior would have changed if every woman who walked through that park had done the same thing, every day—or if even ten women a day had done so.

As Katha Pollitt noted, bus stops, like parks, can be havens for harassers. For economic reasons, women are by far the majority of bus riders in most cities, but at bus stops they are a captive audience for harassers; most women will just endure the abuse, since leaving the vicinity to escape the harasser means missing the bus. However, women are not waiting for the bus companies to take action—they are now reclaiming this public space for themselves. Here's a classic success story from Martina in Philadelphia:

THE BUS STOP

It was about 5:15 on a Wednesday afternoon. I came around the corner to catch the bus and saw seven or eight women and one man in the bus shelter. I could tell that something was going on. I saw him lurching up to one woman, then another, and I noticed that the women were standing very close together, looking uneasy. Then I got close enough to hear what he was saying. It was a steady stream of "Hey, mama, hey, bitch, you look good, I sure would like to lick you, hey, bitch, watsamatter, you don't like it that way, you uptight, how about you, honey. . . . " He was moving in on one woman after another in the group; they kept shifting closer to each other, looking the other way, trying to ignore him. It was really nasty—he was right up against them, in their faces.

I thought, "Boy, is this miserable—can't even catch the bus in our own neighborhood in peace!" So I took a deep breath and marched into the bus shelter. I said to the women, "Is this guy bothering you?" They nodded. I put my hands on my hips, stood there like I owned the pavement, and said, "Stop harassing women! I don't like it, no woman likes it! You get out of here!"

He turned on me, with a surprised look on his face. "Hey, bitch," he growled at me, "what you talking about! I'm waiting for the bus!"

I took a half step toward him. I said, in my best voice-of-command tone, "This is OUR bus stop. You're harassing women. I heard what you were saying, bitch this and bitch that, you want to lick us. Stop harassing women! You want to catch the bus, you go wait down there by the stop sign. GO ON, MOVE!"

He hesitated. The women watched. Nobody breathed. I stood my ground, kept looking him straight in the eye, and repeated: "I SAID STOP HARASSING WOMEN! YOU HEARD ME! GO STAND BY THAT STOP SIGN!" Still no movement. Dead silence. Then he started to say something —it began with the word "bitch" but I didn't give him a chance to get the rest out. I kept going, just rolled right over him: "NONE OF US ARE GOING TO PUT UP WITH YOUR UGLY BEHAVIOR. THAT'S HARASSMENT AND WE ALL WANT YOU OUT OF THIS BUS SHELTER!"

And without another word he walked out of the shelter and over to the stop sign, fifteen feet away.

The women burst into cheers. Some actually clapped. I felt great. We talked about harassment; I told them how I'd learned to confront in the rape crisis center self-defense class. We were all still talking and laughing when the bus came, a few minutes later.

He stood there by the stop sign, looking kind of stunned— didn't say another word, and never did get on the bus.

Like Sharon, Martina demonstrated how one woman can turn even a tough harassment situation around, if she knows what to do. She named the behavior, refused to let him off the hook, ordered him to stop, and kept control of the interaction by interrupting his efforts to intimidate her. It was touch and go for a few minutes. What finally defeated the harasser was her explicit statement on behalf of women in general— she redefined his victims as her allies and multiplied the power of her confrontation when she said that *all* of the women wanted him out of their bus stop. When Martina emphasized their collective strength, she finally demolished his assumptions about his power to control the situation.

Women don't go looking for opportunities to confront harassers, but just walking through the park or down the street often means walking into an incident where confrontation is necessary. In fact, sometimes just stepping out the front door of her own apartment building can bring a woman face to face with a harasser, as K.S. found out:

PITY THE POOR HARASSER

My friend Kate was waiting for me on the front steps of my apartment building one evening, when she got harassed by a man on the street. He said something crude to her; she said something rude right back, and when I got there he was halfway up the steps, making an obscene gesture at her. I jumped in between the two of them, looked him in the eye, and COMMANDED him to stop. I stood up to the guy and yelled, "STOP HARASSING WOMEN! DON'T YOU MAKE THAT GESTURE AT MY FRIEND! GET OFF THESE STEPS RIGHT NOW AND DON'T YOU EVER DO THAT AGAIN!" I was fierce. I actually followed him down the steps, still confronting.

I think his ego was dented. Kate is six feet tall and this guy was even bigger, and here I was—all five feet two of me— leaping to her rescue and verbally hammering away at him. Kate began laughing so hard at the sight, I thought she was going to fall down. Between my yelling and her laughter, well, he didn't have a prayer of saving face. As he slouched off down the street, in complete defeat, the best he could manage was to mumble, "Hey, men have feelings, too, you know." Which set Kate off laughing even harder—gee, we had hurt the harasser's feelings. These guys ought to take a second to think about our feelings before they decide to harass us.

Outdoors or indoors, women face harassment. Whether the harasser is a stranger on the street or an acquaintance in a social situation, women *can* speak up to defend themselves. Here's Amy's story about what her friend Cara did:

CARA AT THE PARTY

My friend Cara is twenty-three, a white woman of medium height and build. She looks nice, not particularly intimidating or anything, but she refuses to put up with harassers. Earlier this year, we were at a party at a friend's house with a lot of people. It was very loud and crowded. At one point *during the evening, a man we barely knew came up and put his hand on her behind.*

Furious, Cara turned to him and said in no uncertain terms, "Women don't like it when men do that! Stop!"

He gave her a stunned look, turned right around, and walked away immediately. He didn't retaliate in any way. In fact, a little while later, he left the party. We weren't sorry to see him go! I thought the way Cara spoke up was just great.

Cara's straightforward statement literally left the harasser speechless. Instead of worrying about whether the harasser might think she was rude, Cara simply called him to account for his own arrogance and rudeness in putting his hands on her—a perfectly appropriate response to his invasive behavior. In social settings, women are often tempted to soften their statements with verbal fluff and excuses, but Cara cut right to the behavior and stopped him on the spot.

And here's Carroll's story about a similar incident, involving a stranger in a hotel lobby in suburban Virginia:

THE HOTEL LOBBY

I was walking through the lobby of the Ramada Renaissance Hotel at the Ballston Metro subway station on a weekend afternoon. It's a large, open space and was fairly empty at that time of day. A few people were seated at the Tivoli, the indoor café in the hotel lobby, including a man who was watching me as I crossed toward the exit, passing right by him. I ignored his gaze but then heard him make a comment about me while I walked past. This made me angry; I muttered a curse at him, under my breath, and just kept going.

But as I reached the exit, I realized that I was in a safe enough place to go back and confront him, so that I wouldn't just have to carry around my anger inside me.

I walked right back over to him, pointed directly at him, and said, "Don't ever do that again!" To my surprise, he actually looked frightened. He said, "I'm sorry."

I walked away feeling I had not only done the right thing, but had won.

Carroll was right—there was no reason to tolerate this harasser's comments. In terms of body language alone, she had the upper hand: He was seated, while she was standing and pointing him out in a public place. What could he say? His action was inexcusable, and he was suddenly being called on it. Carroll's simple, one-sentence confrontation won an immediate, flat-out apology from this harasser—no small accomplishment!

Lacey and Kim were sitting in a café, having dinner, when their harasser struck. They came up with a very inventive way to flip the power dynamics in this social situation:

A WOMAN AND HER BINOCULARS

Lacey and I had been out all day, hiking and talking and just having a good time. We decided to get some dinner at a little restaurant downtown—it was nothing fancy, just a crowded, noisy neighborhood place with the tables all jammed close together, but the food was inexpensive and usually pretty good.

We found a parking place nearby; Lacey decided she didn't want to leave her new binoculars in the car, so we carried them with us. We got a table and ordered our meal. We were both in a great mood.

About halfway through our dinner, a man came in and sat down across from us, a couple of tables away. Apparently the sight of two women laughing and having dinner together was just too much for him. He started making kissing noises and gestures at us, staring and making comments. We felt invaded.

He was on the verge of ruining our good mood when sud-

denly Lacey had a brainstorm. She picked up her binoculars, turned and faced the man, and carefully focused them on him. Then she began to gesture to him, shaking her head and touching her mouth the way you would if you were trying to tell someone he had spinach stuck on his front teeth. He stopped leering and started to look kind of uncertain.

Then Lacey handed the binoculars to me. I too made a big deal of getting them properly focused on him, and then I began making gestures as if he had something on his chin as well.

At that point he lost his cool altogether. He started rubbing his chin and checking his teeth and looking very uncomfortable and embarrassed. We stared at him for a second, then shrugged, put the binoculars down, and continued our meal. The next time we looked up, he was staring down at his table, looking totally mortified. He didn't bother us again for the rest of the evening.

It may not have been a typical confrontation, but Lacey and Kim won hands-down. He demanded their attention, so they gave it to him: very close scrutiny, in distressing detail —not exactly the kind of attention that he had in mind. Without a word, they demolished his dominance agenda and imposed some ego-bruising personal penalties for his obnoxious macho behavior. His "right" to intrude on two women dissolved into public embarrassment.

Construction sites sometimes seem to be staffed entirely by men like this one—males who fervently believe in their innate, all-day, everyday "right" to intrude on any woman going about her business. Men like these have a warped sense of personal identity, the product of a macho, sexist culture. They define their masculinity in terms of control over women and feel free to exert their power at any time to demand any female's attention. Women deeply resent it. For many women, the mere mention of construction workers brings groans about street harassment.

In fact, however, there is no hard evidence that construction workers are more likely to harass than men in other male-dominated occupations. It may be just a matter of location and access. The engineer or business executive who harasses the women in his office is engaging in a particular kind of power abuse, targeting any or all of the women in the workplace. The construction worker who harasses women on the street is doing essentially the same thing—but since the public street is his workplace, he has access to a much larger number of women. If one in five engineers harasses, he may insult three women a day; if one in five construction workers is a harasser, he may insult three hundred.

Most construction workers who do harass women are routine dominance harassers and are actually easier to deal with than bosses, professors, or coworkers who abuse their power. Women have had considerable success in using direct-action tactics to handle construction sites, as Lori A. Roth's story indicates:

LUNCH HOUR: MANHATTAN

I was twenty-two years old. I had just graduated from college and was working at an auction house on Manhattan's Upper East Side. The auction house made a practice of hiring attractive, well-bred young women. At lunchtime, the staff typically ran out to the nearest delicatessen, a block away, and then ate back at the office, while working.

It was spring, and a luxury apartment building was going up on the lot just beyond the auction house. The construction workers took their lunch at about the same time we did, and sat on the sidewalk to eat. As we walked to the deli they'd barrage us with wolf calls and seedy remarks—as if the avenue at lunch hour were a runway in a striptease show. For the stream of young women, it was terribly degrading. We walked blocks out of our way, or went elsewhere, to avoid them. But as a rule we took very short breaks, and sometimes we felt we had no choice but to run straight to the deli and right back to work.

On one particular day I dashed out for a bite. I remember I was wearing a crisp linen blouse and long skirt. It was breezy and warm. Still, I took my sweater and just as I neared the construction site I wrapped it tightly around me, crossing my arms in front of my chest. I braced myself for their comments and set my gaze straight ahead of me.

They whistled, as usual, and offered their comments on my various body parts. I was blocking out the noise as I barreled forward, when one of the workers stepped right in front of me and said, "If you don't want us to see 'em, baby, don't wear those see-through tops."

I was furious. I'd done my best to get by them with my dignity intact. The verbal abuse I expected, but that he'd actually blocked my path was more than I could stand. I stepped back and yelled, "Do you know the meaning of the word harassment? It's one thing to take your slobbering from the curb, but now you have the nerve to do it in my face? Do you have a mother? A sister? A wife?" My heart was pounding but I just stared him down. I felt sick to my stomach. His buddies on the site began to tease him for the lashing he got, and I turned to the rest of them and bellowed, "Does anyone else have something to say?" Apart from traffic, there was silence on the street.

At the deli I saw our receptionist, a beautiful young woman with wavy hair that fell to her waist. We greeted each other and I paid for my order. As I headed back to the office all was peaceful. At the end of the block stood the same construction worker—he was bowing deeply to me, his hard-hat in his hand. It seemed like a good-natured apology and I nodded my acceptance.

I lingered briefly in the lobby of the auction house, and when the receptionist arrived I asked her if she noticed anything unusual. She said, "Yes, it was strange—they were so quiet."

I felt like I taught them something that day. I don't know how lasting the change in their behavior was, but I did make them think, and at least two women were able to walk freely down the block, unharassed. I learned something that day, too. I wasn't a fighter by nature, but I fought back and won. I tasted my own power and it tasted good.

Lori's feelings on initially confronting this man were not unusual. For many women, confronting does feel frightening at first, because it is not the standard, silent-victim appeasement approach most women were taught in childhood. That old ignore-them-and-scurry-past response may be more comfortable on the surface, because it is familiar. But it simply does not work. Women don't avoid victimization when they are silent; they just internalize their anger and feel defeated. Confronters put that anger to productive use, channeling it into a principled public statement, and they end up feeling exhilarated. As Lori found, a well-structured verbal confrontation, backed up with tone of voice and body language, is extraordinarily effective: no obscenities, no insults—just a strong, clear statement of the behavior in a way that holds the man accountable for it. And, as is often the case, Lori's successful confrontation had a broader effect. It freed the receptionist from harassment, too, and probably dozens of other women as well.

Here's another success story about dealing with construction workers, this time from Agnes, in the Midwest:

THE CONSTRUCTION WORKERS

In the mid-1980s I lived in a very nice four-story apartment building on a quiet tree-lined side street near downtown in Cincinnati, Ohio. It was less than a mile from my office, so I could walk to work every day. I really liked the convenient location, and the neighborhood was great.

Across the street, facing my front door, was another four-story apartment building. In 1987, the local university bought it and began renovating it for student housing. The harassment began on day one of the renovation job.

I came out of my building at 8:15 on that Monday morning and stepped out the door into a barrage of catcalls, whistles, hey-mamas, and all the rest. I looked over and saw about forty construction workers putting up scaffolding across the street. They hooted and hollered until I got around the cor-

ner and out of sight. I was furious. So much for my quiet, friendly neighborhood! I steamed all day. The workmen were gone by the time I got home that evening.

The next morning, I was running late. I dashed out the front door, not even thinking about the construction work, and got hit in the face with another barrage of hoots and whistles and catcalls. Crude remarks about my legs, my breasts, my ass. One guy yelled, "Sure would like to see that hair spread out on a pillow!" I stormed up the street and around the corner. It's 8:30 in the morning, I'm late for work, and I can't walk out my front door without having fools laying into me. That evening, I talked to several of the other women who lived in my building. They were all getting the same treatment and were just as angry and upset as I was. It seemed that every woman who came in or out of our building, all day long, was an excuse for the men to entertain themselves.

A couple of my neighbors said that from now on they were going to go out the back door of the building to avoid the abuse. I said that we shouldn't have to go out the alley and past the trash Dumpsters just to get in and out of our own homes! Why should we let these guys get away with that kind of control over our lives?

The next morning, Wednesday, I was ready. I planned what I was going to do, got a good night's sleep, and got up early, ready for action.

I came out the front door, into the bombardment of whistles and comments. But instead of racing up the street and around the corner, I marched over to the curb and planted myself there, looked up at the workers all over the scaffolding across the street, and yelled, "STOP HARASSING WOMEN!"

They were astonished. There was a long moment of complete silence. They looked at me and I looked right back at them. Then a little voice, not very confident, came floating across the street, "Hey, lady, can't you take a compliment?"

I said, loud enough for them all to hear me, "Compliments are something women like. What YOU'RE doing is harass-

ment! This is our neighborhood, and you are harassing every woman who lives here! IT IS NOT A COMPLIMENT AND WE DON'T LIKE IT!"

Long silence number two. I stood there with my head up and my shoulders back and my feet planted like I was the mayor of the city, and just waited.

Finally another little voice, sounding even less sure of himself, said, "Jesus, lady, we're sorry."

I said, "Fine. We accept your apology. Don't do it again. You are in OUR neighborhood and we will not put up with ANY more abuse from you. Now have a good morning." Then I turned and walked up the street to the corner. I heard a few tentative, feeble "good mornings" as I walked away.

That night, my neighbors said the workers had been pretty quiet all day. I told them what I'd done, and they thought it was great. Word spread through the neighborhood. For the next two months, every time the workmen started to say something crude, one woman or another would yell right back at them, "Stop harassing women! We told you we don't like it!"

We wound up with the politest construction workers ever. They certainly treated me with respect. From that day on, I got a couple of very polite "good mornings" when I came out the front door, and not another word. They did a nice job renovating the building, too.

Like Lori, Agnes made a real difference. By talking to her neighbors about what she had done, she also equipped a whole additional group of women with some powerful new confrontation skills.

Women have used many other mechanisms to hold construction workers accountable—for example, demanding to see the foreman every time one of the workers harasses a woman (they hate losing work time to handle complaints and will usually come down hard on the worker who caused the interruption). Women have also written irate letters to the construction firm president; asked the alderman or neighborhood council representative to do the same; and handed out flyers to women in the neighborhood with phone numbers to call to complain about the harassers, including the office numbers of the construction company, the subcontractors, the corporation that owns the property, and even the home numbers of the firms' presidents. In at least one case, a group of women hung a bedsheet out of the window of the building across the street with the words "STOP HARASSING WOMEN" printed in letters two feet high. That cut down the verbal abuse quite a bit. Women who were subsequently harassed on the sidewalk below pointed to the huge sign and yelled confidently, "Can't you all read? Cut the harassment!" With all the options women have devised, no woman should ever again feel helpless when harassed by construction workers.

Judging from women's personal reports, buses and subways are also very common locations for harassment. Many women still have difficulty dealing with harassment on public transportation. Unlike construction workers, the gropers, feelers, flashers, and space-invaders on the bus or subway do not stop at verbal harassment. These are physical harassers.

That alone does not make them harder to deal with; the real constraints are women's own fear and social conditioning, not the nature of the harassers' behavior. Many women feel extremely self-conscious and nervous about making a public scene in a small, enclosed space. They may be able to confront a man on the sidewalk, but doing the same thing on the bus seems impossible. In one case, they are out on an open, public street where they can walk away freely after the confrontation, but in a bus, an elevator, or any other confined space, they feel physically and psychologically trapped, and afraid of negative responses from the other passengers as well as from the harasser.

Mass-transit harassers count on this intimidation factor. Because women silence themselves on buses and subways, the harassers who enjoy physically molesting women can move in on their targets with almost complete freedom, confident that the victims will be too mortified to even consider taking action.

A very clear, matter-of-fact confrontation is the single most effective way to stop these harassers. The first step is naming the harasser's behavior explicitly: In this situation, "Stop that!" is not sufficient. "Take your hand off my leg, stop harassing women, I've never seen you before in my life," is much clearer. In this enclosed space, the confronter should let everyone know *exactly* what is going on, then tell the harasser what to do: "Move back. Go sit over there, and keep your hands off the passengers." That usually ends the harasser's aggression immediately. Most will move in response to a direct, public, businesslike command.

The combination of a strong, principled message and a calm tone of voice is often effective in these encounters, even if the woman and the harasser are the only people on the bus or subway car. Here's a success story in which Ann Mehrten handled just that situation:

RIDING THE SUBWAY

This encounter happened in Washington, D.C., two years ago. I was in my early twenties. It was a Saturday afternoon, and I was on an empty Metro subway car at the Gallery Place station downtown. A guy entered the car and sat down in the seat next to me, making me suspicious, so I wasn't surprised when he began crowding me. At first I gave him the benefit of the doubt and moved over closer to the wall, but he continued to sit right up against me. I debated changing seats, but felt that would send a message that he'd intimidated me, so I didn't move.

Then I felt a nudge against my ribs, but his hands were both in view. He nudged again, and I realized he was poking my ribs with his elbow. I looked directly at him, and he winked at me.

That was it. I said calmly, with deliberate dispassion, "You are making my ride a pain in the ass."

He looked hurt, I didn't change expression, and he moved to another seat. I felt relieved and pleased that I was able to take back my space.

I have sworn at men harassing me in other situations and

it didn't help. It's always a judgment call; in this case, I believe it was the combination of calm voice and angry words that worked.

As Ann concluded, swearing is far less effective than a calm, straightforward confrontation. In this case, she used a stern but simple confrontation statement, direct eye contact, and an unsmiling expression to defend her ground and deflate the harasser. It worked very well. Like Ann, women who face harassers on public transportation should not give up their space unnecessarily. Name his behavior and tell him to move. This is not usually a physically dangerous situation (although it is safer to be on a subway car with at least a few people, rather than an empty one).

If the harasser does not move away when the woman first confronts him, the second stage of the confrontation is to draw the attention of the other passengers. To bring in some reinforcements, stand up at your seat, point to the man, make eye contact with a few of the people around you, and say, "Did you see what this guy just did? He just [describe what he did]. This guy harasses women. Look at this man." They may not say anything, but most will look.

There is no need to shout. A firm voice will work—it is a small space, and people will hear you. There is no need to be verbally abusive. Your confrontation statement should make you sound rational, believable, and completely in control, but indignant at this very bizarre behavior. It is useful to label it as both harassment and abnormal behavior, to say to the other passengers, for example: "What a disgusting thing to do—what on earth would make any man think that he could feel up a complete stranger [or grab a woman's breasts, pull out his penis, or whatever he did, precisely] on the bus? That kind of harassment is outrageous." Use your tone to convey the reaction you expect from the other passengers. Act as if you *assume* they are supporters; any reasonable person would *of course* see this harasser's behavior as repulsive.

In short, if the harasser does not stop instantly, use your

public description of the behavior to isolate him at the same time that you direct a wide circle of negative public attention to him. At that point, the object is to make the harasser feel conspicuous and acutely uncomfortable. Keep describing his behavior and putting public pressure on him until he either moves, sits quietly, or leaves the bus.

Here's a success story in which Karen Crain used this stage-two technique to isolate a panhandler who harassed her in the subway station:

LET THIS BE AN EXAMPLE TO YOU

I'm not into cold weather at all. So when spring comes along and daylight savings time kicks in, I get so happy. It was just that kind of Friday, and my friend Wendy and I were headed for a happy hour at our favorite restaurant.

We were in the subway station, and Wendy needed a fare card. Since it was rush hour, there was a long line, so I just hung out to wait for her. A panhandler came up to me asking for money for the train. I knew it was a scam, but I was in such a great mood, and he seemed like a nice guy, so I gave him some change.

What he did next was one weird way to say thank you. He walked behind me, rubbed up against my back, and said, "Lady, you've got a great body."

I spun around, looked him in the eye, and said, "How dare you harass me! Especially after I did you a favor! Give me back my money!"

He laughed and said, "Bitch, you just don't know how to take a compliment."

Well, that really pissed me off. I decided to declare war. Taking advantage of the rush-hour crowd, I started yelling at the top of my lungs, "This guy's harassing me and I don't like it and I bet you're not going to like it either!" I told the whole scenario to the crowd in a very loud but controlled voice. I just kept telling my story again and again. I brought bystanders into the game, too.

Three college-age guys were part of the crowd that had begun to gather. I said to them, "Boys, don't follow this guy's lead if you want to be successful with women. He harasses us and makes comments about our bodies and all he gets in return is humiliation. And that's all he deserves. So let this be an example to you."

This went on for a full five minutes. After Wendy got her fare card, she went to make a phone call. I decided that I wasn't going to stop confronting until either she had finished her call or I had chased the harasser out of the subway station.

My harasser was such a complete idiot. He must have thought there was still some way he could save face, or else he was paralyzed by shock, because he did not leave, nor did he defend himself. He just stood there while hundreds of people passed. He tried to make a few comments to gain control of the situation, but I don't think that anyone could even hear him over my continuous tirade.

Finally a subway attendant appeared and "escorted" him out of the station. The crowd dispersed and Wendy finished her phone call. When she got to me, I was shaking like crazy. I realized that throughout the whole ordeal my body had been trembling, but she assured me that it was completely unnoticeable to her and the rest of the crowd.

As we were walking toward the train platform, another guy ran up to us and said, "I saw what you did back there. That guy's a jerk and he's here all the time. My girlfriend told me he had harassed her. I'm going to tell her what you did so that she can do it next time."

I didn't hear reactions from any other people, but I know my story made a lot of cocktail party conversations that weekend. I want everyone to know how wonderful it feels to turn an ugly, sexist situation around. Try it—you definitely can do it. I did.

Karen was totally successful in isolating this harasser and drawing the subway station rush-hour crowd into the action.

If the harasser had stopped when she first challenged his offensive behavior, she would not have launched into the highly public, stage-two approach. But when he decided to laugh and call her "bitch," that was it for him.

Ann D. effectively used a stage-two strategy as well. She held a habitual subway groper accountable in the most public way possible:

"RED" GETS WHAT HE DESERVES

My name is Ann, and I'm a twenty-six-year-old legal secretary working in Washington, D.C. My story of sexual harassment is a familiar one, I'm sure. A man on the Metro subway last year slid his hands along the length of my backside as I was leaving the train one morning, leaving me so shocked that all I could do was shout meaningless obscenities in his direction. The effect was a train full of nine-to-fivers staring at me as if I were the one who had a problem.

Afterward, I thought of everything I should have said to the guy, and I felt angry and humiliated all day at work. A friend at work who's been trained in verbal confrontation told me what to do if it ever happened again, and I had the unbelievable opportunity to confront the same idiot months later when I saw him harassing another woman.

My retribution came on a typical ride home at rush hour on a packed Metro train. I was knocked out of my postwork stupor when I saw a woman spring up from her seat, bring her briefcase down on some guy's head, and yell "Creep!" before she rushed off the train. He looked familiar to me—that red hair, the government-issue suit, blue raincoat, the hearing aid . . . yes! It was the same little slug who had grabbed me about two months before, and I found myself actually wishing that I'd been sitting in that seat so I could give "Red" a little dose of "verbal confrontation."

Then I realized I could still do something.

The seat left vacant by Red's former unsuspecting victim was about to be filled by another. A woman was preparing to sit down when I said, as loudly as I could, "Don't sit next to that man. He's a pervert who gets his kicks by feeling up women on the Metro." (OK, I know it's not the most eloquent thing to say, but it's all I could think of at the time.)

The woman thanked me and chose to stand. Then, as the train moved forward, another woman turned around and asked me to explain what had happened, so I proceeded to tell her—loudly—exactly what the guy had done to me previously and that it seemed he had committed some similar outrage a few moments before. Then she got involved. "Which guy did this?" she asked, although of course she knew. "That guy over there in the blue coat," I yelled, pointing at him. He cowered against the window and made no attempt to defend himself.

All the way home—about four more stops—I repeated the story to anyone preparing to sit next to Red. His formerly pasty face was flushed to the hairline and he never said a word.

He probably never expected anyone to confront him. Part of the enjoyment he derived from harassing women obviously stemmed from the utter speechlessness that usually results. I think it probably gave him a sense of power.

I'm sure many women have been infuriated when Red assaulted them, but felt the need to respect that old code of silence. We really don't want to attract any more attention to ourselves and what has happened, but as I realized later, that's exactly what we should do.

Some of the women on the train on the second occasion were supportive of what I'd done, and that felt very good. Other passengers were uncomfortable with the situation. It was clear from the glares I was getting that most wished I would shut up. Some never even looked up, even when I was yelling across the aisle. They were embarrassed, probably appalled, at my "lack of manners," or maybe they were of the opinion that sexual assault and harassment are no big deal—just something we have to learn to live with.

But let me tell you, I felt great about confronting that man, even after he got off at the last station with me when the train *was practically empty. Confronting him gave me a sense of empowerment; this time it was he who was humiliated.*

I did talk to the train conductor (who called me "honey," by the way) and asked about filing a complaint against the man. The conductor told me that because I had no witnesses it probably wouldn't be worth it, but if it ever happened again I could get on the train intercom and ask for the Metro police.

It hasn't happened since, nor, for that matter, have I seen Red. I like to think that he is too embarrassed—or too afraid of outspoken women—to ever use public transportation again.

Women have a range of confrontation options and levels of intensity to use against harassers on public transportation, just as they do in any other setting. For habitual offenders like "Red," the most public, emphatic level of confrontation is entirely appropriate. It does not often happen that one recognizes the very same harasser abusing another woman and has a second chance to confront him. Ann was determined to hold him fully accountable this time, and that she did.

It is a good idea for a woman to be aware of any male who gets off the bus or subway with her, at a relatively isolated bus stop or empty station. If she has any feelings of unease at all, she should take action to protect herself—ask a subway guard to escort her to her car, call a friend to meet her at the station, or stay on the bus until the next stop, for example. In this case, Ann was reasonably safe—no one who had seen her confront "Red" was likely to mistake her for an easy target, least of all Red himself.

Like women on the bus or subway, women on the street must deal with harassers all too often. Occasionally, assertiveness may be enough, but it is usually appropriate—and safer—to go straight to confrontation when dealing with a stranger who verbally or physically accosts women. What a street harasser says is less important than the fact that he felt free to say it. For example, on the surface, "Hey, beautiful!" may seem less offensive than "Hey, bitch!"—but the underlying message is essentially the same: This man believes that he has a right to waylay perfect strangers, interrupt them, comment on their appearance, and demand their attention, simply because they are female. Do all women a favor by correcting that misperception: Confront him. Vary the level of intensity as needed, depending on the circumstances. Aim for a measured response that is sufficient to (1) daunt the harasser, (2) deliver a clear message about the principle at stake, and (3) firmly end the encounter on your own terms.

Like so many other women, Cecile frequently faces street harassers. She and her friends have talked about the problem and have come up with a variety of defense tactics that work to stop harassment. Their anger reflects the frustration many women feel when harassers constantly deny women the right to use public space in peace. Here's what Cecile has to say:

CITY STREETS

All men benefit from the violence of a few. Characteristics I've come to think of as male—a deep voice, a male body—put me on edge, no matter who the individual man.

The force that teaches us is fear. Men put us in fear by physically attacking us, by reminding us they can attack us, by invading our space, by assuming they have the right to engage us in conversation any time they please, by commenting on our bodies uninvited, by pornography. . . .

Verbal attack is the most prevalent form of violence against women. It is one of the first steps on the progression that leads to the ultimate violence, murder. Women are taught to ignore men's verbal assaults. I think men want us to pretend to ignore or not notice their comments, because that makes it easy for them to continue, and they know we can hear them.

Doing nothing rankles me. It makes me feel helpless. Doing nothing is like declaring that I am helpless. I am a white, middle-class, college-educated, able-bodied lesbian in my early twenties, and I am not helpless. I do not make it easy for the harassers.

When I'm on a bicycle I have incredible confidence. On a bike I am unassailable; I can say anything I want and be able to get away. Men must realize this and feel threatened by it, because I am harassed much more on my bike than on foot. It was on a bike that I started yelling back, rather than ignoring catcalls and whistles. I knew I was a physical force to be reckoned with.

Once I learned to yell back from my bike, I became braver in all situations. I have never had a man respond to my response in any way but with surprise. Suddenly, when I confront, they seem disarmed.

I soon noticed that what I wore while biking had a direct effect on how much I was harassed. It angered me that men were clearly using my cool, sensible clothing as an excuse to harass me. Should I have to wear heavy, unrevealing clothing, in the heat of summer, while they go shirtless? No way.

Once, when I bicycled up a hill in Georgetown, a man yelled that he could see down my shirt. I yelled back, but two minutes later what I really wished I had done was stop, pull off my shirt, and yell back, "How dare you tell me what to wear!" He would have been so shocked he would have backed away.

Many of my friends also confront now. Angela uses her "teacher's voice" to explain to men and boys why they shouldn't say misogynist things, and can actually get them to apologize. A friend of Tricia's recently walked right up to a man who was being an asshole, into his space, and said point-blank, "Excuse me, do you have a problem?" A friend in New York City saw a particularly offensive ad on the subway, so, in a subway car packed full of commuters, she ripped the poster off the wall and tore it up. Was anyone going to say anything to her? No way. And Tricia once told a harasser that he could suck her tampon—he was so horrified and astonished, he protested, "Don't say that to me!"

Men who know us personally get away with harassment

the most. I have let too many comments go unchallenged. Well, why not antagonize someone whose sexism makes me uncomfortable? Maybe then he'll go away, because I make him uncomfortable.

I do not condone violence for its own sake. We protest attacks to preserve our selves. I don't harass men who are not bothering me. It's time men stopped harassing me!

There are many different levels of appropriate responses here, from Angela's assertive explanations that prompt apologies from harassers, all the way through Cecile's own sharp confrontations. The responses used by Tricia and her friend border on aggression. "Suck my tampon" is a great line, but all counteraggression should be used with care, to avoid needlessly escalating the incident. Verbal aggression ("fuck you!") and physical aggression (stepping into the male's space) are expressions of anger. They can work in some circumstances, but they do not convey the same clear message that a quick, precise confrontation provides. For example, Cecile's confrontational comeback—"How dare you tell me what to wear!"—has some real content. It challenges the harasser's assumptions and behavior much more effectively than simply yelling "fuck you!" And as Cecile has found, the usual response when women confront is stark amazement from the harassers, with no retaliation.

MULTICULTURAL ACTION

Understanding the power dynamics of harassment, developing a full spectrum of assertiveness, confrontation, and self-defense responses, and becoming comfortable in using them appropriately are especially important for women who travel outside their own cultures. Sexist social practices vary from culture to culture, and any woman who travels frequently will come up against behavioral differences that require some sensitivity and much careful thought.

That is true within the multicultural society of the United

States, and even more so overseas. In Italy and Egypt, for example, street harassment is constant. In Japan, the streets are relatively safe but sex discrimination is pervasive; the first Japanese woman ever to win a sexual harassment case did so only in 1992. In Thailand, women face serious sexual exploitation, but they recently scored one victory: Fed up with mass-transit harassment, they convinced the government to set aside women-only cars on commuter trains. Outside actual war zones, few societies even approach the violence of the United States in terms of rape and murder rates. It is not a question of which societies are more sexist and which can justly claim to be less so, but a matter of understanding the many forms that male supremacy can take. Sexism is sexism, and it limits women's freedom to some extent in every society.

In some cultures, any woman alone is considered fair game for any man: An ordinary, independent U.S. college student can be considered shamelessly brazen. Although effective responses to harassment may differ from one culture to another, the basic social and psychological principles of confrontation apply across a very wide range of situations. Be creative, but think it through and talk to local women before taking action.

Here's how Josephine Withers decided to disrupt the endless stream of harassers she encountered in Italy:

ACTING CRAZY

I am fifty-four years old and a professor of art history. My work and research require that I travel in Europe a fair amount. In 1959 I had such unpleasant experiences traveling alone in Italy that I swore off traveling to that country for many years. I was, for example, almost run off the road and down a steep hill in Florence by two young men circling around me on their Vespa motorbike. Many other experiences, less dangerous but just as annoying, also discouraged me from returning.

In 1974, I decided to have another go at it. I had never been to Rome, which is a sorry confession for an art historian.

I was staying with friends but I was on my own during the day, touring the city. This time, I had a plan. The first time I was seriously harassed, it was by two street hecklers who had driven by in a car and stopped. I turned to face them and started acting crazy. I staggered around, tongue hanging out, making gurgling and other decidedly nonverbal sounds. It worked! I still relish the look of horror and disgust on this one fellow's face. The two of them couldn't get in their car and get out of there fast enough.

I had a renewed sense of confidence after that initial experience, lost whatever lingering inhibitions I had about acting this way, and took great pleasure in improving my act on subsequent occasions.

Josephine's story points up, once again, the serious personal and professional costs that harassers inflict on women. The mobility and freedom that women forfeit because of sexual harassment are not minor losses. In this case, sexual harassment had a direct impact on this art history professor's ability to pursue her profession: She did not return to Italy for fifteen years.

The professor's creative response freed her to go where she pleased. Unlike a confrontation, it did not explicitly challenge the harassers' assumptions about their fundamental "right" to harass women. But Josephine was—quite rightly —determined not to let harassers stop her again. She was more than willing to act crazy, if that was what it took to achieve the freedom she needed. In many ways, it was a liberating experience.

And here's a success story from Shelley Anderson in the Netherlands, about a couple of incidents that can happen almost anywhere:

CONFRONTING ENEMY TROOPS

I'd heard young men say that they had joined the military because they didn't want to see foreign invaders marching down American streets, raping their mothers, wives, or girl-friends, but I was in more danger of being raped on post, by my fellow soldiers, than by any mythical invaders.

First summer on base: I wandered into an area of men's barracks. I was stunned by the hostility. Men leaned out of windows and shouted obscenities; some began to follow me, smacking their lips and exchanging comments on my body. Shaken, and forcing myself not to run in fear, I realized that to my fellow soldiers, I was the enemy.

Perhaps I shouldn't have been surprised. In basic training, my company commander explained that enlisted men would look at us as either whores or lesbians. And just the week before, a friend bitterly told me about being rejected for a better assignment, because she had refused the officer's advances. Another friend, a truck mechanic, was fed up: she found Playboy centerfolds on her truck seat every morning. In 1983, an Army private committed suicide, leaving a note that said she could not handle her sergeant's sexual harassment.

Second summer on base: Four of us are sitting on the steps outside the PX snack bar, eating hamburgers and laughing. A car filled with GIs stops in front of us; the men start shouting obscenities. Feeling safe with my friends around me, I walk to the back of the car and pretend to write down the license number. It's dusk and the GIs can't see that I don't have a pen. But I can see their look of fear as they shout, "Hey! What are you doing!" and roar off, leaving me feeling surprised and powerful.

Later the same evening: My friends and I decide to take a drive—it's a big base with lots of woods and back roads, and you can sometimes spot deer moving gracefully in the twilight. Another car of GIs—not the same crew—starts to follow us down a deserted road, the men grinning and show-

ing us the finger. We fall silent. Then one of my friends says, "We'll fix these guys," and whispers something to the driver. She drives for about a mile, makes a sudden turn and stops. The second car slows down—then roars away when they realize we have just parked in front of the military police station.

Shelley's experience is a sad commentary on the ethics of the U.S. troops involved. But her tactics for dealing with the harassers in these two cars—pretending to take down the license, and driving straight to a police station when followed—will work in or out of the military, in many different countries. Because both of these tactics put the harassers at some risk of being identified and held accountable, they worked like a verbal confrontation to disempower the GIs: The men took off instantly.

Other women traveling overseas have encountered similar problems—including an epidemic of street harassment—and have come up with additional solutions. Here's one from K.S. and her friend Charlotte, a very resourceful pair of women:

THE SIGN OF THE HATCHET

Char and I were traveling in Europe one summer, and we were getting harassed every time we turned around. We were two American women in our late twenties, and it seemed like we couldn't ride a train, visit a museum, or walk down a street without some fool inflicting himself on us. It was really aggravating. Men seemed to feel completely free to impose on us. They interrupted us at every turn with crude remarks, kissing and lip-smacking noises, flowery fake "compliments," whistles, catcalls, comments about our anatomy—the whole spectrum. They blocked our path on the sidewalk and invaded our table at restaurants. And yes, they grabbed, fondled, and rubbed up against us, too.

Well, Charlotte and I are pretty creative. We came up with "the hatchet sign," and you know, it seemed to work in every language.

It's hard to describe this exactly, but what we did was a quick three-part sequence of hand gestures: first, an unzipping motion, then a pulling-something-out motion, and then a quick decisive chop, using the side of our hand like a hatchet.

Every time we got hassled, we'd look straight at the harasser and do the hatchet sign.

It was amazing. Once we started applying the hatchet, we were back in control of our lives. Men everywhere stopped in their tracks, got a queasy look on their faces, and backed off immediately. They stopped in midcomment, they stopped in mid smacking noise, they stopped in midgrab as they reached for us. Smug leering faces turned shocked and horror-stricken at the thought. Nonverbal communication certainly is powerful! We had a great time for the rest of the trip, and we are proud to share our invention, the noble sign of the hatchet, with women everywhere.

Around the globe, women like K.S. and Charlotte are coming up with ingenious ways to defend women's human rights, devising new tactics that not only stop the harassers but challenge the fundamental premise that men have a right to harass women in any society. Ending sexual harassment is a multicultural project; there are as many ways to eliminate the societal rewards of sexual harassment and hold harassers accountable as there are varieties of sexism. Wherever women travel—down the block or around the world—we will, for the time being, have to deal with men who harass. Speaking up and sharing our strategies with one another, we create the tools for change. And the more resourceful we are, the fewer harassers we will all have to face in the year 2000.

When Your Minister Is a Molester, Your Professor Is a Lech, or Your Landlord Is a Sleaze: Stopping Harassers in Power Positions

On the street, on the subway, in the park, and throughout the community, harassers turn women's daily lives into an obstacle course of insults and sexual threats. On one corner are the casual dominance harassers, "merely" amusing themselves by flexing their gender dominance at the expense of women's freedom. On the next block there may be strategic harassers who aggressively defend public areas as male turf, sexual-pastime harassers who get a thrill from the act of harassment, or cold-blooded assailants who engage in rape-testing. All of these men violate women's fundamental civil rights. On a whim, they can make the simplest encounter an experience of anger, fear, and humiliation. They can transform the most routine daily activity—walking out of the grocery store or riding the bus—into an ugly, threatening episode the victim will remember all her life.

The experience can be even more traumatic when the harasser is not a stranger on the street but a man who exercises some official power over his victim's life—a man who can target the same woman, over and over again, using the power and authority of his position. These predators can conduct a sustained campaign of harassment that amounts to nothing less than sexual terrorism.

When the landlord, the professor, or the minister is the harasser, women must stand together to stop the abuse. Individual strategies rarely stop this kind of harasser. Avoidance, appeasement, and counteraggression do not work; even a strong one-on-one confrontation, while it may make him back off from one victim, is not usually enough to stop his overall pattern of behavior. These powerful predators will continue targeting victims at almost every opportunity, until women finally break the silence and, together, hold them publicly accountable for their actions.

Men who abuse their positions of authority get off on both the sexual access they achieve and the exercise of power involved. Because they hold respected positions in the community, they expect to be able to bulldoze their way out of any accusation. They deny their own behavior and try to demolish the reputation of any woman who comes forward. They expect that the woman will not be believed, and they often use every resource at their command to try to ensure that she is not.

But even in these situations, women have succeeded. It takes courage, planning, and determination to stop these powerful harassers. Here are the stories of just a few of the women who have done it.

Mollie McLeod was up against a formidable harasser: the minister of her family's church. Because both she and her family trusted and admired this man, she experienced a deep sense of betrayal when she realized the extent of his predatory behavior. Like many victims of childhood abuse, she repressed the memories of what he had done; then, as a young adult, she began to remember. And she took action. Here's how Mollie did it:

WHEN THE PASTOR IS THE HARASSER

My parents were members of Grace Baptist Church in San Jose, California, before I was born. My younger sister, Diana, and I grew up in the church. But after Reverend Andrew Kille became the youth minister, the church was no longer a safe place for me.

He became the director of the children's choir in 1975, when I was ten years old. The kids under his supervision called him "Andy." In 1979, he was called by the congregation to be the pastor. He served for nine more years and, in 1988, left to begin a doctoral program in theology.

*In the beginning of 1991, I began reclaiming memories of
sexual violations during childhood. . . .*

I was lying on my stomach on the orange carpet. The living
room was dimly lit. My parents were nearby, in the kitchen.
Andy, my pastor, massaged my back. I was surprised when
he told me to take off my shirt. He said it was getting in the
way and he couldn't reach my shoulders.

I didn't even think the word "no." I took off my shirt.

Next, he told me to roll over, and I did.

I felt frozen. His hands rubbed back and forth across my
breasts.

*Andy molested me in many different places, including my
home, the church, the food pantry of another church where
we fed homeless people, the field at the lodge where annual
church trips were taken, and on many church outings.*

*Andy was the leader of church-sponsored backpack trips
every summer. I went on four of these trips between 1978
and 1981. I was thirteen years old on the first trip—one year
younger than the age limit, but Andy made a special exception for me. During these trips, Andy coerced the kids under
his supervision to swim naked in the lake, took me alone
with him skinny-dipping, gave me full-body massages, slept
naked next to me, walked around naked much of the time,
and watched the girls use the exposed outdoor toilet. Once,
he took some youth group members (age fourteen to sixteen)
to a nude beach.*

*My sister Diana figured Andy out and took action to protect
us. Sometimes we would come home and find him sitting in
our kitchen: To keep him out, Diana hid the spare house
key. Of course, hiding the key didn't prevent Andy from
having access to us; he just found other ways. Nevertheless,
it was an important effort at resistance and I'm proud of her
for doing it.*

*Andy represented God. He was the pastor, the highest reli-
gious authority in our congregation. I buried the knowledge
of Andy's violations in my head. Doing anything else meant
facing up to the betrayal by adults I loved, people I wanted
to believe had my best interests at heart. I went on being a
good church member, musician, and student. I did not leave*

Grace Baptist Church until I began attending college in Oregon.

In 1991, as I began to uncover my memories of what happened, I had violent nightmares and bouts of uncontrollable shaking. On June 17, 1991, I wrote a letter to Andy. It reads, in part: "I know you sexually abused me. I feel the effects every day. Now, I'm going to describe some of the horror you brought into my life. You must become aware of how your touch damaged me. I will no longer be silent. I cannot bury the shame while you are still a threat." I sent a copy to Andy's wife at her work address.

After I mailed the letters, I was amazed at my audacity. I was acting as if Andy did not have the right to hurt me or any other kid.

The next day, I called Child Protective Services. But when I talked to a police officer, he explained that the criminal statute of limitations for sexual battery (six years in California) had expired.

I decided to contact Andy's peers in the hope that they would hold him accountable for his professional misconduct. On June 26, 1991, I filed a complaint with a minister at the regional office of the American Baptist Churches of the West (ABCW). Professional recognition of ordination in the American Baptist Church is conferred by regional associations like this one. I specifically asked about their policy for responding to allegations of sexual abuse of a minor by a member of the clergy. Six months passed before I received any acknowledgment of my complaint.

The first response was unofficial: An ABCW staff liaison person told my father that Andy "confessed." Soon afterward, however, we received official notification that the wrong word had been used in that conversation, and Andy denied wrongdoing.

On New Year's Day 1992, I sent out a letter to almost one hundred "friends and family of Grace Baptist Church," informing them that I had filed a complaint of professional misconduct against Andy. One month later, a committee from the ABCW was finally convened to investigate my complaint.

During the hearing process, I wrote letters stating my allegations, responding to the procedures, requesting information, and objecting to delays. Mostly, I was ignored. I kept adding pages to my binder of correspondence and resources. Two days before the preliminary hearing, I still did not know where it would be held or who would interview me. I was angry that nobody cared enough to let me know what they planned. There were also moments when I felt relieved— maybe I wouldn't have to go through with it. But then the telephone would ring with another call from friends or family, and I thought about how I would feel later on if I didn't persist.

I cultivated several helpful habits during the hearing process. I still keep a notebook of telephone calls, for example. I write down the names of people with whom I speak, dates, times, and summaries of the conversation. I also save my telephone bills so that I can confirm the number and length of calls I make regarding my case. And I insisted on going to all the hearings and bringing a tape recorder. A word of caution: Always ask where official copies of your tapes and written statements will be kept. In the midst of the process, one minister called me to ask for another copy of my tape because his tape had been stolen from his car five days after the preliminary hearing. (What was it doing there?)

Carefully consider whether you want to give the perpetrator or the authorities any written or taped statements, because the exchange may not be equal. Andy was never required to submit any written response to my allegations, and his testimony was not taped during the hearings.

The conduct of American Baptist leaders seemed designed to make me feel presumptuous and insignificant. Throughout the hearing process, which lasted four months, many ministers said they wanted to protect me, they didn't want to revictimize me, or they wanted to tell me something in confidence. What they really wanted to do was persuade me not to go to any more hearings. Be skeptical about promises made by friends and colleagues of the perpetrator. Don't be stopped either by accusations that you are a rude, hysterical, vindictive bitch, or by "friendly" advice to give up.

Diana and I did many things to keep our spirits up. We sang the Sweet Honey in the Rock song, "We Who Believe in Freedom Cannot Rest," again and again. I also started to draw. I'm glad I found a creative way to express how I feel about the resurging memories of abuse and the hard work of disclosing sexual violations.

A few days before the final hearing, a friend of Diana's came to town for a bridal shower. The three of us met and talked for the first time in many years. She agreed to make a taped statement about Andy's conduct during two backpack trips she attended as well as the nude-beach trip.

Afterward, Diana and I decided to destroy everything in the house that reminded us of Andy. We didn't act recklessly. We took pictures of gifts made by Andy and souvenirs of church events he led. We made copies of Andy's letters. Then we ripped, smashed, hammered, shredded, and tore. It felt immensely satisfying. We placed the remnants in a three-gallon Ziploc plastic bag and sent it to Andy by certified mail.

The ABCW committee issued its hearing report on May 5, 1992. After four months of ecclesiastical hearings, the committee suspended professional recognition of Andy's ordination for at least two years, and required him to enter therapy with someone trained in sexual abuse issues.

But this was only a partial remedy, and it was not enough. The extent and duration of Andy's sexual abuse were minimized. No other victims were acknowledged in the report. By their own admission, the hearing committee members excluded from the report any allegation of professional misconduct that Andy denied.

I wanted Andy's ordination revoked, not just suspended, because he used his power and position as a pastor to exploit me and other kids.

I found out that the members of Grace Baptist Church are the only ones with the authority to revoke his ordination. After the ABCW committee suspended professional recognition of Andy's ordination, I made a written request to the lay leadership of Grace Baptist Church. I asked to present my allegations against Andy before the entire congregation so that members could vote on whether Andy should remain ordained.

The local church leadership declined my request.

So on May 31, 1992, we held a protest outside Grace Baptist Church. We arrived before the worship service and stood quietly on the sidewalk as members drove into the church parking lot in their cars. We came prepared with educational pamphlets, "No Excuse for Sexual Abuse" buttons, and drinks in an ice chest. The sun was shining and I held my sign up high. One of my favorite signs read: "If you can't trust your pastor with your body, how can you trust him with your soul?" My friends and family held other signs: "Stop Sexual Assaults by Pastors" and "Fathers Say Stop Sexual Abuse!"

Afterward, I talked with the other sexual abuse survivors who picketed with me. We agreed that it was a relief to shed another layer of shame and secrecy. We also felt tremendously proud of ourselves and decided to picket again one week later.

The leadership of Grace Baptist Church decided that it might be possible after all for members to consider the issue of Andy's ordination, since the congregation had already seen the protest signs. Some books on abuse by clergy were purchased and set out in the church library. A few small group meetings were scheduled to allow members to discuss the "situation."

I decided to contact the Metro, our local weekly paper. I knew it might be possible to get the story published with both my name and the name of my former pastor because I had the written ABCW hearing decision in my possession. Andy agreed to be interviewed, and a long news article appeared on July 23, 1992. The headline read: "Out of Touch: When a church fails to properly address charges of sex abuse, the result is further pain for both the accuser and the accused."

Later that day, I called a radio station to find out if they would be doing a talk show on sexual abuse by clergy any time in the near future. I explained that my story had just appeared in the Metro. The operator connected me with the news section. I didn't realize that the radio station was affiliated with a television station. I got a call back informing me that an anchorwoman and a cameraman would come to my home in one hour. The opening local news story at 11:00 P.M. was, "A San Jose woman accuses her former pastor of sexual abuse. . . ."

As this book goes to print, I am waiting for the congregation to revoke his ordination. Other victims are coming forward informally; they may file charges as well. Unless congregations are willing to listen to the experiences of clergy-abuse survivors and evaluate the process used to call pastors to account for professional misconduct, there will be more victims.

Andy himself could be a powerful voice within the church for change, for progress. And that's what people should be holding out to him, saying, "You can do this. You, too, can be healed, by facing what you've done and making restitution for it." And if he does that, and I get justice from the church, it's a lot more likely that I am going to be able to forgive.

Going public with my name and face means that I will not protect Andy with my silence any longer. And I refuse to be ashamed about being a sexual abuse survivor.

Mollie's story is a classic example of how one courageous survivor, coming forward, can not only reclaim her life but begin a process that moves an entire institution forward. She could not have done it alone. Her family and friends stood by her, other witnesses and victims began to speak up, and together they forced the church to face what Andy had been doing. Mollie used all the tools she had—everything from a personal letter confronting the harasser to formal church procedures, a picket line on Sunday mornings, and media visibility—to name Andy's behavior and hold both him and the church accountable. Step by step, she was creative with the tactics she applied as well as the ways she dealt personally with the trauma: singing, drawing, talking with her sister and friends to keep her spirits up throughout the long, grueling process. Her demolition of all reminders of Andy, toward the end of the hearing process, was a psychological catharsis —a symbolic end to her status as a helpless victim. (She was careful not to destroy the documentation she needed.) She also regained a sense of control over her life by being very organized, keeping a binder with resources, a telephone log, and copies of all letters and documents.

Mollie's experience of repressing the conscious memories of an intolerable situation was not at all unusual. Incest survivors and other victims of severe childhood abuse (sexual and nonsexual) often find themselves first remembering what happened to them only many years later, as adults, when it is finally safe to do so. In some cases, a specific event may trigger the memory.

Once the memories return, recovery can take months or years. Because recalling the violations can be so overwhelming, skilled counseling, support groups, and support from family and friends are important. Many women also find that they want an acknowledgment of wrongdoing from the abuser, some indication that he understands the horror of what he did and regrets the harm he inflicted. Taking action to confront the molester is never easy, and sometimes not even possible, but it can be a significant step in overcoming the experience of powerlessness and victimization. For Mollie, Diana, and their parents, taking action was essential. The entire family felt victimized and betrayed by Andy's behavior.

However, Mollie's goal was not just individual healing, but institutional change. She wanted to make sure that Andy would never be in a position to do this again. Any organization that has placed a harasser in a position of authority has a responsibility to take prompt, decisive action on several levels: (1) to ensure that the harasser cannot continue to exploit and abuse new victims (not just hope that he won't do it again, once he gets some counseling); (2) to recognize the real extent of the injury done and make amends to the survivors; and (3) to implement strong public measures to end the problem within the institution. That means creating accessible administrative avenues that encourage victims to step forward, instead of disempowering them—procedures that include much more than a cursory investigation, and that impose visible and meaningful penalties for this kind of abuse of power. Because of Mollie's action, the regional ABCW association revised its procedures to address future clergy-harassment cases.

Anyone in an organization that is dealing with a charge of sexual harassment should understand that it is not enough to interview the harasser and his accuser. Because authority figures count on their power to deny what they have done, as well as their power to intimidate potential witnesses, the investigation must be extensive, independent, and immediate. Like the federal official in Chapter 2 who persisted in his denials despite the testimony of twenty witnesses, "respectable" harassers use denial as a weapon and expect their distorted, self-serving versions of reality to prevail. But this type of predatory harassment is a pattern of behavior that poisons the organization; there are almost always additional victims, witnesses, and corroborating evidence. Look for the witnesses, including women who have left the church. Taking the harasser's denial at face value does *not* constitute an adequate institutional response.

And when the harassment charges are documented, minimizing the problem is never a solution. No matter how much discomfort the organization's officials may feel, the only way out is swift, honest action.

The higher the harasser's status—a minister, a pastor, a bishop—the less likely the church is to want to come clean about the situation, and the more essential it is for church officials to do so. Secretive, face-saving "solutions" that attempt to protect the institution are worse than a mistake. To slap the harasser's hand and sweep the problem under the rug is a moral failure, irresponsible both to the victims and to the organization. That approach is also a time bomb; when the explosion comes, as it eventually will, the destructive impact on the institution is ten times worse.

In this case, as in many others, the church leaders' reluctance to face up to the situation damaged the church far more than prompt, effective action would have. Far too many organizations try to silence the victim; when that fails, they may discipline the harasser secretly, behind closed doors, as if the individual victim and the harasser were the only ones involved. But the destruction caused by high-ranking predatory harassers is always wider than that. The entire congregation needs the healing that comes only with acknowledgment of the damage, amends to the victims, and a public commitment to see that it never happens again. The only way to protect a church—or any other community institution—from sexual harassment charges is to STOP THE HARASSERS.

Like Mollie and her sister Diana, Kimberly G. ran up against a powerful, persistent, predatory harasser. In Kimberly's case, the harasser was the university professor who supervised her academic work. He had enormous power in her life—he was in a position to demolish her success in graduate school and derail her future career. But Kimberly stood up to him. Unlike Mollie, she had to do it almost single-handedly, because the women around her were afraid to come forward publicly. Here's her success story:

TOMORROW COMES

It is morning, and the sun finally begins to peek through the dark curtains of the night. Waking from a dream, I watch the sun rise. I am amazed that life can be so simple and so peaceful.

Through my ordeal, I have learned to appreciate the simplicities of life. I find tranquillity in nature; I find strength in all of the broken places. When tomorrow comes, I will be a stronger person still.

My ordeal began two years ago, when, as a twenty-two-year-old fresh out of college, I made the decision to pursue graduate study. I was thrilled to receive a full scholarship to attend a well-known master's degree program. The money was essential, as the sudden death of my father three years earlier had left me with very limited resources.

As that summer drew to a close and I prepared for my first semester, I dreamed of what would follow. I imagined myself writing late-night term papers—searching through the endless halls of the library—cramming with buddies on the night before a midterm. What I did not imagine is that I would be battling with a monster.

That monster is sexual harassment—a vicious beast that lives in a dark cave called society, where it is often hidden, making its capture all the more difficult. Many find it much easier to deny its existence than to battle it.

My harasser, a forty-two-year-old professor, carried the beast within himself. His clearly schemed plan of action was to win the victim's trust, seduce her, then abuse her. Such a plan is very simple to carry out when one is in a position of authority. I, having attended a small women's college, was unaware of the dangers that awaited me at this large urban university. I trusted my professor, and I paid a high price.

Throughout the seven months I was enrolled in his classes, I was subjected to seduction, violent threats, and emotional abuse. Nearly every day, he commented on my looks and my sexuality. In computer class, he put his arms around me and rubbed his body back and forth against me. He told the class he was taking ten points off my grade because he thought I was "pissy." He gave me a lower final grade than I'd earned "so that [I'd] have to come and complain." He coaxed me into bringing him expensive chocolates, which he said he deserved because he was "protecting" me from my boss, whom he accused of "wanting to have sex" with me in his office. He made repeated references to "whipping" and "handcuffing" me, and to the pleasure he would receive from "punishing" me. (These were more than idle threats; he kept handcuffs and a saw in his office.) One day, he called me into his office, and when I got there, he told me he wanted to push me out his fourth-story window. All of this was "fun" to him, and he repeatedly told me how "special" I was that he had chosen me.

There was more. He inappropriately confided in me about his personal life and his colleagues. He ridiculed students behind their backs, calling them his "fucking fan club." He showed me his drawer full of pornographic greeting cards, which he attributed to "female students." He was happy as long as he was in control; whenever I challenged him about his mistreatment of me, he called me "immature" and "a baby."

Ironically, it was his most frightening threat that gave me the strength to stand up to him. When I finally told him that his behavior was becoming obvious to other students, he became enraged. He threatened my life if I told anybody what he had done. He was being considered for tenure and knew that his misconduct, if reported, would put that decision in great jeopardy. As his voice uttered those four words —"I will kill you"—my mind flooded with recollections of the horrible abuse I'd suffered as a child, at the hands of my father. Suddenly, it all became clear to me. The reason I had endured this man's mistreatment for so long was that it was familiar. Abuse from men in positions of authority was what I had been accustomed to. But this time, there was a difference. I was no longer a helpless six-year-old. This time, I could stand up for myself.

I first reported the situation to the director of the graduate program, who happened to be the perpetrator's best friend and a sexual harasser himself. His advice to me was: "There's nothing you can do about it. He's just flirtatious, that's all." The director told me that I would have to take the perpetrator's class the following semester, so I might as well "forget what happened."

I could not, and would not, forget. My determination grew stronger. Standing up to this injustice was more important to me than any degree.

I reported the matter, including the director's lack of assistance, to the deans of the college. The deans immediately referred me to the office of affirmative action, which is designed to handle such complaints.

The two investigations that followed revealed substantial

evidence to support my complaint, but those months brought intense pain and fear. I was diagnosed with post-traumatic stress syndrome and suffered from frequent stomachaches and nightmares. I knew that the next ordeal—a long review hearing—was yet to come.

That hearing was, in a sense, a revictimization. I was petri-fied just being in the same room with the perpetrator, never mind having to look at him sitting across from me. He, of course, denied everything, accusing me of having a "fatal attraction" and being "a woman scorned." He brought in a number of students, some of whom had even witnessed a few of the events I'd described. The vulnerability of these students became apparent when they entered the hearing room and had to face their powerful and angry professor. Suddenly, they had "no recollection" of any misconduct on his part, and instead accused me of having "asked for it" by wearing skirts and having long hair. One young woman praised the harasser, describing him as "a ten professor," although she had previously complained about his mistreat-ment of her (calling her "stupid" and refusing to assist her in class) to one of the deans.

During the hearings, one administrator reported receiving anonymous phone calls from women claiming to have been sexually harassed by the perpetrator at his former university. (He had mysteriously resigned from his position at an Ivy League school during his sixth—and tenure—year.) In addi-tion, other professors had been approached by students over the years with sexual harassment complaints against this man. Unfortunately, none of the other victims would step forward.

When I felt like giving up I thought of these women. I realized how angry I was that not one of them came forward, thus leaving me to fight the battle alone. I made a vow that I wouldn't give up—that I had to fight this, with the hope that this man would not be allowed to strike again.

After examining all the evidence, the review committee recommended dismissal of this untenured professor. The university, however, took no action. He continued to teach.

He was even scheduled to receive tenure, based on his academic accomplishments.

I am pleased to announce that in March 1992, the university president finally acted on my behalf, opening up a more thorough investigation into this man's gross misconduct. As soon as the harasser was notified of this investigation, he resigned from his position. Since all of his colleagues now know about the sequence of events that led to his downfall (including several allegations of harassment at his two previous places of employment), it seems unlikely that he will ever receive tenure at a university.

So this really is a hard-won but very satisfying success story. It is not every day that justice prevails and a known sexual harasser is finally put in his place. And to me, my very coming forward was a success in itself. If it happened again, I'd probably think twice, but my final decision would remain the same. I realize that my well-being and that of womankind depend upon the determination and the courage to speak out against sexual harassment.

It was a painful process; I doubt that the pain will ever fully subside. The wound has left a scar. It will grow nearly invisible with the passage of time, but every once in a while, something—a place, a name, a feeling—will remind me of its existence. Even so, that scar does more than tell me I've been a victim. It tells me that I'm a survivor. And tomorrow comes.

Kimberly demanded responsible action from the university, and she finally got it. She used a variety of institutional and personal resources to confront the harasser, marshaling the evidence, documenting the incidents, and relying on her own determination to see this through. Once she began to stand up for herself, she was systematic and resourceful. She faced moments of real despair—the harassment had been unbearably ugly, the harasser denied his actions, and the administrative process was physically and emotionally exhausting—but like Mollie McLeod, she knew that she would feel far worse in the future if she gave up. The university's failure to act on the review committee's recommendation must have been a particularly low point: Here she'd won her case, but still the university did nothing. Finally, when the appeal had gone all the way to the president, the breakthrough came. Despite all the obstacles, despite the fear that kept other women silent, Kimberly succeeded in putting this harasser's behavior on the public record and removing him from his position of authority.

Kimberly's success was not only a vindication of her rights, but a victory for all the women who had been too afraid to call this professor on his actions. Her perseverance spared many young women who would have been targeted as "special" victims at the university in the future, had this harasser been allowed to continue.

But next time, it is up to us—all of us, male and female— to find the courage to speak up when we see this kind of harassment. Kimberly succeeded through the strength of her own character, but no woman should ever again have to stand up alone against a habitual predator like this one.

The importance of united action against a persistent predator is also clear in Catherine Hanson's story. When a professor is the harasser, school and career are at risk. But when the landlord is a predatory harasser, even the most basic notion of "home" loses its meaning. In Catherine's case, only a concerted effort by a determined group of women could produce a victory: The harasser was the resident manager of their apartment building, and he terrorized the women under his control for almost four years, until they finally stopped him. Here is Catherine's success story, which led to a landmark legal decision:

RECLAIMING OUR HOMES AND OUR LIVES

My name is Catherine Hanson. After my divorce I was left penniless and eventually homeless, with two small children. Because I was receiving no child support from my ex-hus-

band, I tried working two jobs to pay the rent and put food on the table. I also tried to live with roommates to minimize the cost of rent. That's when everything fell apart. One of my employers closed his business, I was suspended from my other job because I didn't have reliable transportation, and I lost my home because my roommates didn't pay their share of the rent.

I had to make a decision, and I decided that I needed better skills to get a better job. I turned to public assistance, enrolled full-time at Solano Community College in California, and worked part-time at the local high school.

I also depended heavily on the rent-subsidized apartment that I had been lucky enough to find. My friend Molly McElrath lived at the same complex. Feeling that anything was possible now, Molly and I founded an organization to assist other single parents who wished to further their education and get off the welfare rolls. Our life certainly wasn't easy, but it was definitely getting better as our goals came closer and closer to being realized.

Then, in 1987, along came Jim Skinner, the new resident apartment manager. His reign of terror began. He entered apartments without permission, snooped through personal belongings when no one was home, gossiped about women tenants, and made sexual innuendos. Soon, his activities turned to blatant sexual comments, asking women tenants to watch pornographic movies with him, grabbing women's breasts, and patting buttocks. All the while he reminded the women that it was he who held the keys to their apartments.

He told women like Vonney Lindsey that she and her children would be sleeping in the park for Christmas if she didn't consent to posing in lingerie so he could take pictures. She refused and was evicted. He loaned other unsuspecting women money and then told them that he was involved with the Mafia and needed the money back immediately. If they didn't have it? They could pose for him. He humiliated others like Karen Deards by grabbing her breasts in front of other people. When Elizabeth Howard walked out of her bedroom in her nightie, she found him standing in her living room; when she rejected him, he threatened to turn her in to Child Protective Services because her toddler was given to screaming fits. She was so frightened by Skinner that she found herself sitting in a closet with her hand over her child's mouth whenever he had a temper tantrum.

Some women hid in their apartments, afraid to come out and fearful that he would come into their apartments with his keys. Others took a more direct line of defense. When Viola Gardner was fondled by Skinner and she pushed him away, he asked, "What's the matter, you don't like to be touched by men?" She replied firmly, "No, I don't want to be touched by you!" Nine months after Viola moved out, he tracked her down and harassed her at her new job, telling her, "I can always find out where you are."

Another tenant, Debra Kalloff, was grabbed by Skinner at the pool. She gathered her courage and screamed at him, "You touch me again and your arm will be a bloody stump!" Soon after this, Debra awoke in the middle of the night to find Skinner standing over her bed, undressing himself. She jumped out of bed and pushed him out the front door and down the stairs. "I'll get you for this!" he threatened. He had her and her children evicted, and then continued to harass her at her new home.

Women walked out of the shower to find him standing in their apartments. He began threatening women and children with a gun. He enforced an 8:00 P.M. curfew for single mothers.

It was apparent that he was not going to stop and that we needed help from someone. But who?

We had already called the property management company several times to complain. They told us to either send a woman into Skinner's office with a tape recorder strapped to her or stop calling.

Molly and I had tenants knocking on our doors day and night. Because of our Single Parent Support Group, women assumed that we would find some way of helping. After several run-ins with Skinner myself, I drafted a three-page letter of complaint to the owner of the apartment complex and managed to get eleven tenants who weren't afraid to sign it. Because some women were afraid to be seen talking with us, Molly and I had to sneak around the complex, going to the women who had gotten word to us that Skinner had harassed them. Many women met in the laundry rooms to try to talk about it without Skinner knowing it.

The owner acknowledged the letter, but according to his investigation (which did not include talking with any of the tenants who signed the letter) there was no proof of wrong-doing.

At this point, because Skinner's actions went unchallenged and virtually ratified by his employers, his pattern of harassment escalated. He seemed to find particular satisfaction in retaliating against those of us who sent the letter, threatening other tenants not to associate with me and referring to Molly as "the blonde with the big tits."

He apparently also began turning friend against friend. He coerced tenants into writing false letters of complaint against other tenants he wanted to evict. He made bogus complaints about us to the Welfare Department and Child Protective Services. He towed our cars away. He threatened Molly until she cut off all communication with me. I was devastated. Not only was I losing a special friendship, but my single parents support organization as well. He accused me of running an illegal business out of.my rent-subsidized apartment, then spread malicious rumors that I was actually running a prostitution ring.

All of us struggled to make sense out of this outrageous series of events. Our lives were being turned upside down by a man who seemed to be consumed with the need for power and control over our lives. Many of us had nightmares about what was occurring and what we were afraid would happen next. But we couldn't give up. We had the right to be safe in our own homes.

Annette Sandford had sent over one hundred letters and documents to support her complaints to government housing agencies, only to discover that all of her evidence had been turned over to Skinner's attorney. Other women called housing agencies and were told that there was nothing that could be done by their offices.

Annette arranged for a meeting with Legal Assistance attorneys and tenants at her apartment, knowing that she was risking retaliation from Skinner. Fifteen tenants showed up, even though Skinner knew of the meeting and had threatened tenants if they attended. We got little advice, no help, and even overheard one of the attorneys joke that "Skinner had quite a harem."

We contacted every government agency that we could think of. We called the police, but their hands were tied because sexual harassment is not a criminal offense in California. We contacted our government representatives and were told that it wasn't a congressional matter. We contacted private attorneys, the local chapter of NOW, and every social agency that we thought could refer us to someone who would intervene.

With each disappointment, we felt a growing sense of frustration, anger, and disbelief that nothing could be done by the "powers that be" to protect women in their homes. I believe it was that same feeling of anger and disbelief that fueled our fierce determination not to allow this to continue, and not to allow it to go unnoticed or unpunished.

Eventually, the Department of Housing and Urban Development (HUD) contacted us and began an investigation. Paul Smith, an investigator for HUD, came to the complex to try to talk with women. Dressed in a suit and tie and carrying a briefcase, he found only a few women willing to talk to him. They were afraid of Skinner finding out and putting them and their children on the street, as they had already seen him do to others.

Finally, after almost two years of not speaking to each other, Molly and I were able to reconcile our friendship. Molly had just moved out of the complex, and I had remarried and was now living elsewhere. Until this time, I never knew that Skinner had threatened her into halting our friendship and ending her association with the parents organization.

We were out of the apartments but we couldn't get the situation out of our minds. We knew that other women were still being harassed. So, when the investigator from HUD had little luck in gaining the women's trust, we came up with a plan. I was very ill at the time, so Molly risked her own safety to go back to the complex alone, to go door to door, talking with women and collecting statements for the HUD investigation.

She was afraid to go by herself, and she doubted her ability to convince women to talk. She said, "Why would they listen to me? Who am I?" I grabbed a clipboard and shoved it at her, saying, "Here, take this with you. People will listen to you if you have a clipboard." Then I waited nervously, thinking of how unsure she looked as she walked out to her car, clinging to that clipboard.

After three weeks of going door to door, she was cornered and threatened by Skinner. He asked if she had a petition against him for sexually harassing tenants. It was usually Molly's nature to avoid confrontations with Skinner, so she meant to say "No" when he asked her—but out of her mouth came "YES!"

Skinner threatened to physically remove her from the property. She went to another apartment and called the owner one more time. She threatened the owner with pickets and press coverage if he refused to meet with her immediately. After two years of effort to get the owner to take action, he finally agreed to meet with her on the following day.

The owner showed up for the meeting to find fifteen irate women, one male tenant, and a Welfare Department fraud investigator (he was there incognito—we invited the fraud investigator because Skinner had stolen welfare checks from many of the women).

The meeting was hostile. We demanded that he fire Skinner. When the owner said this was the first time he had heard of these complaints, I waved the letter of complaint, now over two years old, in his face. How could he say that? He still denied that Skinner had done anything wrong and refused to fire him.

Elena Fiedler stood up and recounted her first experience with Skinner. After coming from a battered women's shelter, she had gone to pay her first month's rent and deposit to Skinner. As she handed him the money, she said, "I have this for you." In front of her eight-year-old daughter, he reached over, placed his hand between her legs, and said, "Baby, I'll take anything you've got." She was in shock. He already had her money. There was nowhere else for her and her three children to turn.

The owner asked who else had been sexually harassed and almost every hand in the room went up. His response was, "I guess what we have here is women who have been sexually harassed." Finally, he agreed to fire Skinner.

He did let Skinner go, but gave him three months' salary and a letter of recommendation. We were livid. Skinner was now free to go to another complex and prey on other women. We vowed to publicize this story.

We soon learned that Jane Clark, Debra Kalloff's mother, had been waging a private battle with the Department of Fair Employment and Housing over her daughter's eviction. She, too, was frustrated and angry that nothing was being done through the appropriate agencies. She had finally managed to find two feminist attorneys, Leslie Levy and Amy Oppenheimer, in Oakland, California. Even though all of the other attorneys we had collectively contacted wouldn't take our case, they did. What happened next made history.

Fifteen of us sued Jim Skinner, the owner, Mark Chim, and the property management company, Dana Properties.

The case of Fiedler v. Dana Properties was settled through mediation in federal court for an unprecedented $850,000. The U.S. Justice Department became involved because of HUD's investigation and sued on behalf of another eight women, winning an additional $384,000. The owner also had to pay $45,000 in fines. All in all, the damages awarded totaled $1.6 million for twenty-three women and their children.

Skinner disappeared as soon as we filed the lawsuit. After the case was settled and we followed through with our plans for publicity, two women went to Rape Crisis and filed crimi-

nal charges that Skinner had raped them at the apartment complex. Shortly thereafter, because of the publicity, an anonymous caller notified our attorneys that Skinner was working at an apartment complex in Cupertino, California, as a maintenance man. And he carried keys to all of the apartments there.

We notified the local police department. Detective Harold Sagan, who had taken the rape complaints, drove the two hours to Cupertino to arrest Skinner himself. The television news show Exposé was there to film his arrest at gunpoint.

When he was brought back to the Solano County Jail, we were waiting. When Detective Sagan pulled up with Jim Skinner, we approached the unmarked car in a show of solidarity and shook our keys at him. The sound of those keys represented Skinner's extortion tool—the keys to our homes. Now the jail held the keys to his home.

Molly and I have formed a new nonprofit organization, WRATH—Women Refusing to Accept Tenant Harassment. WRATH is dedicated to promoting public awareness of sexual harassment in housing. We provide information and referrals to women concerning their rights under the Fair Housing Act, Title VIII. We offer our experience and support to other women who are sexually harassed by their landlords. Sexual harassment in housing is still not widely talked about; that silence demonstrates the extent to which our society is willing to allow women to be victimized. So we feel it is our responsibility to speak out and provide other women with the information they need to fight back.

We have developed an intervention program specifically geared toward empowering women and providing them with options of recourse. When possible, we meet with tenants who are being sexually harassed and use our experience to help them develop their own plan of action against the harasser. It is the primary goal of WRATH to bring this issue out publicly, as we cannot be quiet, nor should any woman have to endure this type of harassment. WRATH can be contacted by writing to 607 Elmira Road, Suite 299, Vacaville, California, 95687.

We are still awaiting the outcome of Skinner's rape trial.

We have promised to stand by the side of the rape victims throughout the trial to lend our support. Most of us have been subpoenaed by the prosecution as witnesses who can establish a pattern of Skinner's behavior. This criminal trial is going to take its toll on both the victims and the witnesses, some of whom are still afraid of Skinner. It may be difficult to win because there is no physical evidence and the rapes happened so long ago. Luckily, at this point, all we know how to do is to forge ahead and try to leave our fear behind.

The story is not complete without an acknowledgment of Leslie and Amy, our attorneys. Their belief in all of us and their willingness to take a case of this magnitude on a contingency-fee basis gave us our first ray of hope and our long-awaited victory. When our landmark harassment case was settled, they continued to believe in us, and struck another blow against harassment by donating $10,000 to WRATH.

I am proud to have been part of this historic effort, proud to be a cofounder of WRATH, and proud to share our success story with women everywhere.

WRATH's victory is a historic breakthrough for women. Their success established an important legal precedent that can now be used by women across the country. The large fines they won should be a convincing incentive for landlords everywhere to act promptly to stop sexual harassment. If your landlord fails to act, let him know about this lawsuit —and don't be afraid to insist on your rights.

In this case, the predatory harasser was an employee of the firm that managed the apartment complex, and both the apartment owner and the management company were found legally liable. Sexual harassment by a neighbor is also against the law, as Debbie Chalfie explains in Appendix B. While the legal remedies are slightly different, the basic steps are the same: Confront the neighbor, report him, find allies, and file charges if he doesn't stop. As Catherine Hanson says, we have the fundamental right to be safe in our own homes.

onfronting Muggers and Burglars: Self-defense in a Robbery

When women are harassed the best solution is strong, immediate action: individual confrontation on the spot, group confrontation and legal action if the harassment continues. Report the harasser to the authorities, talk to the other women around, and stand up for yourself like the women of WRATH did.

But defending your possessions—at the risk of your life—is a very different proposition. While it is sometimes possible to confront an unarmed thief successfully, it is almost never a good idea to use direct confrontation tactics with an armed robber. If you have any reason at all to suspect that a mugger on the street or a burglar in your home has a weapon, the safest thing to do is to stay calm, give him the money, and get yourself out of there.

Although a robbery may leave you feeling violated and angry, it's important to keep your priorities clear. Do NOT engage in heroic action for the sake of money, television sets, cameras, stereos, or jewelry. They can be replaced. You can't. A robbery is *not* equivalent to harassment, and you must adjust your tactics accordingly.

Why shouldn't you confront an armed robber? Whether he is on the street or in your home, he is likely to be a very jumpy young man. He's probably fourteen to twenty-five years old, not a cool, clear-thinking adult. He may be on drugs; he is certainly desperate. At the moment of contact, he is just as tense as you are. Don't startle him, corner him, or give him any excuse to panic and escalate the situation. The psychological dynamics involved, combined with the presence of a lethal weapon, mean that confronting him directly could escalate the level of violence.

Moreover, unlike harassment or sexual assault, a robbery is usually over quickly: fifteen to thirty seconds in a street robbery, a matter of minutes in a home burglary. The assailant wants to get in and out fast, to minimize his risk of getting caught. There is no reason to prolong an encounter with an armed man by fighting to defend yourself, physically or verbally, if all he wants is your money. *It's only money.* Here are tactics you *can* use, however, should this happen to you.

ROBBERY ON THE STREET

If you're held up on the street, move slow and easy (no sharp, sudden sounds or gestures), cooperate by placing your purse, wallet, knapsack, or briefcase on the ground, and then take off—run for safety, to the nearest place where there are other people.

However, deciding not to confront an armed robber does not mean that you're a helpless victim. It just means that your strategy must be a little different. Try to identify the man. Look for facial features, haircut, jewelry, shoes, clothing, height, weight, scars, mannerisms—anything that you can use later to describe him. Assailants have been identified from the shape of an eyebrow or earlobe, a slogan on a T-shirt, a class ring on the hand holding the gun, and a hundred other tiny details their observant victims noticed. Look quickly for identifying marks, get yourself to a safe place, and report the incident to the police. Let them deal with him; that's their job.

There's one more step to take. Let your neighbors know about it. They're at risk, too, The street mugger is probably working the neighborhood; the odds are that you are not the first or the last person he'll hold up. Tell your neighbors when and where the robbery took place, what he looks like, whether he used a knife or a gun, and anything else you know about him. Tell them how to respond, if they've never taken a self-defense class.

You may find that some of them have already encountered

him. Ask them to help you describe him. Did they notice any additional details about his clothes, or voice, or face? Did he smell odd or use some kind of cologne? List everything you can think of. Working together, you may be able to put together a very good description.

Then take some responsible community action. Put a flyer with his description up around the neighborhood—in the Laundromat, grocery, library, liquor store, bus stop, and church—wherever people will see it. If you were robbed on your way home from school or work, put the flyer up there.

Keep it simple. Describe him in detail and describe what he said and did—that's all. Don't use obscenities, racial slurs, or ethnic stereotypes in the description. Don't be insulting or melodramatic; just lay out the facts. There's no need to put your name on the flyer or identify yourself in any way; the purpose is to warn your friends and neighbors. Let everyone in the vicinity know about this man. The more alert they are, the safer they're likely to be. He may even decide to leave the neighborhood alone, once he sees his description up on every corner.

What about an *unarmed* robber on the street? Is it ever safe to confront him? The answer is yes, sometimes, but only if he has an escape route and you are absolutely sure that he has no weapon. If there is any doubt in your mind, assume that he is armed and act accordingly. Most muggers carry a gun these days, so err on the side of caution—a robbery is a dangerous situation.

An unarmed mugger is just as nervous and panicky as an armed assailant. He is just as likely to be young, tense, unpredictable, or on drugs. The psychological dynamics are similar, with or without a weapon; the only difference is the level of physical danger that you face. The absence of a weapon reduces your risk of injury but does not eliminate it entirely.

Cornering a mugger on the street (or a burglar at home), even an unarmed one, is *always* a bad idea. Being trapped makes people violent, so before you decide to confront this assailant, make sure that he has a clearly visible path to get away. The purpose in confronting him is to interrupt the attack before he has a chance to injure you (and perhaps make him think twice before he tries it again). Let him get away—you want him *out* of here.

Take these cautions seriously. Do not confront without thinking, just because you're angry! Size up the situation very carefully. If (1) he has a clear, open escape route and (2) you're *sure* he has no weapon, you may be able to stop an unarmed robber with a confrontation.

Here's an example in which Kim did just that:

BALTIMORE STREET SCENE

I was leaving my office in downtown Baltimore at 7:30 one evening. The section of downtown where I work was deserted at that hour, and since it was winter, the streets were dark. I have a four-block walk from my office to my parking garage. This evening I noticed a couple of people leaning against a wall ahead of me. The first thing I do in a situation like this on the street is to look the people straight in the face, but when I did that, these two were looking down at the pavement, not at me. I looked at them carefully. As soon as I passed, I heard them start walking behind me. I was aware of their closeness. I immediately started focusing on them and began to weigh my options, but I didn't turn around. Then as we passed a glass shopfront, I saw the reflection of a hand up in the air just above my shoulder, reaching for my purse strap. I spun around and shouted, "What are you doing? Stop it! Back off!"

The shorter one, who'd been reaching for my shoulder, was a woman, I think (they were both dressed in unisex punk style and wearing hats—it was hard to tell). The woman cowered. I stepped right up to her and her taller (male?) companion and continued at an angry volume: "What do you think you're doing! Keep your hands to yourself!"

She said weakly that they were "just walking" and they both started to back away. "You were not!" I yelled. "I saw your hands reaching for me! Get out of here!" She and her friend crossed the street and began walking the other way. I stood stock still and watched them, and yelled, "Don't you dare do anything like that again!" I didn't have the feeling that they were likely to hurt me—I think they just wanted to grab my purse and bolt.

I was glad I'd acted so fast, but it was still a shock. After the shock wore off, I trembled for several hours. But I did succeed in confronting them and foiling their robbery attempt.

Kim's action was successful because of several factors: (1) She sized up the two unarmed muggers and the situation accurately; (2) she trusted her instincts about them, and was not only alert, but already mentally preparing to take action when they made their move; and (3) she had the benefit of taking *them* by surprise when she saw the reflection in the store window and was able to whirl around and challenge them. That got the muggers off balance, unsure about what would happen next. And at that critical moment, Kim was careful not to corner them in any way; in fact, she yelled at them to "get out of here," which made it clear to them that they could get away. In the face of her strong, angry presence, getting out of there was a sensible decision, and that's exactly what they chose to do.

It's always preferable to confront before the situation fully develops. The earlier you act, the less the mugger has invested in the encounter, and the more likely you are to succeed in breaking it off. However, it is sometimes possible to confront an unarmed mugger after the fact. Here's Sarah's success story, about a robbery in upstate New York:

WINTER STREET ROBBERY

I'm a young white woman, from a working-class Polish-American family. I won a scholarship to attend Syracuse University in upstate New York, and that's where this incident took place.

In January of my junior year, I was taking an evening exam in a building about two blocks from my dorm. I finished early and decided to head back to the dorm by myself. It was 9:30 P.M. I bundled up in my parka and wool hat and mittens and headed out the door.

The building where I had the exam was at the bottom of a long block of low-rise buildings—old houses and apartments that the university had converted into classrooms and academic offices. At the top of the block was a T-intersection. My dorm was at the top of the hill, just out of sight, off to the left on the cross street.

Now, Syracuse in January means snow—snow up to your knees, snow up to your waist sometimes. We had about two feet of new snow on the ground that night. The snow was six to eight inches deep on the streets and sidewalks, packed down and salted, and the plows had pushed the excess into huge mounds that lined the roads and the paths. Walking up the sidewalk was like walking through a tunnel.

The street was completely deserted when I stepped out the door—nobody out walking and no lights on in most of the buildings.

I was about halfway up the block when I saw two young black men come from the right side of the cross street up ahead, turn, and start down the long block toward me. As soon as I saw them, I thought, "They're going to rob me." All I had with me was a small purse over my shoulder and a notebook in my right hand. (I never carried much money—I never had much money.)

Then I thought to myself, "Wait a minute. If these were two young white guys walking toward you, you wouldn't jump to the conclusion that they were going to rob you. You'd expect them to hassle you, maybe, but not rob you. What are you thinking? What a racist assumption!" I decided that I was not going to let racism control my actions. I deliberately did not turn around, run, or even switch my purse to my other shoulder. I just kept walking up the narrow, snowy sidewalk, with my purse on my left and a huge snowbank on my right.

As I got closer, I could see that they were boys, really—
one was about my size (five foot three) and the other only a
few inches taller—maybe fourteen and sixteen years old, I
guessed. I felt even more chagrined about the racist reaction
I'd had. I was almost at the top of the hill, and I smiled at
them as they approached.

In the next instant, without a word, the big one shoved me
into the snowbank and the little one grabbed my purse,
broke the strap, and dashed past me; they both took off running down the sidewalk, back the way I'd come.

I was beside myself. I couldn't believe it. Here I'd gone
through this whole mental process about not being a racist
and not prejudging young black men and not assuming the
worst—and they went and did it! I was as angry as I'd ever
been. I thought for one split second, then I knew what I was
going to do.

I jumped up out of the snowbank, snatched up my notebook, and took off after them. They had a head start but my
boots had soles like tire treads—great traction in the snow. I
started gaining on them. And all the way back down that long
snowy block I yelled at the top of my lungs, "Goddammit,
give me back my wallet! I need my driver's license! I need
my school ID! Who do you think you are! I can't believe
you did this!" I never shouted "help"—I pounded down
the sidewalk, running hard and roaring, "Stop, goddammit, I
want my wallet back!"

We ran past the building where I'd taken my exam—no
one came out. We kept running. At the end of the block they
stopped and turned to face me. I was only ten feet behind
them, still yelling blue murder and coming fast.

I marched past the little one and up to the bigger one, who
was holding my purse at this point, and demanded, "What
the hell did you do that for? Give me back my purse!"

They both just stood there, dumbfounded. I launched into
a tirade about how I was a scholarship student and what the
hell did they think they were doing and people like me
busted our butts to get into college and worked our tails off
and it would cost me ten bucks for a new ID card and five

bucks for a new license and if they wanted to rob somebody why didn't they go rob some rich person downtown instead of robbing a student like me. . . .

Halfway through this verbal barrage, the big one silently handed my purse back to me.

But I was on a roll; I didn't stop. The taller one was facing me. The little one never said a word—he just stood there with his mouth open and his eyes wide with amazement, looking at me and then at the big guy and back at me and back at the big guy. My adrenaline was pounding and I was going strong. I yelled about race and class and privilege and education and jobs, and poor people robbing poor people— I was really fired up.

I demanded again, "Why did you do this!" and the taller one muttered, "Well, jeez, lady, we needed the money." I said, "Well, I need the money, too! You think all students are rich?"

I opened my purse and took out my wallet. I had all of two dollars in there. I said, "Look at this! Were you guys really going to take my last two dollars?"

He said, "Jesus, no, lady!"

I put my wallet back in my purse and said, "Well, all right then. Good night. Don't you ever do that again!" Then I turned on my heel and went striding back up the block.

I didn't hear another sound from them. When I looked back, they were still standing there on the corner, staring at me and looking completely stunned. I looked back again when I got to the top of the street, at the T-intersection, five or six minutes later. They were still standing where I'd left them. Deep in shock, I think.

Again, it was the fact that Sarah was mentally prepared that made this confrontation work. She assessed the two critical aspects of the situation accurately: The two young men were unarmed and not cornered, out on an open street. Sarah decided to do the unexpected, and she was very loud and clear about it.

Like Kim, she had consciously focused on the assailants

beforehand and was ready to act. Sarah didn't trust her instincts entirely; she may have picked up on something in their body language as they turned down the street, but she really thought about *why* she had the feeling that these two would rob her. Racism is a reality in our society, and it does distort white women's judgment about who is and is not a threat.

Analyzing her feelings about racism did not prevent Sarah from reacting decisively when the time came. That she'd looked closely at the young men and thought carefully about her own behavior helped to put her in control of the encounter. Her choice of action after the robbery was clearly a product of her analysis beforehand. And it was a clear choice; angry as Sarah was, she thought before she acted.

Delivering an impassioned sociology lecture on race, class, and poverty to a pair of muggers is not a typical response to a robbery. It was an excellent confrontation, however. It was strong, direct, and honest—not only appropriate to the circumstances, but downright overwhelming.

THE OBSERVATION CIRCLE: A SIMPLE EXERCISE

The habit of observation is essential to effective confrontation. In the cases above, noticing the assailants before they made their move gave Kim and Sarah an important advantage in sizing up the situation and deciding how to respond successfully. To practice your skills in basic street observation, try this exercise: For the next week, draw an imaginary circle twenty feet around you, every time you're out on a public street. Actually *look* at the people on the street, and name (to yourself, not out loud) at least three distinguishing characteristics for each man who moves into that circle: glasses (what kind?), blue suit, fiftyish, overweight; young kid, punk haircut, red "Megadeath" T-shirt; baseball cap (what does the logo say?), white T-shirt, overalls torn at left knee—whatever. If you like, you can do the same thing with the women around you, too.

There's no need to stare or be rude in any way; just take

half a second to really look at every man within that twenty-foot circle and mentally register at least three descriptive facts. Notice their body language and mannerisms as well as their physical appearance. You don't have to remember the details for more than a moment; there's no quiz at the end of the day. Once you get used to doing it, make the circle a little bigger. The point is to get into the habit of *observing*, to really know who's moving around anywhere near you. Practice this consciously for a week and then check yourself from time to time. Once you start doing it automatically, it takes little or no mental effort, and you've given yourself the kind of streetwise early warning system that Kim and Sarah used so effectively.

After all, it's one thing to trust your instincts when you're assessing a situation—you have to *notice* the situation first.

And it is useful to think about racism, as Sarah did, when you're evaluating a potential threat on the street. If you're a white woman who automatically flinches whenever a black or Hispanic man approaches, think about where and why you learned to do that. Do you unconsciously tense up, clutch your purse, move away if he's black? Do you automatically relax if the man is white? As you practice the observation exercise, notice all the African-American and Hispanic men who pass by and do *not* harass you on the street, steal your purse, or otherwise molest you. Observe your own behavior. Begin countering stereotypes for yourself.

Eliminating racist stereotypes is not just a matter of morality and social justice. On a strictly practical level, your safety in a street robbery may depend on having accurate reactions, undistorted by racism. Whether or not you ever decide to confront an unarmed mugger, it's important not to overestimate the risk from men of color on the street—and not to minimize or dismiss the potential threat from white males.

ROBBERY AT HOME

What if you have to deal with a burglar in your own home, instead of a mugger on the street? Don't assume that he is unarmed; there are plenty of weapons in the average house or apartment, from baseball bats to kitchen knives. If there's a gun in the house, he may have found it. Go out the back door, the window, the fire escape, wherever you can; use any emergency exit that you'd use in case of fire. Get out immediately and call the police from next door.

Although confrontation is not the first choice in this case, you can use your verbal skills in other ways. As frightening as this situation is, you are not helpless. Draw on all your resources: mental preparation, verbal skills, escape routes, and neighbors. That's what Kimberly F. did, in this success story about a midnight burglary at home:

THE INTRUDER

My name is Kimberly, and I'm a white female, single, age twenty-three. This incident happened earlier this year, just two weeks after I'd taken a short self-defense class at the rape crisis center.

I was sitting downstairs in my two-level townhouse apartment in Washington, D.C. It was approximately 12:30 A.M., and my roommate was upstairs in her bedroom asleep. I heard a noise coming from the top of the stairs. Assuming it was my roommate, I called out to her. When there was no response, I went over to the stairway and started up. I saw two legs in dark gray sweatpants just above the landing, and as I climbed up a few steps, I realized that it was an intruder. He was about five feet seven, wearing a dark-blue hooded sweatshirt with the hood pulled tight over his head. He had something in his hand—I couldn't tell if it was a gun, but I assumed it was. I was terrified, but I didn't freeze. I immediately started yelling, "Oh, my god, oh, my god!" and ran back down the stairs toward the front door.

He was stunned for a moment, but then he came after me, fast. In my panic, I couldn't get the door unlocked. However, as I felt him getting close, I remembered my self-defense session. I calmed down, got out the door, and began scream-

ing the karate yell I'd learned, "KIYA! KIYA! KIYA!" over and over. I ran across the open concrete porch to the next townhouse, a few feet away, and began pounding on my neighbor's door, still screaming, "KIYA!"

The intruder hesitated, just inside my front door. Once I got outside, I wasn't afraid that he'd hurt me, but I wanted him out of my house and I kept yelling and banging on my neighbor's door. There was a long second while the intruder was deciding what to do next. Then he bolted, running right past me and down the street, as fast as he could go. He didn't even touch me as he raced past.

Within moments, there were half a dozen people on my front stoop. A couple of my neighbors even chased him partway down the street.

The police were there in less than two minutes—a woman in the apartment complex later told me that she had called them immediately when she heard me screaming "Kiya!"

After it was all over, I felt angry, relieved, and smart, at the same time. I knew what to do, and I did it—fast. My roommate didn't wake up until I was already outside, yelling, but she and I were both fine. And my neighbors' response was just great. They realized from my karate yell that this was something serious and they leaped into action. I don't think that guy will be back on our block any time soon.

Like Kim and Sarah in the street robberies above, Kimberly found that her preparation and presence of mind paid off in this situation. She did not confront; she was absolutely right to get out of the townhouse as fast as possible. But she used her verbal skills very effectively to stop the burglary almost before it began. By reacting immediately, and then using a karate yell (not just crying "help, help"), Kimberly made it clear to the intruder that he was up against more than he'd bargained for. This was no helpless female. Kimberly got herself to safety, roused her neighbors, and acted like a formidable opponent. The intruder had an open escape path, and it took him only a moment to decide that he'd better use it.

Kimberly was able to get outside and to a neighbor quickly. But what if the intruder is blocking your only exit? In that case, confrontation is one option to consider. Yelling, "Get out of here! Get out right now!" is a way to startle him for a moment and try to give yourself a chance to get past him and out. It may or may not work; use your judgment before you yell. DO NOT startle a man who is holding a gun directly on you. Whenever a weapon is involved, a sudden confrontation can be very risky. But if you're trapped with the intruder between you and the exit, a confrontation may give you an opportunity to escape. In the best possible outcome, he may be so startled that *he* takes off. This is a dangerous situation: Think before you act and be ready to move fast. What you say does make a difference; telling him to get out lets him know that he is not trapped and makes it clear that you will not try to stop him if he takes off.

Negotiation is another verbal option. If the intruder has a weapon and has your escape route blocked, it is sometimes possible to talk your way out the door. Keeping your voice calm and steady, look at him as you say: "Look, I'm going to get out of here, I just want to get out the door and out of your way. I'm going to walk out that door and not come back, so you just stay calm. I'm not going to touch you, I'm getting out of your way here, don't worry, I won't be coming back. . . . " Move gently, with no sharp gestures, but keep moving toward the door as you speak. Watch his hands and his face. Keep your hands in plain view. Try to keep your body language neutral: neither helpless nor threatening. Don't beg or plead, but keep talking, keep negotiating, and keep moving. Once you get out, run.

Neither confrontation nor negotiation will work in every case; they are options to consider, depending on the circumstances. The safest strategy with a burglar is to assume that he has a weapon and avoid him altogether: Like Kimberly, use the closest exit and get out of the house immediately.

onfronting Rapists: Self-defense in a Sexual Assault

There are some very critical differences between a robbery and a sexual assault. While a robbery is a relatively simple crime with a simple motive (cash), a sexual assault is far more complex. The rapist's motive is power and control; he seeks to dominate his victim, and is likely to find her fear and humiliation sexually exciting. While a robbery is usually over in seconds or minutes, a rape often goes on for two to three hours (and sometimes even longer). While most muggers and burglars are armed, many rapists still carry no weapon—they assume they will be able to terrify and overpower their victims. A robbery is usually an impersonal crime—he holds up the first person who comes out of the supermarket, or breaks into the first house that has a window unlocked. A rape is usually planned—he has been stalking the area, watching women, sometimes even using harassment as rape-testing to select potential victims. More often than not, the rapist is no stranger in a dark alley; he is an acquaintance, someone the woman knows, perhaps someone she has seen in class or around the neighborhood.

Sexual assault is a reality for an estimated one in every three women in the United States. It is a crime committed against children, against young and middle-aged women, and against women in their seventies and eighties. It takes place in the victim's home, in the assailant's home, at school, at work, almost anywhere: in a car, a stairwell, a laundry room, a parking garage, an elevator, a public park, or a woman's own bedroom. Rape is a crime of both sex and power, a means of ripping power away from a human being, stripping away her sense of self and personal safety and control over her life. It is a sexual turn-on for the assailant, and a life-changing experience of terror for the victim. And it is an effective method of social control: When one woman is raped, one hundred women may stop working late, avoid their local park, or drop their night classes—living in fear in their own homes and communities. A robbery is a frightening experience, but the societal and psychological effects of rape are far more lasting.[1]

Because rape and robbery are so different, the best strategies for stopping rape are very different from the safest tactics in a robbery. What's at stake is *you*—not just your cash, your watch, or your television. Calm cooperation may save your life in a robbery, but it is no defense against rape. Because most rapists are cowards and bullies, are not carrying a lethal weapon, and are looking for victims they can control, a strong verbal confrontation at the outset can often succeed in breaking off the attack.

No two sexual assaults are identical, no single self-defense tactic will work every time, and women should always use their own judgment in deciding whether and how to fight back. Submitting under threat is not the same as consenting! Confrontation, like other forms of self-defense, is a choice, one strategy among several. Only the woman herself, at the moment of an impending attack, is in a position to assess that particular assailant and decide what is most likely to work. Confrontation, however, can be an extremely effective method of self-defense.

At the earliest stages, when the assailant is still engaged in rape-testing, confrontation can sometimes prevent an attack altogether by making it absolutely clear that the potential victim will not be a passive, helpless target. Here's one example in which confrontation made all the difference: a rapist who selected his victims by stalking women in supermarkets. In the first aisle, he would merely stare at the woman from about forty feet away, with that invasive, predatory look that almost every woman has experienced at some point. Many women noticed him at that point, but just took evasive action, moving over to the next aisle. Following his prey into the second aisle, he again stared at the woman, now from only ten feet away. If she confronted him at that point ("Stop staring at me! Get out of here! Stop harassing women!"), he backed off and looked for another victim. If the woman still did nothing, he continued to test her: He followed her into the third aisle and deliberately ran his cart into hers. Even at that stage, many women, trained in feminine politeness, actually said, "Oh, excuse me!" instead of confronting him—despite the fact that *he* was the one who had run into them. Those were the women he chose to follow into the parking lot, where he assaulted them. The women who confronted him in the safety of the supermarket prevented a rape; the women who reacted passively and politely left themselves open to attack. He used the technique over and over again, and raped at least ten women this way before he was caught.

Cultivating the mental habit of maintaining a twenty-foot "observation circle"—as described in Chapter 11—discourages sexual harassment (including rape-testing) and gives the intended victim the chance to confront a potential rapist before the situation develops into an assault. Even in the worst case, the observation circle gives a woman a few extra seconds to think and get ready to act.

According to the research on actual sexual assaults, once an attack begins some self-defense strategies generally work much better than others. Crying, begging, and pleading are usually ineffective; they play right into the rapist's power trip. Telling a rapist that you are pregnant, have VD, have AIDS, or have your period rarely works. Nor does throwing up on him, peeing in your own pants, or other self-demeaning behavior; if his motive is humiliation, humiliating yourself is not likely to dissuade him.

What does seem to work, more often than anything else, is a four-part strategy:

- *Resist immediately.* The beginning of an attack is the point at which women can most often succeed in fighting off the assailant. In terms of preventing both completed rapes and other serious physical injuries, fighting back right away is often safer than submitting, and almost always safer than cooperating with the rapist for a while, then trying to fight in the middle of the assault.

- *Yell and keep on yelling.* Do not scream "Help!" It doesn't work. Hollering "Fire!" is often ineffective, too; it doesn't work at all outdoors, and even inside a building, people may simply open their doors, see no smoke, and go back inside. Shout "No!" directly at the attacker, or use a karate yell like "Kiya!" to startle him and get your own adrenaline flowing. Then start telling people what is going on, at the top of your lungs: Yell, "This is an attack, call the cops!" People are much more likely to take action if you tell them what to do. Keep on shouting as long as possible, to let people know where you are.

- *Use a combination of tactics.* To break free from the assailant, use every combination of basic physical self-defense tactics you know, as well as your verbal skills. If one move doesn't work, try another; don't give up. Take a self-defense course at the local rape crisis center. Learn, ahead of time, the kinds of moves that work.

- *Once you get free, run.* Head for the nearest place where there are people around—bang on doors, keep yelling, get out in the middle of the road and stop traffic if necessary. Take a walking tour of your neighborhood *now* to locate dead ends and other traps, as well as safe places to run to; know who is likely to be around to hear you if you yell and which way to run in case of an emergency.

With unarmed assailants, these four steps frequently succeed in getting the intended victim out of the attack unraped and otherwise uninjured. The average rapist is only five foot nine and is unarmed; he is terrifying, but he is not invulnerable. Some studies show that, using these techniques, women have as much as an 80 percent chance of escaping unharmed.

If the rapist has a lethal weapon—a knife or gun—the safest strategy usually involves negotiating to try to get the weapon away from your body before you begin to fight. Although some women have done it successfully, yelling at a man who has a gun trained on you or a knife right against your skin is risky. Use your judgment. The odds of success increase substantially if you can get him to put the weapon down, even briefly.

Negotiating means using firm, repetitive statements and commands—the "broken record" technique. Again, the more specific the command, the more likely it is to be followed: "Put that knife on the table right now. I hate knives. I want you to put it on the table by the lamp now, before we even talk about anything else. I can't stand knives, I've never liked knives. Put it down on the table. . . . "

One woman in Washington, attacked at gunpoint on a downtown street, did exactly that. As she was walking down the street at 9:30 P.M., a van pulled up beside her. The driver jumped out, grabbed her by the arm, held the weapon to her temple, and said, "Get in the van, bitch." She realized immediately that this was a rape attempt, not a robbery, and that she was much more likely to survive if she resisted right then and there. She began negotiating: "Put the gun down, put the gun in the van. Put it on the passenger seat. I hate guns, put it in the van now. . . . " After a minute or more of this, she finally said, "If you're going to shoot me, you'll have to do it right here downtown. I'm not getting in that van as long as you keep waving that gun!" He said in disgust, "Fuck you, bitch," let go of her, got back in the van, and drove off. She was shaking with fear, but observant enough to get part of his license plate number as he took off.

Another woman, cornered in her three-room school when she was working as a teacher in Central America, negotiated her way out of a rape by a young soldier armed with an M16 rifle. Early one evening, as she was preparing class notes at her desk, she looked up to see the man standing in the doorway of the classroom. She was alone with him in the building. He raised the weapon and ordered her to lie down on the desk. She looked him in the eye, stood up, and began to speak in her firmest teacher-in-command voice: "That is shameful, you should be ashamed. I am a *teacher*. I will teach you to read, I will teach you to write, but I will not let you do this shameful thing. Put that rifle down over there in the corner. This is a schoolroom! What were you thinking of, to say such a thing to a teacher! Put that rifle down now." He walked into the room, still aiming the rifle at her. She went on talking and lecturing him about what a shameful thing he had suggested, as she gathered up her papers. Then, still talking, she walked past him and out of the room. He followed her out into the long hallway. He had the rifle in his hand as he watched her march down the hall and right out of the building to safety.

Both of these women used strong negotiating tactics to confound their attackers and escape. Good verbal tactics—confrontation and negotiation—are as much a part of effective self-defense as knowing how to break out of a front choke or any other physical hold. Your brain and your voice are self-defense tools—use them!

Mosi Harrington successfully confronted an assailant—unarmed, but a real lunatic—who threatened both her and the kids she was supervising, in an assault that took place on an isolated country road in Ohio. Here's Mosi's success story:

MAD DOG

It was in the sixties and I was working hard in a camp in southern Ohio, trying to integrate white middle-class kids with black kids from the south side of Columbus. I had taken eight twelve-year-old girls on an all-day hike. We were trekking back to camp in a remote rural area. We were hot and we were tired. Our route was a winding back road; there was a lot of tall brush along the sides, which made it impossible to see around the curves behind or ahead of us.

Then one of the girls said, "There's a man back there."

"Yep," I said, looking back into the brush.

"He has a couple of dogs."

"Oh, it's probably Woodie," I answered. Woodie was a

counselor who was always picking up stray dogs and went around with a pair of Levis on and a bare chest—and by now the man was out far enough that we could see he had no shirt on.

He took a few more steps and one of the girls said, "He doesn't have any clothes on."

"You're right. He doesn't," I responded. "We won't run. We'll walk calmly unless he starts to chase us."

He started to chase us.

We started to run. He was gaining on us.

"Get in the woods," I shouted to the girls, and I turned to face him. His arms were high over his head and his eyes were bulging as he ran toward me.

"Stay right where you are!" I said in as normal a voice as I could manage. He kept coming. He was about ten feet from me and coming fast.

I was holding a cardboard box with a first-aid kit in it. I threw it at him and it hit him in the chest. He kept coming.

Now he was right on me. I put my arms up to block his and attempted to knee him in the groin. Apparently misplaced, the knee had no effect, but I screamed when I did it and he had started some at the scream. I knew I couldn't fight him off, so I thought maybe I could scare him off.

I put my arms up in the air and I made my eyes big and I screamed, "I'm a mad dog!" He turned and I began to chase him down the road. I kept screaming, "I'm a mad dog! I'm a mad dog!" as I took off after him.

When I had chased him back around the curve in the road, I ran back and pried the girls out of the woods where they were hiding—not an easy task after the amazing performance they'd seen their counselor put on—and we ran back to camp.

The girls were convinced I'd saved their lives. In actual fact, we had him outnumbered and could probably have handled the situation in a variety of other—though probably less colorful—ways. But the story of "mad dog" became a camp legend.

Bravo! Mosi was magnificent. Her quick, decisive verbal and physical response turned a dangerous and potentially tragic situation into a complete rout for the attacker. At the same time, she provided an example to every one of those girls. She showed them that she thought that their safety and hers were well worth fighting for, and that they were not powerless in the face of an assault.

That kind of immediate action is usually the strongest, safest way to respond to an impending attack. Cecile successfully confronted rapists in two separate incidents in the same year, when she was stalked by men on the street. Here's what Cecile has to say about her experiences:

ESCAPING RAPE

I have escaped attempted rape, and it clarified a lot for me. It's sad that it was a man who radicalized me on this issue, but then again, if it weren't for people like him, there would be no need to be radical.

In the first incident, I pretended to ignore the man when he first came to my attention. Then I varied my pace to see if he was really following me. I pivoted and walked away in the other direction. I walked past some people (I didn't say anything to them), hoping that the mere presence of other people would protect me. I walked more assertively than I have ever walked in my life. None of this worked at all. He kept following me.

I tried talking nicely to him, trying to diffuse his hostility by appearing harmless myself. Then I didn't respond to his comments, so as not to escalate the situation. But my silence allowed him to escalate the situation—a man's first comment starts the cycle of violence. At this point, we were in an alleylike setting, where I felt trapped. The only thing that worked was confrontation. I managed to take him by surprise. I suddenly turned, charged, sprinted past him, and escaped.

Six months later, on Valentine's Day, Farar and I found

ourselves being followed by another man as we walked to my car. We did not stop at the car, so as not to make ourselves more vulnerable (many women are attacked while getting into a car). But after we passed by my car, I got exasperated. I faced him and shouted, "Stop following us! Go away!"

He did not deny that he had been stalking us. "I just wanted to help you into your car, for Valentine's Day," he whined. Yeah, sure. Farar backed me up, and it was amazing: Her anger at him made me feel completely unafraid. "No!" we said, and he left—off to try to "help" another woman into her car, no doubt.

If I sound like I know I'm right, and show no fear, I am safer on the street. Men, like dogs, are bullies and can smell fear. Any kind of unusual behavior can work as a deterrent. I once heard a woman yapping at a man like a small, angry dog —it was frightening. Whenever I'm walking in the city alone at night, I sing loudly in my off-key voice; it's not "normal" behavior, it makes me more visible, and it makes men uncertain about what to expect from me, so I'm a less desirable target.

Women need to stop letting fear disable us. We can take action. A woman at the Michigan Womyn's Music Festival this year told me that, three times in her life, she has awakened to find a strange man standing over her. Each time, she yelled in rage and he ran away.

Cecile's success in confronting these two stalkers may have saved her life. A swift response can make all the difference. Because of Cecile's prompt action in the second case —admirably backed up by her friend Farar—that incident was much less dangerous than the first one. She and Farar stopped the potential rapist cold, before he had a chance to escalate the interaction into a major threat. By contrast, the first stalker kept following Cecile, undeterred by her evasive strategies, her attempts to defuse the danger with conversation, or her subsequent silence. Only when she turned, physically confronted him, and sprinted past was she able to get

free. Once she decided to confront, she moved fast and succeeded.

Many women, when followed by a stalker, try to pretend
that they aren't really aware of the threat. They pick up their
pace and scurry down the sidewalk, they may even cross to
the other side of the street, but they never turn and confront
the assailant—as if, by not looking at him, they could make
themselves invisible. This does not work.

It is usually much safer to confront the man as soon as you
are aware of his presence. Don't ignore him—something set
off your alarms. Take immediate action to protect yourself.

One of the simplest ways to do that is to turn around, look
him in the face, and say in a loud, clear voice, "Are you
following me?" There are only two possible answers. If he
says yes, get ready to run or fight. (At least he is honest about
his intentions, and now that you are facing him, you can
identify him and are in a much better position to fight him
off physically if you have to.) If he says no, you need to take
a second step. His answer may or may not be true. Tell him,
politely but firmly, to walk past, and then to walk in front of
you. Stand out by the curb or even in the street as he goes by
—where you can't easily be grabbed or shoved into a doorway. If he is not stalking you, he will understand your request and comply immediately. You can thank him, if you
like, as he goes past, and then simply continue walking down
the street, behind him. If he refuses to comply with this
simple, direct request, you now know something very important: His original answer was false. Prepare to run or defend yourself, just as if he'd answered yes to your first
question.

As frightening as it is to be stalked by a stranger on the
street, acquaintance rape is sometimes even more difficult
to deal with. These rapists can be smooth, persistent, and
extremely manipulative. Like most predatory harassers, they
count on women's reluctance to make a scene, especially
young women's fear of looking foolish by "over-reacting." In
fact, a date rapist or acquaintance rapist will often accuse his
victim of "over-reacting" when the woman first expresses

some uneasiness or concern about his actions. Denying his own intentions and leveling that charge at his victim is a skillful technique to overcome her objections and keep her from taking effective action against him. Don't be fooled. Trust your instincts about what's going on. If he denies being aggressive and mocks you for getting tense, that does *not* mean that your intuition is wrong. Get yourself to a safe place immediately.

Barbara learned the hard way about the kind of manipulation that acquaintance rapists often use. She ran up against one in college, but she did not confront him when she first began to feel uneasy. Here's Barbara's story:

THE CAMPUS TOUR

This is the story of how I fought back successfully against a rapist.

It was 1970 and I was a college freshman, celebrating my eighteenth birthday by visiting a number of bars in the Greenwich Village section of New York City with some classmates. At one point in the evening we dropped in at the student center at New York University (NYU) for a bite to eat.

While there, we met a pleasant-seeming guy named Bob. He latched on to our group and went to one or two bars with us. He appeared OK, and we told him he ought to visit our brand-new college campus in New Jersey. I casually offered to be a tour guide and gave him my dorm address, and then I went home with my friends.

Imagine my surprise a few nights later when he showed up at my door with a sleazy-looking friend, asking for his tour of the campus. Unlike my first encounter with Bob in New York, this time something didn't seem right about their behavior, so I tried to get my roommate or somebody else to join us. Nobody wanted to, so I nervously began taking the two men around the well-populated areas of the campus— the student center, the dining hall, the library.

I got more and more uncomfortable. Bob started coming on to me and the sleazy sidekick vanished. I tried to tell Bob I was tired and I started to head back to my dorm, but he didn't take the hint. I couldn't get rid of him. When I finally got back to my dorm, he pulled me into the cleaning closet across from my dorm room, began removing my clothes, and unzipped himself.

I was a virgin and terrified. I remembered my mother's advice about how to fight off men. Mama was a European immigrant who had lived several years in a displaced persons camp after World War II.

She didn't tell me much in the way of sex education, but she did teach me two things: Watch out for guys who try to get you drunk, and, in a rape situation, kick or knee the attacker in the groin.

As Bob started rubbing against me, I kneed him hard in the groin, opened the closet door, and hopped across the hall to my dorm room, screaming for help. Luckily my roommate was there. She opened the door, I scrambled in, and we slammed and locked the door. Bob began pounding and pushing on the door. We shoved a dresser in front of the door and another in front of the windows and shouted at him to go away or we would call the police.

At that point he began begging us not to report him. A short time later, he left. I never saw or heard from him again.

I never notified the police because I felt so stupid and ashamed of myself for letting the situation develop. This was back in the hippie era when we were supposed to treat our fellow hippies with love and peace. (Bob apparently felt no obligation to treat me that way!) I was afraid—probably rightly—that the police would berate me for stupidity and accuse me of instigating it. Back in those days, people were even more unenlightened about rape than they are today and it was common for a woman to be blamed for a rape. And as a hippie type, I didn't stand a chance in the justice system.

Oddly enough, the story doesn't end there. Years later I spoke about it to a childhood friend who had briefly attended NYU. When I described Bob, she told me that she had met

him and had had a similar narrow escape. He had lured her
to his apartment near NYU on some pretext. She managed to
get the door open and flee. Like me, she had felt like such a
fool that she never reported it to the police. Neither of us
knows if Bob was ever arrested or prosecuted.

I realize now that I was extremely fortunate that my roommate was on hand to help me escape the attack. It was years
before I could even talk about the assault, and until recently
I felt very badly about it.

But when I read an article about confronting harassers, it
made me think about the entire incident in a new way. Suddenly I did not feel so dumb. I had been an inexperienced
eighteen-year-old; he was a sexual con artist. I had sensed
something wrong, tried to protect myself by seeking help
from others, and finally fought back physically and won.
Since I have never been much of an athlete or a fighter, I feel
proud that I thought quickly, hurt my attacker, and escaped
uninjured.

I'm now the mother of two daughters. In thinking back on
all this, I can see how vulnerable teenage girls can be, and I
hope that confrontation tactics and women's success stories
become required reading in every junior high school across
the United States.

Like many women, Barbara was reluctant to be rude to a
man who was clearly imposing on her. He used her politeness to gradually maneuver her into a situation in which he
could rape her—as he had clearly done to many women before. Faced with the assault, Barbara fought back beautifully
and won. She is right, in retrospect, to be very proud of the
way she defended herself. She is also right to talk to her
daughters about the dynamics of date rape and teach them
confrontation skills, so that they can react much faster if it
ever happens to them.

Given the choice, it is always safer to confront an acquaintance or date rapist at the beginning. Don't wait until the
attack is under way. Confront when you first sense that his

behavior is inappropriate, to avoid having to fight your way out later. And, if possible, report the incident. At the very least, let other women around you know about your experience with any man who behaves in a predatory or manipulative way. Identify and describe him, and tell your friends exactly what he did. Don't let them walk into the same ambush.

Women have stopped both acquaintance and stranger rape in many different ways. Jennifer Womack, a young African-American woman, prevented a rape when she was only fourteen. She was asleep at her grandmother's house in Galveston, Texas, sharing a bed with her sister. In the middle of the night, a sound woke her up. She opened her eyes and found a man standing beside the bed. He put a gun to her head, told her not to make a sound, and ordered her to unzip his jeans.

Jennifer kept calm and thought hard. She didn't yell, since the gun was right there. She very slowly reached out and began fumbling with his zipper. She pretended to have trouble getting it unzipped. All the while, she was madly kicking her sister under the covers, trying to wake her up.

Her sister didn't wake up. Jennifer kept stalling, fumbling with the zipper. And she kept kicking.

Finally, finally, her sister stirred and rolled over.

The assailant was so startled to see that there was another person in the bed that he jumped back, dashed across the room, and went right back out the window he'd come in. He never even got his zipper unzipped.

Jennifer used her intelligence and the best resource she had at hand—her sister's presence—to make the rapist flee. As soon as he was gone, she yelled, woke everyone up, and told her grandmother and sister what had happened.

Not every fourteen-year-old would have Jennifer's presence of mind. But her strategy—stay calm and use your resources—is the key to succeeding in many dangerous situations.

Confrontation skills are one important kind of resource. The people who are around when an attack begins are an-

other. Women have stopped rapists by using all kinds of resources: negotiation skills, verbal and physical self-defense
abilities, and all kinds of weapons—everything from keys to
a pen, a pair of scissors, or even a book or an umbrella. Think
about what you might use; practice the kind of mental preparation that will help you to react quickly if you need to.

The decision about what tactic will work best depends on
the circumstances of the attack. Because, over the past
twenty years, rape survivors have spoken up about their experiences, we know much, much more about effective self-
defense than we did a generation ago. In the final analysis,
whether or not it is possible to prevent the attack, any woman
who survives a rape should consider herself a heroine: She
used her resources and her skills to save her life. A black
belt in martial arts, a knife, a gun, or another weapon is not
the crucial factor in survival. The single most important resource for any woman during an attempted rape is her own
intelligence.[2]

In some cities, feminists have stenciled the sidewalks with
a logo that says, "A woman was raped here," marking each
site where an attack took place as a way of increasing community awareness. In the 1990s, perhaps we all should design a new sidewalk logo: one that says, proudly, "A woman
was attacked here and fought back and won."

If you are a rape survivor, don't waste a minute second-
guessing the decisions you made at the time. Whatever you
did that enabled you to survive that attack was correct, and
the fact that you are here today to read this book means that
you did something very right.

There Is Strength in Numbers: The Power of Group Confrontations

One of the most powerful responses to sexual aggression is an organized, well-planned group confrontation. The basic technique is discussed in Chapter 4, and the impact of a group confrontation is tremendous. If harassers do not expect individual women to stand up for themselves, they are altogether dumbfounded when women actually get together and take forceful collective action to stop abuse. It is, in fact, a very frightening experience for the harasser.

There are several factors that make group confrontation so effective. First, there is simply the shock of it—women are not "supposed to" get organized and cooperate this way. It violates all the sexist stereotypes about women being catty and unreliable for each other, women being willing to sell each other out to please a man, and women being too fearful, too disorganized, or too incompetent to ever carry out a successful action together.

Second, the women are presenting a unified force—not one is smiling, acting deferential, making any excuses for the harasser, or offering him any emotional or psychological escape from facing up to what he did. Together, they have seized control of the situation, and there is no weak link that he can play on. Sexist men count on being able to divide women, to set them against each other—but this time, there is no out. The women are united.

Third, they are angry, blunt, and disciplined. They are furious but entirely in control. Anyone who abuses power fears retaliation from his or her victims. Sexist males have a deep, subconscious fear of what would happen if women ever really decided to get together and take revenge, retaliating in kind for all the rape, battering, and incest, let alone the political and economic discrimination. (What else did you think all those male castration anxieties were about?) Confrontation is *not* revenge, not violent retaliation-in-kind, but the harasser doesn't know that. Like individual confronters, confrontation groups make no idle threats—they name the harasser's behavior, hold him accountable, and let him sweat it out, pondering in his imagination and his nightmares just what might happen if he ever does it again.

And finally, a group confrontation demolishes the harasser's sense of safety in privacy. His actions are *known*. It is humiliating to have one's morally bankrupt private behavior publicly labeled as despicable and exposed to the community. Just the fact that the eight or ten or twelve women in the room, confronting him, know exactly what he has done strips away his sense of safety and entitlement and leaves him feeling deeply at risk. The possibility that they may take further public action is a chilling threat, unspoken but very real.

All of these factors come into play, in addition to the fundamental power of the confrontation itself: the "truth force" of the women's direct statements; the use of language that condemns the abusive behavior as a matter of principle, on behalf of all women; and the absolute insistence that the behavior will stop. The women leave him no face-saving excuses, no possible exceptions, and no other options—the behavior is over.

Retaliation is virtually impossible—too many women are involved. Continued harassment is virtually impossible—too many people know about his behavior and are now watching him. And personally, emotionally, the power of a group confrontation must be felt to be believed. As with individual confrontations, the more sexist the harasser, the more devastating the impact. A group confrontation is so far outside the realm of expected female behavior for a harasser that it can be a life-changing event, a psychological shock right down to the core of his most basic beliefs about how the world works.

As noted in Chapter 4, a group confrontation requires detailed planning, a carefully designed scenario for the action, and very disciplined behavior on the part of the women. It is not hard to command control of the event at the outset, since the harasser will be initially stunned, but to maintain control it is important to plan the entire sequence of the confrontation, including closing lines and departure. A rehearsal is a good idea, to make sure that all of the women involved know exactly what they will do at each point in the action. Each woman should be prepared to carry out her part with controlled determination, without breaking the discipline in either direction (neither giving in to relieved laughter at the harasser's fear and powerlessness nor giving in to rage and revenge and committing violence against him).

Group confrontations work even with groups of harassers who are more than a little scary themselves, as Crindi Loschinkohl's success story demonstrates:

THE HOUSE BY THE HIGHWAY

I was working on a mailing one day at the Women Against Rape office in Columbus, Ohio, when a woman called in, very upset. She had been driving on the outerbelt highway. When she got off at the Hudson Street exit, there was a house with a group of men sitting on the porch. One of them was holding up a big sign that said, "Show us your tits." She was outraged. He was holding the sign to point toward the highway ramp, so that everyone getting off the exit saw it. She wanted to do something about it and she wanted some help.

We gathered up the women who were working in the office, called a few others, and when the woman who'd called came in, we planned out a confrontation. There were twelve of us. One woman was to be the major spokeswoman; the caller was to back her up; one woman got an old, broken camera out of a closet; one found a pad of paper and pen to write down everything everyone said during the confronta-

tion; and one took paper and pen to write down the names on the mailbox. The rest of us were to be (mostly) silent support.

We drove over in three cars, the woman caller leading the way. We parked, got out, and walked up to the house together. Sure enough, there were six or seven men, dressed in leather and chains, looking mean and laughing as people driving by reacted to their sign. When we walked up the steps, they looked a bit taken aback. (To tell the truth, they looked a little afraid. It occurred to me that they probably thought we were going to beat them up.)

The woman with the camera pretended to take their pictures; she kept snapping away the whole time we were there. One woman went straight to the mailbox and wrote down all the names. The rest of us walked right up to the men.

The spokeswoman took the sign away from the man who was holding it (by then he was holding it face down—they knew why we were there). She ripped it up. She told them something like: "We are outraged at your behavior. Women have to take enough crap without you going out of your way to harass us. We will not put up with this. If we ever hear of any harassment in this neighborhood again, we'll be back." The woman who had called us added: "I felt slapped in the face by your sign when I drove by. I will not tolerate this. You had better not do anything like this again." A couple of the men tried to make feeble excuses, but the spokeswoman interrupted them, to reiterate that we would not tolerate this and they had better watch themselves in the future, because we would be watching them.

Then we left. The men just sat there, stunned.

We went back to the Women Against Rape office and debriefed. We felt great! We put the notes and their names in the files and planned what we would do in case we needed to confront them again. All of us went out of our way to drive by that house for the next few months, and never saw or heard a peep of sexism from those men again.

This was our first group confrontation, but not our last. And every one was just as successful as this one.

In only a matter of hours, these women planned and carried out a formidable confrontation. They may have felt fearful as they walked up to the house, but they maintained their discipline, stuck to the structure of their confrontation, and were immediately effective in controlling the situation. Although the harassers were a group of tough guys in chains and leather and were on their own home turf when confronted, the women had no trouble reversing the power dynamics—their action left the men in shock. The confronters' clarity and precise, principled statements were essential to the success of the action. And, as Crindi notes, the effect was long-lasting. One experience of group confrontation was enough to persuade even these guys that they did not want to risk it again.

Even without a full-scale confrontation, women's collective action is often an effective tool against sexual abuse. Here's another success story from Kathleen Hopwood, about a two-woman tactic that she and a friend developed when there seemed to be no way to organize a group confrontation:

THE PHONE CALL STRATEGY

I was working as the only woman painter on a plant maintenance crew. One of the painters was harassing the secretaries whenever we painted offices. He only picked on black women.

I began to notice a certain pattern: The women would be friendly at first, as we set up to paint their office, and then they would start avoiding us like we had the plague. It only happened when this one particular guy was on the crew.

One day I watched him carefully as he approached a woman who had offered us coffee. He was asking her something in a whisper, so I moved closer to hear.

He was offering her cash for "some good black pussy."

The woman was shocked and immediately left the room. I followed her to talk with her, but she didn't want to talk about it. I knew from my own interactions with this man that he was one of the most vicious sexists on the crew. I had narrowly missed being "accidentally" hit by him many times when we were moving painting equipment.

There was no way of reporting this incident to anyone in the administration. There was no antiharassment policy, and I was already considered a troublemaker.

I found out that everyone on the paint crew, including the supervisor, already knew what this man was doing. He would boast about it in the shop. The rest of the guys seemed to think it was funny and were betting on who he could get to take up his offer.

I talked the problem over with a female friend, and she suggested that she could report it anonymously, over the phone, to the physical plant director. She decided to make the call when I was in full view of my own paint crew members so they would not assume that it was me calling. Over a period of a few weeks, she made several anonymous calls to both the paint shop supervisor and the physical plant director.

It took a while, but finally the harasser was called into the office and given a chance to explain his actions. I don't know all the details of exactly what happened in there, but I do know how it ended: He yelled at the physical plant director, threatened to hit him, and quit.

Although it would have felt better to have had a more direct solution, the phone call strategy did work. Those calls forced the upper management to take notice and deal with this harasser.

Working creatively with other women is one of the most basic steps in stopping sexual harassment. In situations in which a group confrontation does not seem possible because none of the victims wants to confront, other women can still take action—either with an indirect strategy like the phone call technique, or with a group confrontation of their own, speaking up as women who have witnessed the behavior and object to it for their own reasons. In instances of combined racial and sexual harassment like this one, the African-American women who are targeted may feel not only threatened but isolated. It is not their responsibility alone to stop such harassers—the white women who witness the behavior can and should intervene to hold the harasser accountable, just as Kathleen and her friend did. The two-person phone call strategy was a way to take responsible action and report the harassment without jeopardizing Kathleen herself, since she had to deal with these men every day. It didn't work quite as fast as a confrontation, but it succeeded in the end.

Here's another story from women who took group action short of confrontation, but managed, through their joint strategy, to prevent a harasser from abusing them:

THE ACCOUNTANT

My name is Sonia. I'm a twenty-three-year-old Latina; I've got two years of community college and I'm taking evening classes to get a degree in accounting. I work in a secretarial pool with five other women in a large accounting office. We all sit in a big, open, central room, and the accountants' private offices are around ours; their doors open into our room. All the accountants here are men, and some of them are really nice guys. But about two years ago, this new manager, "Mr. Brown," was promoted into our division. He started harassing all of us.

Of course, at first we didn't know that he was doing it to all of us, but then we started talking to each other. I told Susan how he'd propositioned me twice in the past month and how he kept making these remarks about how I was too pretty to want to be an accountant. She said that she'd had about enough of his comments, too, and said every time he called her into his office, he managed to put his hands on her one way or another. So then we asked Alice if he'd ever been out of line with her, and she said, yeah, he made comments about her breast size when she brought him a stack of reports the week before, and that wasn't the first time, either. By lunchtime that day the word was out—he'd been hitting on all six of us. He never did it in front of anyone—but every time he had one of us alone in his office, he'd pull some kind of stunt.

We were pretty sure that we wouldn't get anywhere by filing a complaint. We were really afraid to try that. He was a rising star with some big clients, and we figured that a complaint wouldn't accomplish much of anything except to get us fired or reassigned as troublemakers. I know that most of the time in this kind of situation, the women just end up getting disgusted and quitting. None of us wanted to quit, although he was getting to be really obnoxious.

So we got together to develop a plan. We worked out a mutual defense strategy—we watched his door, and every time he got one of us in there alone, one of the others would find some excuse to go in and break it up. If he had Barb in there, Alice or Mary would jump right up, open his door, and say, "Oh, Mr. Brown, here's that memo you wanted"—and leave the door open. If he got me or Alice in there, Susan or Barb would come to the rescue with a note about a telephone message or some other piece of business. We just set about the job of keeping that door open and making it impossible for him to get any of us alone.

And it worked. He got really frustrated, and after six months, he quit.

This was a purely defensive plan. Unlike a confrontation, it did not compel Mr. Brown to face up to his harassment, and it did not create the kind of social penalties or psychological incentives that would force him to change his behavior in the future. Sonia and her colleagues simply stymied him. They analyzed Brown's specific pattern of harassment and came up with a way to prevent him from implementing it. To make the plan succeed, they had to work together—first, making his behavior visible among themselves by telling each other what he was doing to them in private, and then, once they'd come up with their "mutual defense strategy," making a group commitment to look out for each other, watch that door, and intervene instantly. They very neatly eliminated the opportunity for him to abuse his power over them.

Once he left for another job, the next step would be to call the women in his new office and warn them as well.

A mutual defense strategy is an excellent start, but a straightforward confrontation is a much stronger form of group action, on the job or on the street, as one persistent harasser on a New Jersey sidewalk found out. Here's Linda's story:

THE SOCCER TEAM

I love soccer, and between the games and the practices, I play three or four times a week. The field where we usually play is down the street from some old yellow brick apartment buildings. The parking spots closer to the field are always taken by the time I get there, so I always end up parking up by the buildings and then walking down the block in my shorts and T-shirt. This older man, in his late thirties, I'd guess, was always hanging out in front of one of the buildings when I'd come by, and he always felt compelled to make some stupid comment about me. It was, "Hey, baby, nice buns," one day, and "Looking fine, baby," the next.

I just kept trying to ignore him, but it seemed like I had to walk past him, coming and going, every single time. Then I realized that he had figured out when we would be out there playing and was waiting for me every time. That started to feel dangerous, not just annoying. Made me start to take it personally, especially when he worked his way up to really charming sentiments like, "Mmm, mmm, sure would like to have those legs wrapped around me." This guy was getting creepier every day. It kind of worried me, and it was so unpleasant that it was ruining my game.

The day he said, "Baby, I sure would like to lick that sweat off your body for you," I decided I'd had enough. I talked to my teammates about it. A couple of them had taken self-defense classes, and they suggested a group confrontation. They explained what that involved and we all loved the idea. We laid our plans for the next practice, the following Monday evening.

That Monday, I parked in my usual spot at the usual time and started down the street. My teammates were tucked away in alleys and doorways all around, out of sight. As I got to this guy's building, he was out there as usual, and he said, "Oh, baby, that is a fine little shirt. I love the way your breasts bounce when you walk by."

For the first time, I turned and faced him. My teammates materialized out of nowhere. In an instant, there were fifteen women beside me. I looked him in the eye and took a step toward him. He backed up against the building, looking absolutely terrified.

We all just stared at him for a second, to let him get good and nervous. Nobody smiled, nobody made a sound. We just kind of loomed around him in a semicircle, glaring at him, with our arms crossed. Then I said (I'd practiced this, so I had it down, in a real cold, stern voice): "You have been making offensive comments about my body all summer long. That is harassment. I hate it. It is disgusting, insulting, sexist behavior. You are never going to say anything but 'good evening' to me ever again."

Then my first buddy chimed in: "You are harassing women. No woman likes it, not one of us. As of right here and right now, you will stop harassing women."

Then my next teammate: "All women have a right to walk down this street, or any street, without your comments. You are violating women's rights. We are here to make sure that you never harass a woman again."

He turned kind of green when she said that. He hadn't said a word since his initial comment about my shirt and breasts. I'm sure he thought we were going to kill him.

My next buddy said: "Nod your head if you understand this." He nodded. Then she said, "Are you going to say 'good evening' when we walk by?" He nodded yes. "Are you going to say or do anything else?" He shook his head no.

My next teammate (a particularly tall, strong woman) then said to him: "We are all going to be watching you from now on. You are never going to harass another woman!" She roared at him, "Is that clear?"

He nodded again and inched further back against the wall. Then I spoke: "You've been warned. Don't make us come back and deal with you again." He just stared at us all. I thought he was going to faint dead away.

Then we turned and walked briskly down to the field and had a great soccer practice. We all felt wonderful. We whooped and hollered and talked about the look on his face and how the whole thing had gone just exactly the way we planned it. I felt like I was finally free of this jerk. Liberated from a burden and free as a bird.

Just to be on the safe side, two of my buddies walked me back to my car after practice, but he was nowhere in sight. None of us saw him again until the end of the summer. When I did finally run into him again, he swallowed hard and said, "Good evening." I said, "Good evening to you," and he dashed into his apartment building.

This harasser's belief in his "right" to harass was utterly demolished. Linda and her soccer buddies reclaimed the street and changed his behavior in three minutes flat. Their teamwork in the confrontation was superb. If they play soccer half as well as they confront, they've probably won the city championship by now.

The final success story in this chapter is from Annie McCombs, one of the women who helped to invent group confrontations.[1] Annie played a pivotal role in organizing one of the grandmothers of all group confrontations. It took place in San Francisco in the late 1970s, when fifty women confronted a man who had made two rape attempts on the same young woman. Here is Annie's story:

A SUMMER EVENING IN THE ROSE GARDEN

I stayed aboard that morning while the rest of the crew went ashore to breakfast at Pier One. I had just finished polishing the brass bell up forward and had gone down below to stow the rags and cleaner when I saw Patrícia walking up the gangway. Patrícia's visit during my shift on the San Francisco waterfront was not ordinary. She worked shore-side on the dock, supplying us with necessaries, managing assembled passengers, following capricious orders from too many agents of management.

Patrícia was very young, and had just come to work for the company. She was Native American, a lesbian, and disabled by epilepsy and dyslexia. Any of these things could have made her the target of any one of the waterfront bigots, but what was done to her was specific to her being female and accessible: She could be raped. As I was finishing my work on board after the ferry docked that Tuesday morning, Patrícia came to tell me that Willie, a young white man, had terrorized her for two nights in a row.

Those of us who had broken into the male-dominated world of inland waterways, tugs, and ferries had learned about sexual harassment firsthand. We knew the tactics of terror in all their manifestations: verbal threats of violence, actual physical assaults, pervasive pornography, sexual innuendo, and outright demands. It was incessant. We were also told that we would not be taught the seamanship skills that were ordinarily passed on to new hands by so-called old salts. Women had begun to work on the waterfront only after organizing, filing a sex-discrimination lawsuit, obtaining a federal consent decree, and repeatedly proving that we were willing and able to do the job. Not every man actively participated in the hostility, but few openly opposed it. The few who did cross the line drawn by hatred made it possible for us to succeed in learning what we needed to know.

When Patrícia walked up the gangway that morning, I had been working on the waterfront for five years. Those years had honed my skills in dealing with abuse, and everyone knew that I viewed sexual harassment as intolerable. Patrícia sought me out because of my reputation. I listened to her story. . . .

At night, the waterfront is not romantic; it is desolate. Patrícia had been working with Willie on the night shift, after everyone else went home—everyone except the night watchman who doggedly made his rounds, punching in at intervals to document his passage. Patrícia and Willie were supposed to split the work of cleaning the restrooms. Patrícia had gone into the women's head to do her half of the work; she needed to use it as well. She didn't hear Willie come in, and was startled when she looked up to see him peering into the stall through the wide crack in the door jamb. He laughed when she yelled at him. With the choice of remaining trapped in the stall or coming out, she zipped up her coveralls and stepped out. He backed her up against the wall and suggested what they ought to be doing together. When the night watchman called out to Willie from beyond the room (Willie had locked the outer door), the struggle was over. Patrícia got away. But it happened again the next night, this time in the tiny supplies room. Patrícia fought hard and broke free on her own. When he threatened to keep at her until he got what he wanted, she decided to come to me.

I promised Patrícia that I would record her story after work, since her dyslexia made it extremely difficult for her to write. When I met with her later that day, she reconstructed the events in detail. I asked questions about what had happened, how she felt, what she did, what outcome she'd be happy with, what she wanted to happen next. I even cautioned her not to let my questions lead her in any direction that was not absolutely right and true.

I also interviewed Robin, Patrícia's roommate and partner, for corroborating details. Next, I approached Patrícia's shop steward, Abby. We combed the deposition for inconsistencies, studied the problem, considered the possibility of a false accusation, and discussed credibility issues. I was determined to be fair to Willie. In hindsight, the way I questioned Patrícia seems ludicrous—worrying about extreme fairness for perpetrators, in a world where the body count of women hurt by men grows higher every year.

The following day, Abby and I brainstormed. The company and union were both hostile to women; it wouldn't be easy to file and win a union grievance. We also discussed approaching the superintendent, with us accompanying Patricia as advocates. If the super didn't respond satisfactorily, we could take the case to the company's Equal Employment Opportunity (EEO) office. Then we called Patricia and asked her what she thought of these options. She decided to talk with the super, if I would go with her.

When Patricia and I walked into the super's office, Mr. L. was cold, wary, and sarcastic. But he made a mistake by suggesting that, if it had been attempted rape, she would have called the police. At first, she and I were stunned: it had never occurred to us to call the cops, whom we mistrusted. But, in that stunned silence, something clicked for me: I told Mr. L. that filing a police report was a fine idea; maybe he would be good enough to call them right away so that they could come over and take Patricia's statement. He freaked at the thought of having to explain an attempted rape to the police and then reporting to his boss that it had been his idea to call them. We finally left his office with a commitment that Willie would no longer be assigned to work with Patricia. So far, we had succeeded in putting some distance between Patricia and her assailant. Patricia felt better, but not whole.

After Patricia and I left Mr. L.'s office, we picked up Abby and visited Mary B., the company's EEO officer. We wanted formal recognition that Willie had done something seriously wrong. Mary immediately threw out Abby, but inexplicably allowed me to stay. After listening to Patricia for a few minutes, Mary said that she intended to bring in Willie so that he could face his accuser; she wanted to evaluate them together in her presence—without me or Abby. The threat triggered a response: Patricia had an epileptic seizure. As I knelt beside her, Mary coolly stated that, when Patricia recovered, I could relay her responses. She then walked off. I was too shocked to reply or be angry. That came afterward.

Patricia made it plain that she would not submit to being in the same small room with Willie. She also refused to talk further with Mary B. Our options were narrowing fast: The police were out, the union was no help, the super had done what little he was going to do, and the EEO officer was a washout. The three of us—Patricia, Abby, and I—were left to our own devices. We needed a new idea. Out of necessity, we invented one: a direct confrontation with the perpetrator, on our terms.

For the next week, Patricia, her partner, Robin, Abby, and I charted the course for Willie's introduction to feminism. The four of us researched what feminists had written about sexual harassment. We talked to experts as well as other victims. Robin toured Willie's haunts, photographing him at work, his car, and his house. We discussed what our objectives should be and where the confrontation should take place. I called various women with whom I'd previously done politically radical and feminist work; their response was overwhelmingly supportive. A quick explanation was enough to get their interest.

Thirty women showed up at our initial meeting, where they met Patricia, Robin, and Abby for the first time. Many of these women had already worked together on events protesting injustices, so it was a meeting of easy respect and strong focus. We discussed broad issues as well as tactical details. After an extended discussion, a veteran activist named Grace spoke up. She said that our original plan of confronting Willie in the parking lot at work could not be pulled off without his becoming suspicious or without intruders inadvertently stumbling on the scene. Grace was persuasive; it was the wrong approach. We needed to confront Willie somewhere of our own choosing at a time that suited us. The confrontation needed to be on our own ground.

We agreed with Grace's analysis, but no alternative plan leaped to mind. Grace then suggested that someone could simply pick him up for a date. The room gasped, but with her usual understatement and droll humor Grace replied, "What! We've all been trained to do it all of our lives." (Grace later remarked that she was probably "doomed" to be the bait: She had suggested the idea, was closest to Willie's age, was small enough not to intimidate him, and could pass as the traditional girl next door.) A concrete, workable plan began to evolve as the group regained its composure. We chose the Rose Garden in Golden Gate Park as the site of the confrontation, and dusk as the time. The Rose Garden is a rectangular plot between the intersection of Fulton Street and Park Presidio, at one end, and Kennedy Drive, at the other. What roses mean in the everyday lives of women, the fundamental joy they bring to women who love growing things, made it a place that we wanted to reclaim. I visited the Rose Garden to reconnoiter and drafted a map of the area to help us with our strategy.

At our second meeting, someone raised the possibility of Willie's having a weapon. I knew that some deckhands routinely carried handguns in their seabags, so it was not a foolish fear. We anticipated this danger by recruiting women martial artists familiar with disarming techniques; half a dozen experts volunteered. Over the next two weeks, our group rehearsed the confrontation. We drilled; we practiced; we gained new confidence each time. We were ready. It was none too soon for me, because I had the dubious distinction of playing the role of Willie in our practice sessions. I was genuinely sick of being yelled at, jerked around, disarmed, and thrown to the ground with karate yells blasting in my ears. I had bruises, but beyond the discomfort, the focused anger of these women scared me, even though I knew that it was just a rehearsal that I had helped plan.

The confrontation was to take place in four coordinated phases. Phase one involved Grace riding a ferry while Willie was working on it. The tactical problems were twofold: first, how to know when he would be aboard, since he worked only part-time; second, how Grace would recognize him. We solved the first problem by having Abby serve as lookout; when she spotted him on one of the ferryboats, she'd call me and I'd call Grace, who would rush down to catch the ferry. The identification problem was solved by one of Robin's photographs of Willie; Grace taped it inside a paperback novel that she would carry with her. Grace was to call me if anything went wrong or when she had successfully completed her mission of setting up the date.

Abby's call soon came: Willie was on board. When Grace boarded the ferry, she quickly located him, but delayed approaching him until the return trip in order to limit their conversation as much as possible. On the return trip, Grace found Willie sitting just outside the fo'c's'le. She boldly sat next to him and started a conversation about his job. She claimed that her brother had worked out of the union hiring hall several months earlier, had said that it was a good job, and that a few women did it, too. She wanted to check it out, since she had just moved to the area and needed work. Willie agreed that it was a good job, but said that she wouldn't like it. Why not? He hemmed and hawed and finally remarked that only "dykes" worked on the job. How did he know this "terrible" thing? He gave a manly shrug of worldliness and merely replied, "You know!" As the ferry came into view of the San Francisco terminal, Grace decided that if he didn't soon ask her out, she'd have to ask him. Willie, however, came through like a champ: He asked for her phone number. She replied that she was staying at the YWCA and didn't have her own phone yet, but perhaps he'd give her his phone number. He did. Grace promised to call him in a couple of days.

The group had already decided that we would need three or four days of lead-time to contact everyone involved and arrange the final details. Grace called Willie two days later, and told him she'd taken an apartment near the beach, had gotten a temporary job at the De Young Museum, and there was a party Friday night. Would he like to go with her? Willie jumped at the offer. She arranged to meet him in the museum's parking lot at nine Friday evening. She added that she'd like him to see her new apartment after the party. He was thrilled.

That Friday evening, Grace and another member of our group, Lillian, posed as coworkers chatting in the museum parking lot, waiting for Willie to show up. He eventually pulled his car into the space next to them. Grace introduced Willie and Lillian; she then told Willie that she needed something from her car, which was on the opposite side of the Rose Garden, just a short distance away. Would he walk with her? Sure. They bid good-bye to Lillian. As Grace and Willie walked around his car, he stopped to open the trunk. He reached in, took out a shirt, sniffed the armpits, decided that it was clean enough, and put it on. Grace recalls thinking that he was in serious need of some tips on dating.

Phase two of our plan involved monitoring Grace and Willie as they walked. Each step of their way was watched by women in pairs—sitting on a bench enjoying the summer evening, strolling along smelling the roses, hiding behind giant eucalyptus trees. Another woman jogged by and reported back to the rest of us. Willie was not allowed to walk with Grace unwatched; we did not intend to have another victim.

Meanwhile fifty women—more than we had dared hope—were assembled at Haight and Stanyon streets. We had kept the actual site of the confrontation guarded on a need-to-know basis until now. To my amazement, however, a vanload of country women from Mendocino suddenly pulled up; they had heard about our plans through the grapevine. We then drove to the intersection of Fulton Street and Park Presidio. This was the spot—at the end of the path leading through the Rose Garden—where Willie thought Grace's car was. Willie would never get this far.

The gathering spontaneously assumed a mood that felt very volatile. We had all agreed on a nonviolent confrontation and were prepared to force Willie to remain nonviolent, too. (Less of a contradiction than it sounds.) Troubled by the jagged edge of anger among the women in a situation in which we clearly held the upper hand, I addressed the group in the strongest possible way about our intention: No one was to touch Willie unless he made a sudden or aggressive move. I reinforced that commitment, but I know to this day that one wrong word could have changed the dynamics completely. Willie was blessed that summer evening with a disciplined and principled group of women who had purposefully organized to instruct him but not to hurt him.

Abby and I then headed for our stations to watch for cops

and stray strollers; we were the lookouts, one at each end of the Rose Garden. The rest of our large group split up into two smaller ones, positioning themselves on either side of the path and vanishing behind tall hedges. Everyone waited in silence for the signal.

Phase three began when Frankie whistled loudly from behind a cypress tree as Grace and Willie passed her on their way into the Rose Garden. Willie was startled by the sound and turned to see where it had come from. Finding nothing, he turned back to discover that he was surrounded by fifty strangers. Grace was whisked away from the scene at once.

Willie was ordered to remain still and silent. He was told to nod his head if he understood. He did. In case Willie was armed, one martial artist was assigned to check each of his limbs: Frankie his right arm and Mary his left, Lori his right leg and Phyllis his left. He was to be disarmed and immobilized if he made a wrong move. Another martial artist was to give him a head-to-toe inspection and alert the others if she discovered anything. A fifth woman was charged with helping him from behind if he forgot to nod his understanding of our instructions. He didn't forget.

The confrontation was designed to allow Patrícia to say whatever she wanted to say to Willie. Her face was the only one he recognized as she emerged from the wall of women enclosing him. She was backed up by her partner, Robin, who was prepared to speak if Patrícia chose not to. In fact, Robin did speak for Patrícia, and then spoke for herself in no uncertain terms. When Robin finished, others stepped up to Willie to express themselves on the subject of violence against women and what he had done. Several women held up Robin's zoom-lens photos, now blown up into posters and illuminated by flashlights, so that Willie could see himself, his car, his license plates, his house. The purpose of these photos was to inform him that we not only knew where to find him, but had already been closely watching him and his activities. We meant these photographs both as a graphic reminder of male vulnerability and as a warning.

After each woman who wanted to address Willie had done

so, he was told to never again harass Patrícia or any other woman. His knees were shaking visibly. He was also told not to reveal this confrontation to anyone. Finally, he was told to turn around and walk normally back to his car without looking back, to get in it, and to drive away immediately. He did as he was told.

At dusk, on a gorgeous summer evening, a solitary man, surrounded by fifty angry strangers and his victim, learned that what he had done was not acceptable behavior to be tolerated by women. It took just a few minutes to accomplish, once he was face to face with the group. It was short, sweet, to the point, and powerful.

From my lookout post, I watched Willie retreat from the Rose Garden. I did not hear the jubilant yell bursting from the participants as he left, but the police may have. As Willie disappeared into the museum's parking lot, an SFPD patrol car pulled up alongside me. I expected the worst. I carefully did not react, and after several long minutes, they drove off without a word. Perhaps it was just an unnerving coincidence. Two things might have caused them to cruise the area: the improbable massing of fifty women who were not exactly "touring" the garden, or the hue and cry of celebration. If we ever do this again, we might want to hold off on the hollering and have some obvious and plausible pretext for our presence.

The fourth and final phase of the confrontation was simple but crucial. Everyone promptly went to the waiting cars and left the vicinity. We all drove to a prearranged place to count noses, see how Patrícia felt, discuss security measures for her and Robin, compare our experiences, be excited, congratulate each other, and cheerfully decompress. Patrícia was disappointed that she hadn't said anything to Willie herself, but told us that she felt great about everything else. Our confrontation had come down exactly as planned.

As for Willie, he avoided the waterfront for a while. Grace had previously voiced a concern that a confrontation might intensify his misogyny; we had decided to take that chance, but it didn't happen as far as we could tell. Grace even came to feel a little sorry for Willie, with his ordinariness and pathetic ineptitude, but Patrícia knew him for the sexual bully he was.

When he did finally take another part-time job with the company, he kept his eyes on the ground whenever Abby and I were around, although he hadn't seen either of us at the confrontation. Within months, he vanished altogether.

Two weeks after the confrontation, we threw a party to celebrate our success. We handed out "Order of the Rose" awards. Grace presented one to me: "For Conspicuous Leadership," it read. Her own award, with its fading ribbon, still hangs on her bulletin board.

One of the women audiotaped the confrontation, and the public radio station, KPFA, later played it for the edification of the greater Bay Area. It created an urban legend that eventually reached all the way across the country to the Rape Crisis Center in Washington, D.C., and became part of the herstory of women confronting harassers and rapists. Then and now, all of us feel very good about what we did. We have one recommendation for all women who are facing the problem of male violence: do something about it and do it on your own terms.

Where Do We Go from Here? Community Strategies for Ending Sexual Harassment

All of these success stories—and the many thousands more that take place every day—are part of a larger process of social change. On the job, on the street, in universities and high schools, in public parks and playgrounds, in every imaginable setting, harassers are learning that they can no longer abuse women with impunity.

Instead of reacting with fear and silence, women are making harassment visible, naming the behavior and holding the harassers publicly accountable for their destructive actions. Using everything from direct confrontations to administrative procedures and lawsuits, women are changing the culture—eliminating the social protection harassers have enjoyed for so long and raising the costs both for the harassers and for the institutions that fail to take responsible action. In some cases, women are now being joined by men who speak up against harassment—allies in the effort to rid our schools, workplaces, and public streets of this unjust and inexcusable abuse of power.

Each sexual harassment lawsuit filed and each decision to confront a harasser is part of this larger effort. Individual action is essential: Every woman who holds a harasser accountable with a confrontation or a lawsuit contributes to the safety and well-being of all women. Every man who speaks up makes it harder for other men to harass. Group action is equally important: We all need to be allies for each other when harassers strike. In some instances—dealing with predatory harassers in positions of authority, for example—a group effort may be the only way to stop the harasser's pattern of sexual abuse.

But women need to think about preventive strategies as well. How do we create a society in which harassment does not occur? We can confront individual harassers until they find harassing women so risky and unrewarding that they simply give it up. We can begin to multiply our successes, bringing to bear the cumulative impact of thousands of lawsuits and individual and group confrontations. And we can take the next step: organizing a community effort to stop sexual harassment as a social practice.

That's what women in Washington, D.C., did in 1985, when they launched the "Hassle-Free Zone" campaign. They were disgusted with the barrage of verbal and physical abuse on the streets of Washington, and they decided to do something about it. Nkenge Toure was one of the women who organized the citywide campaign. Here's how she describes it:

THE HASSLE-FREE ZONE CAMPAIGN

The Hassle-Free Zone was an action-oriented concept, a way to link the energies of a broad cross-section of the community to educate the public about street harassment, empower women to stop harassers, serve as a catalyst for men to re-examine their behavior and attitudes about harassment, and create a climate for change in which sexual harassment is no longer a social norm. We wanted to declare all of Washington, D.C., a harassment-free area and put our harassers on notice that their days were numbered.

Fed up with street harassment, an interracial group of women from half a dozen community organizations—the Rape Crisis Center, local NOW chapters, and the D.C. Women's Law Center, among others—came together to form the Hassle-Free Zone Coalition. We were quickly joined by women's groups from the area universities and other local activist organizations, including D.C. Men against Sexual Violence.

Linda Leaks and the African-American Women's Committee for Community Education had already produced posters and flyers advocating an end to street harassment. The Rape Crisis Center's self-defense instructors were teaching confrontation classes for women, and local law students were interested in doing some research on statutes that might be used to prosecute street harassers. We wanted to pull all the pieces together and create a community education campaign that would really have an impact.

In September 1985, we made street harassment the focus of the Take Back the Night March and the annual Anti-Rape Week program. We persuaded the mayor to issue a proclamation calling for all citizens to work to make D.C. a Hassle-Free Zone. The City Council passed a resolution supporting the campaign. We got the coalition rolling and began publicizing the issue at every opportunity.

By the spring of 1986 we were ready to rent a generator and a microphone and begin organizing speakouts on harassment in public parks and at subway stops—we knew where some of the worst harassment was happening, and that's exactly where we went. We scheduled the sessions at lunchtime and right after work, to reach the maximum number of people on the street. In addition to speakers and pointed street-theater skits about harassment, we held open-mike sessions to give women a chance to sound off about their harassment experiences. We got quite a response. Speakouts are quick and direct (sixty to ninety minutes in duration), the expense was minimal, and the impact was substantial. Women lined up at our microphones to talk about harassment and reported that the level of harassment in the vicinity deceased, at least temporarily, after each speakout.

At the same time, we offered free harassment-confrontation classes for women in neighborhoods throughout the city. We produced brochures about street harassment and confrontation techniques and sent instructors and speakers to every section of the city.

When our legal research team reported that harassment was actually on the D.C. law books as a misdemeanor but the statute was never enforced, several women also began to try to develop a test case. They photographed and tape-recorded harassers and reported them to the police. We never got a case to court, but we certainly did educate the local police about the issue—and we sure scared some harassers.

We enjoyed several waves of press coverage, all of it very positive. The campaign generated interviews on a lot of local radio and television talk shows, as well as articles in every newspaper in the city, from The Capitol Spotlight to The Washington Post. Several national women's newsjournals also carried stories. Off Our Backs reported on the Hassle-Free Zone, and so did The New York Times.

We held our final public speakout in October 1986, wrapping up the public campaign eighteen months after we started. Did we succeed in ending street harassment once and for all in Washington, D.C.? No. That may take a few more years. But the Hassle-Free Zone campaign put the issue of street harassment front and center on the public agenda for our elected officials, the media, and the entire community. We empowered a lot of women, gave a lot of harassers a good reason to think twice, encouraged men to speak up as allies for women, reclaimed some public parks and subway stops, and had a pretty good time doing it.

Perhaps most important, women experienced some real victories over harassers as a result of the campaign. The spirit of empowerment is alive, the classes and seminars continue, and every year more and more women have inspiring success stories to tell about ways they've confronted and stopped harassers on the streets of Washington, D.C.

As Nkenge suggests, none of this was particularly difficult or expensive to do. The Hassle-Free Zone campaign took a fair amount of energy, time, and planning, but it's the kind of community effort that could be done almost anywhere. How about your community?

Unions, enlightened management, or a committee of women employees can organize the same kinds of speakouts, classes, and publicity about harassment in any large government agency or corporate workplace. Universities can do the same on campus. Churches can provide a focal point for a hassle-free zone strategy in their communities. Neighborhood organizations can start a very effective hassle-free campaign on a smaller, local scale. Talk to your friends, neighbors, and coworkers, and start by reclaiming your local park as a harassment-free zone. What's holding you back?

We have all had more than enough of sexual victimization, in all its forms. We know what harassment is—and we know what a destructive impact this abusive behavior has on women's lives and freedom. Eliminating sexual harassment from our daily environment at work, at school, and on the street is no small accomplishment, but it can be done. It is time to break through the fear and powerlessness that sexual harassment produces, and take a good clear look at what women (and men who care about women's lives) can actually do to stop the harassers. We need to start creating communities where women feel comfortable and harassers feel nervous.

From administrative remedies to formal lawsuits to direct confrontation tactics to community-organizing strategies, we have more tools today than ever before. Because women are using these tools to take action, harassers are at far greater risk for their behavior now than at any time in history. At this point, women know more about harassers' motives and methods than the harassers themselves do.

And women have succeeded against all kinds of harassers, in all kinds of situations. Some of their success stories are funny, some are moving, and some are downright amazing. In many cases, it was a tough battle, but every one of these success stories is an example of what women can really achieve, individually or collectively, when they engage in well-planned direct action or use the other resources at their disposal. From an eight-year-old in the schoolyard to an organized group confrontation by fifty women in response to an attempted rape, the women in this book refused to be helpless victims.

It's time to give some credit to all the women who win—

the thousands of ordinary women who manage to fight back with great intelligence and resourcefulness and leave their harassers dazed with the shock of it. Women's successes are no small part of our history; we cannot afford to let them remain invisible. Women's successes are just as critical to our future; we need to share our victories, if we are to succeed in ending sexual harassment.

You are part of that future. Practice the confrontation scenarios, the body language, and the verbal techniques. Script out your own confrontations. Envision yourself as a hero in your own life, dealing calmly and decisively with the harassers you encounter. Speak up when women around you are harassed, and teach your children how to confront harassment. Understand that the way each woman handles this kind of sexual power abuse can make a revolutionary difference in the daily environment that all women face.

The women who have shared their success stories here are creative, valiant, and resourceful. But, admirable as they are, these women are no braver or smarter than you—they managed to stop harassers because they knew how to do it. They have broken the silence about one crucial aspect of women's lives: our hidden history of everyday resistance. Step by step, they have created a new direct-action strategy that shifts the balance of power, frees women from the "victim" role, and transforms the social dynamics of sexual harassment. Individually and collectively, on the job and on the street, they have refused to tolerate injustice—and they've left a trail of truly astonished ex-harassers in their wake. But their achievements are only the beginning. The next success story is yours.

THE CONFRONTATION SURVEY

Turn and face the harasser. Look him in the eye. In a calm, businesslike voice, **YOU SAY:** "That's very interesting. You have just harassed a woman. Women are conducting a research project on sexual harassment, and I want to include you in this survey. I want to take just a minute to ask you a few questions. This is important research."

1. **VERBAL HARASSMENT. YOU SAY:** "I want to get your exact words down. You just said [repeat whatever he said], is that right?" Write down what he said:

   NONVERBAL OR PHYSICAL HARASSMENT. YOU SAY: "I want to get this exactly right. How would you describe what you just did?" (Examples: kissing or sucking noises; hand on some part of woman's body; exposing himself.) Write what he says he did:

   Now write down what he actually did (be specific—note where he touched you, etc.):

THEN ASK THE HARASSER:

2. (OPTIONAL) What's your name?

3. In general, can you say why you do this?

4. What other kinds of things like this have you sometimes said or done to women or girls?

5. How would you describe the way women or girls usually react, when you do this?

6. How do you feel when you say or do this kind of thing to women or girls?

7. How do you think women and girls feel about it when you do this?

8. Do you usually do this kind of thing when you are by yourself, or when you are with a group of male friends or coworkers, or both? (Check the answer that applies.)

Alone _____   With group _____   Both _____

9. Do you do this to all kinds of women, or do you pick out certain kinds?

All kinds _____   Only certain types _____

10. Which of the following kinds of women do you harass? (Check all answers that apply.)

Black _____   White _____   Hispanic _____   Asian _____   Arab _____   Jewish _____
Women under 15? _____   Women you know? _____   Women alone? _____
Women 16–40? _____   Strangers? _____   In groups? _____
Women over 40? _____   Both? _____   Women who look rich? _____
Women who look poor? _____

Any other particular kinds of women?

11. Are there any types of women that you never harass? Who?

12. Do you remember how old you were the first time you said or did something like this to a woman or girl?

Age: _____   How old are you now? Age: _____

13. About how many times today have you done this to a woman or girl? _____

14. About how many times this week have you done this to a woman or girl? _____

15. Where else have you harassed women or girls? On the street _____ At work _____
    At school _____ On the bus or subway _____ In the park _____ What other places? _____

16. Has a woman or girl ever told you to stop it, or let you know that she doesn't like it?

    Yes _____ No _____
    (If yes) What did she do? _____

17. Do you have a wife?   Yes   No
    A steady girlfriend?   Yes   No
    Any sisters?   Yes   No   How many? _____
    Any daughters?   Yes   No   How many? _____   Ages: _____
    Any sons?   Yes   No   How many? _____   Ages: _____

18. Do you ever harass women or girls when you have a woman or a child with you?

            Yes   No

19. Do you think most other men harass women, too?   Yes   No
    In your opinion, why do men harass women? _____

20. What do you think a woman should do if she doesn't like this behavior?

THEN YOU SAY: "Thank you. Most women do not think this behavior is a compliment. I expect you not to do it again, to anyone. I appreciate your cooperation with this survey. Good-bye."

AFTERWARD, FILL IN THE FOLLOWING INFORMATION:

1. Time of incident: Date: How many harassers?

2. Describe location of incident:

3. Your age: Your race: Harasser's race:

4. How did the harasser react to the survey? Surprised? Polite? Rude? Apologetic?

5. Were there any witnesses? How did they react to the incident and the survey?

6. How did you feel about the incident? How did you feel about using the survey to confront the harasser?

7. Any other comments or information to share?

THANK YOU! PLEASE MAIL YOUR COMPLETED (OR PARTIALLY COMPLETED) SURVEYS TO:

CONFRONTATION SURVEY, C/O D.C. RAPE CRISIS CENTER
P.O. BOX 21005, WASHINGTON, D.C. 20009

YOUR LEGAL OPTIONS: SEXUAL HARASSMENT AND THE LAW

Deborah M. Chalfie

Where Does the Law Fit In?

Direct confrontation and lawsuits aren't completely separate strategies for combating sexual harassment; both in theory and in practice, they go hand-in-hand. In fact, pursuing legal strategies can be seen as just a more formal way of confronting sexual harassment. By naming the harasser's behavior as sexual harassment, asserting your and other women's[1] legal rights, and holding the harasser publicly accountable for his actions, lawsuits accomplish many of the same objectives as direct, verbal confrontation. In turn, a direct confrontation can be an important prerequisite to building your legal case, because it helps you prove that the harasser's conduct was "unwelcome." A group confrontation can later turn into a class action lawsuit.

Even before you confront or decide whether you will ever take legal action, knowing the law governing sexual harassment gives you important advantages. First, being able to cite the law implicitly threatens legal action, which helps make your direct confrontation more effective. If a harasser or his higher-ups don't take you seriously after an initial confrontation, they may indeed listen better upon learning that this behavior is illegal and could result in bad publicity and damages.

Second, by knowing what the law requires, you can be better prepared if you later decide to sue. If you keep the law and your option of suing in mind, you will probably do a better job of documenting the harassment, finding witnesses, proving that you confronted it, or showing that you "went through channels" but didn't get anywhere. All of these things will help you settle your case successfully or win your case if you end up in court.

Should You Sue?

The great thing about directly confronting sexual harassers is that it's quick, inexpensive, empowering, and almost always works. By contrast, lawsuits are lengthy, expensive, and emotionally grueling, and the outcome is uncertain. Still, there may be many good reasons why you should consider legal recourse.

Bringing a lawsuit may be your last resort to make persistent harassment stop. It is also probably the only way you will get compensation for the losses and injuries you suffered due to the harassment. In addition, for many women, bringing a lawsuit is empowering. It allows the woman to go on the offense against the harasser. In addition to making the harasser accountable for his behavior, this can help overcome the feelings of powerlessness and anger women experience as a result of sexual harassment. Finally, bringing and winning a lawsuit strikes a blow for sex equality. Not only does it improve the lives of women like you, it can also set a precedent that can be used to help women in other ways. For example, the law developed for workplace harassment is now being used to fight sexual harassment in housing and education.[2]

There are, however, definite drawbacks to suing. It is often difficult to find a competent lawyer who is experienced in sexual harassment or civil rights cases (especially in small towns) and who is willing to represent you at a reasonable price. Once the lawyers take over, you lose an element of control over this part of your life. Thus, you must stay actively involved in managing your lawyer and your case.

Lawsuits are also expensive and take a long time—it can take several years to exhaust preliminary channels, complete discovery, resolve motions, and get a trial in a backlogged court. If you win, you may be able to get the defendant to pay your legal fees (but in some cases this is difficult). Win or lose, however, you will be responsible for paying the litigation costs, such as filing fees, the lawyer's travel expenses, transcription fees from depositions, and expert witness fees. Finally, winning a judgment in court may not be the end; you may have to defend your verdict on appeal, or take additional measures to make sure that the judgment is enforced and that you collect your award.

As women too often discover, having the law "on your side" doesn't mean that the outcome will be too. Sexual harassment lawsuits are hard to win. As with other forms of sexual violence, there is a large gap between law and reality. Sexist attitudes—blaming and refusing to believe women who have been victims of sexual violence—are as prevalent in the courts as in the rest of society, making sexual harassment cases (especially the "she said–he said" ones) difficult to prove.[3] Also, even if you are ultimately vindicated by a lawsuit several years from now, that may not be much comfort if filing a complaint makes you lose a good job or an A in a course *now*.

There is one other option for pressing your rights of which you should be aware. Any kind of case, including sexual harassment cases, can be resolved through out-of-court channels such as mediation and arbitration. Mediation is a process by which a neutral "mediator" lets each side have its say and helps the parties reach a settlement themselves. That settlement can include any conditions and remedies the parties agree to and need not follow the law. If the parties can't agree, the victim can still go to court. Arbitration, by contrast, involves a neutral "arbitrator" who holds a hearing and imposes a decision on the parties, just like a judge but outside the courtroom. Arbitrators generally follow the law, use hearing procedures that are slightly less formal than those used in court, and issue binding decisions. Both of these dispute resolution methods are voluntary and are much cheaper and quicker than litigation. Private mediators and arbitrators, who are paid by the parties, may be found by consulting your telephone book or a local bar association.

Carefully weigh the pros and cons and decide what's best for you. If you are interested in pressing your rights through the legal system, there is a list of legal resources in Appendix C to help you further.

SEXUAL HARASSMENT IN EMPLOYMENT

What Is Sexual Harassment?

In a nutshell, sexual harassment is unwanted sexual attention. According to guidelines issued by the Equal Employment Opportunity Commission and endorsed by the courts, sexual harassment is defined as "unwelcome sexual advances, requests for sexual favors, and other verbal or physical conduct of a sexual nature."[4] This encompasses a wide range of behavior, from repeated requests for dates, comments about a woman's body or clothing, comments or jokes of a sexual nature, and the posting of pinups or other pornographic pictures, to making women wear provocative uniforms, unwanted touching, assault, and conditioning promotions or other job benefits on sexual favors or putting up with harassment. This last category also allows women who don't submit to sexual demands and harassment to complain when women who do are given preferential treatment.[5] Because such behavior would not occur "but for" the victim's sex, sexual harassment is a legally recognized form of sex discrimination.

Unwelcome means that the woman didn't want the attention; a woman may "voluntarily" put up with harassment to keep her job and still claim that the attention was unwelcome.[6] Although the courts have never defined the term "sexual" in sexual harassment, it is clear that harassment need not be of a sexual nature to be considered sex discrimination. Just as racial epithets and harassment violate the law, hostile, sexist remarks and discriminatory behavior amounting to harassment that is aimed at making women feel unwelcome and unequal in the workplace is also actionable as harassment based on sex, even if it's not called *sexual harassment*.[7] In reality, women are often subjected to both kinds of harassment in the workplace, and some behavior encompasses both. For example, if a workplace is filled with "girlie pinups," this is sexual harassment *and* harassment based on sex—it conveys the message that women are sexual objects, not equals.[8]

There are two types (or legal "theories") of sexual harassment recognized by the law, nicknamed *quid pro quo* harassment and *hostile environment* harassment. Quid pro quo ("this for that") covers situations in which a woman is made to feel that she must trade sexual favors to get ahead or keep her job. A sexual proposition is made or implied (usually by a superior) in a way that makes submitting to sexual attention a condition, for example, of employment. If she refuses the demands, she suffers negative consequences, such as getting a bad job evaluation or losing a raise. With this kind of harassment, the woman suffers a concrete economic loss, such as losing a promotion or being fired.

With hostile environment harassment, on the other hand, there may be no sex-for-jobs trade-off, nor any tangible economic loss. Rather, women must "run a gauntlet of sexual abuse in return for the privilege of being allowed to work and make a living."[9] The work environment is so " 'heavily polluted' with ... sexual abuse"[10] that it interferes with job performance or poisons the workplace. Isolated or "trivial" harassment doesn't count; it must be so severe or pervasive that, when looked at as a whole, humiliation and aggravation become, in effect, a "term" of employment.

These two types of harassment aren't as distinct as they first appear. For instance, if, instead of refusing, you submit to sexual demands in order to keep your job, you may not have any financial loss. Thus, even though it's a sex-for-jobs situation, the lawsuit would probably proceed under a hostile environment theory. Similarly, if a hostile environment gets so bad that you feel forced to quit, your case could proceed under a quid pro quo theory—you suffered tangible economic harm as a result of refusing to tolerate the environment.

Whether the environment is hostile or whether a sexual demand has been made or implied is often a matter of contention. A man may believe that his sexual jokes or repeated requests for dates are not harassment, yet the woman indeed feels harassed. Whose definition of reality wins the day? Cases used to be decided from the perspective of a reasonable *person*, which often translated into reasonable *man*. However, recognizing that women and men have different experiences with sex inequality and sexual violence, courts have begun to judge the facts based on a reasonable *woman's* (or victim's) perspective; the victim's feelings and perceptions of reality matter.[11]

Finally, from a legal standpoint, who the harasser is doesn't make much difference in determining whether sexual harassment has occurred. Although harassment may be most threatening when it comes from a supervisor, harassment by coworkers, subordinates, and even customers is also illegal.

Who the harasser is, however, does make a difference in whom you can sue and under what laws. Under the federal civil rights law, the company that employs the harasser typically will be liable. This is especially true if management participated in the harassment (if management makes women wear skimpy uniforms, or if a supervisor is the harasser) or if it knew about the harassment (received a complaint) but didn't take effective action to stop it. Even when management doesn't actually know about the harassment, it may still be liable if it *should have* known about it but refused to see it, for example by having no antiharassment policy or complaint procedure. The harasser himself will only be liable under the federal civil rights law, though, if he is an "agent" of the employer, namely a supervisor or manager.

Important note: If your employer *retaliates* against you for filing a complaint, for example by giving you a bad job evaluation or giving you a bad recommendation after you quit, that is a separate, additional violation of the civil rights law. If you've suffered any form of retaliation for filing a complaint, make sure you include it in or add it to your original sexual harassment complaint.

Legal Options, Complaint Procedures, and Remedies

CIVIL RIGHTS LAWS

The main federal law that prohibits sex discrimination, and therefore sexual harassment, in employment is Title VII of the 1964 Civil Rights Act.[12] Almost all employers with fifteen or more employees are covered by it, and it is enforced by the U.S. Equal Employment Opportunity Commission (EEOC). There are also Fair Employment Practices (FEP) laws at the state and even the local levels, which generally cover the same things—sometimes more, sometimes less[13]—and which are enforced by state or local FEP agencies.

This dual system is important to remember for two reasons. First, even though you may not have a valid claim under federal law (if, for instance, your workplace only has eight employees or you didn't file the complaint on time), you may still have a valid claim under a better state or local law. Second, the federal, state, and local agencies work together, with state and local agencies usually having first crack at your case. Thus, even if you file your complaint with a regional EEOC office, be prepared to work with your local or state agency, if one exists, for the investigation and preliminary stages.

Whether you file with the EEOC or a state or local agency, if your complaint is made (at least in part) on the basis of federal law, you only have 180 days, or six months, from the date of the *last* discriminatory incident to file your claim. Ideally, however, you should complain within 180 days of the *earliest* incident of harassment. Although courts may look at incidents that occurred before the six-month period to discern a pattern of harassment, for *remedial* purposes the law only covers the incidents that occurred within six months of the complaint. In some states, the EEOC will allow a longer time limit (300 days), but it's best to file within 180 days just to be safe; otherwise, your complaint can be dismissed as untimely. Even if you also choose to use a nongovernmental complaint procedure within your company or union, you should make sure to meet the EEOC/FEP deadline —that complaint can always be withdrawn later if you resolve it another way.

Important note: If you are a government employee,[14] you may have a much shorter deadline for filing your claim. In the federal government, employees have only 45 days from the date of harassment to file complaints;[15] state employees may face similarly short deadlines. Efforts are under way to extend that deadline to the same 180 days that employees of private companies have, but for now, act quickly!

Once you file a complaint with the EEOC/FEP agency, the basic process is simple:[16]

- *Investigation:* The agency takes statements from you and your employer, interviews witnesses, and collects other evidence. It may also hold a fact-finding conference—an informal discussion with both parties.
- *Determination:* After collecting all the evidence, the agency will make a "cause/no cause" determination. If it finds no cause to believe you've been harassed, it will dismiss your complaint. You can still appeal or sue, but the odds are probably against you. If the agency finds cause to believe you were harassed, you go to the next stage.
- *Conciliation:* If the agency finds for you, it will try to settle the case informally. You can ask for anything you could normally get in court. If the employer agrees to your request, your case is over. If you can't reach a satisfactory settlement, the next step is a lawsuit.
- *Lawsuit:* The EEOC can sue on your behalf, but rarely does. It's more common that you are given a "right-to-sue letter" which allows *you* to sue. You can't sue without this letter, and once you receive it, you only have ninety days to get your lawsuit filed in court.

You must give the EEOC/FEP agency first crack at resolving your complaint, but if it fails to do so, then you can take matters into your own hands. The agency is required by law to resolve your complaint within 180 days of your filing. Because antidiscrimination agencies are often backlogged with complaints, this rarely happens. Thus, if the agency hasn't completed its work within 180 days, you can either wait for it to finish and sue later or request that it issue you a right-to-sue letter so you can proceed without further delay.

If you prevail in court, there are several kinds of remedies available from the harasser, the company, or both:

- *Lost wages and benefits:* If you were fired, were demoted, lost a promotion, or were forced to quit, you can collect the lost wages, pension contribution, and monetary value of other benefits you would have received but for the harassment.[17] In addition, the court can order the employer to rehire or promote you, with back pay and other lost benefits.

- *Compensatory and punitive damages:* If you experienced physical or emotional injuries, you can seek reimbursement for your actual, out-of-pocket expenses. You can also collect punitive damages (to punish the harasser). Both kinds of damages, however, are limited to a total of fifty thousand to three hundred thousand dollars; the maximum varies depending on the size of your company's workforce.[18]

- *Injunctive relief:* You can also ask the court to issue an "injunction," or court order, requiring the employer to do certain things. For instance, it can order the employer to stop the harassment, change its policies, create new complaint or workplace procedures, post notices about its responsibilities, devise a training program for employees, and take other preventive steps.

- *Attorneys' fees:* If you win, you can also usually get the court to make your employer pay your attorneys' fees and other legal costs.[19]

OTHER LEGAL AVENUES

In addition to federal, state, and local antidiscrimination laws, you may also be able to bring a tort lawsuit, either separately or in conjunction with your civil rights claims. *Tort law* is designed to redress physical, emotional, and financial injury and is usually based on judge-made law instead of statutes. Depending upon the facts of your particular case, you may be able to sue the harasser and employer for such *torts* (civil wrongs) as intentional infliction of emotional distress, defamation, interference with a contract, wrongful discharge, or assault.

Besides having no "coverage" limitations, tort suits offer two major advantages: time and money. The deadline for filing such a lawsuit—usually two or three years—is much longer than the one for civil rights actions. You also gain time in that you don't have to go through the civil rights agency process or wait for permission to sue before taking legal action. Moreover, unless your state has enacted special limitations, damages under tort lawsuits aren't nearly as restricted. You can collect for intangible losses, such as pain and suffering, and punitive damages, without limit. There are, however, a few disadvantages too. You usually can't get relief that requires the employer to *do* things, such as reinstate you or stop the sexual harassment. Also, even if you win, tort law makes no provision for the award of attorneys' fees.

Finally, there is one other legal avenue you may want to consider. If you've been physically assaulted—molested or raped —you can file criminal charges for sexual assault against the harasser (but not the company). It makes no difference whether an assault takes place at work, at home, or on the street; under the criminal law, it's still an assault. A few states also have general criminal laws against intimidation or harassment, or specific "hate crime" laws against intimidation, harassment, or assault based on sex. Check with your local rape crisis center, state or local human rights agencies, or a lawyer about these options.[20]

Building Your Case

As soon as possible after the first incident of sexual harassment occurs, you should begin documenting your case. You never know whether you will need that documentation later.

The first step in building your case occurs when the sexual harassment begins. Confront it directly and verbally if you can, at the time or as soon as possible after the incident, then reiterate that confrontation in writing, preferably with a letter to the harasser. Remember: Confrontation not only usually stops the harassment, it also draws the legal line of "unwelcomeness," making further incidents actionable.

Document everything and keep your documentation at home. Keep or make copies of objectionable notes and pictures. If the harassment only occurs when you are alone, you might also want to consider tape-recording the harasser. Keep a journal and write down everything you can remember about each incident

—exactly what he said and did, exactly what you said and did, when and where it happened, whether there were any witnesses, their reactions, and so forth. Be as complete and specific as possible. Make and keep copies of all correspondence and documents that mention or are related to the harassment. Also, if you think it's likely that you will suffer reprisals from refusing sexual demands, confronting the harasser, or filing a complaint, document your job performance. That way, if the employer retaliates and takes unfair action against you, you have a better chance of showing that his action was really prompted by your objection to harassment, not by your actual performance.

If possible, try to talk with other women in your office to determine whether they've also been harassed. Whether or not others have been harassed, these women may be willing to join you in a group confrontation, and can later serve as witnesses. In some cases, male coworkers may also be allies or helpful witnesses. If you don't feel comfortable talking with your coworkers, tell some people outside the office about what is going on. Telling others what happened helps corroborate your case even when there is no written evidence of the harassment.

Finally, check with your personnel office about your company's discrimination policies and complaint procedures. If your company or union seems to have a good complaint mechanism in place, consider filing an internal complaint. Often, the matter can be quickly resolved this way. Even if the process seems useless, however, it's a good idea to file a complaint anyway. It notifies the employer of the harassment; if the employer then does nothing about it, the employer can also be held legally liable. Whatever you do, make sure you keep track of and meet the deadline for filing a discrimination complaint with the EEOC/FEP agency.

SEXUAL HARASSMENT IN EDUCATION
What Is Sexual Harassment?
It is clear that federal law prohibiting discrimination in education prohibits sexual harassment of students by a school's employees.[21] If an instructor, a guidance counselor, an athletic coach, or other employee sexually harasses a student, school officials and the school district will be liable for the harassment if they knew or should have known about it and didn't try to halt

it.[22] The law covers sexual harassment in any elementary school, high school, and university that receives government assistance, and retaliation for filing a complaint is a separate violation.

Most of the court cases on sexual harassment within educational institutions have looked to and applied the law developed for the workplace. Although the scenarios are played out a bit differently, virtually all behavior that constitutes sexual harassment in employment also legally constitutes sexual harassment in education. There is no question that incidents following the quid pro quo formula violate the law. Typical examples of quid pro quo harassment would be a teacher threatening a student with a lower grade or a student loan officer threatening a denial of financial aid unless the student sleeps with him. In such cases, the student has lost a tangible educational opportunity or benefit.

It is less clear, however, whether the law on sex discrimination in education will protect students from sexual harassment by other *students*.[23] It is also unclear whether the hostile environment theory so well-established in employment law is also applicable to school programs and activities.[24] It certainly isn't difficult to envision what either form of harassment would look like—a professor repeatedly makes sexual jokes about women in class, a student writes the name of a female student on a pornographic picture and circulates it in school, a vocational school teacher persistently tells his mostly male class that "women's breasts will get in the way of their being good mechanics," a teacher sexually assaults a student, or a high-school student grabs a classmate's breasts.

These cases may be just around the corner, though.[25] Pervasive or severe behavior poisons the educational environment for women and should be actionable. If anything like this has happened to you, don't let uncertainty about "legal theories" stop you from complaining about it.

Legal Options, Complaint Procedures, and Remedies
CIVIL RIGHTS LAWS[26]
Title IX, the federal law that prohibits sex discrimination (and sexual harassment) in education, wasn't added to the law until 1972.[27] By its terms, it applies only to schools that receive fed-

eral financial assistance. In reality, however, this covers almost all schools—most public schools are partially funded with federal monies, and private schools often receive indirect assistance in the form of federal loans to their students.[28] If the school is covered, all of its activities and programs from the athletic program to the zoology department are covered.[29] As with civil rights laws regarding employment, there may also be laws in your state that you can use that prohibit discrimination in education.[30]

The complaint process for educational discrimination cases is very different from the one followed for employment discrimination. There are three places to file a complaint and, unlike the procedure with employment complaints, you are not required to exhaust out-of-court procedures before you can go to court. First, because schools that receive federal funds must adopt an internal grievance procedure for handling complaints, you can file a complaint with the appropriate division in your school. Second, you can file a complaint with the Office of Civil Rights of the U.S. Department of Education (DOE). Finally, you can bypass both of these and file a complaint directly with a court. Obviously, there may be advantages to trying the out-of-court processes first: They may quickly and cheaply solve the problem.

Each of these complaint channels has a different filing deadline. Check with your school about the deadline for using its grievance procedure. If you want to file a complaint directly with the DOE, you have 180 days from the date of the discriminatory incident. If you want to go directly to court, the deadline is the same as it is for personal injury actions in your state (usually two years). Both your school and the DOE will investigate your complaint and try to reach an informal settlement relatively quickly. You can ask for any of the remedies that would be available to you in court. Be aware, however, that the DOE has no power to order a school to agree to a settlement. Its only enforcement "club" is to cut off all federal funds to that school. If you can't reach a settlement, you can still go to court and, contrary to the rules for employment complaints, you don't need any right-to-sue letter or permission from the DOE to do so.

Students who have been sexually harassed can suffer a variety of injuries. For example, there can be physical injuries and emotional damage that require medical treatment or counseling. In addition, if refusing sexual demands results, for instance, in a failing grade, that could mean having to pay to retake the class, delaying graduation, and losing a job or later educational opportunities. A college's denial of admission or financial aid based on a student's refusal to have sex with a school official certainly has economic ramifications. Finally, if a woman feels compelled to drop out of a program or transfer to another school, there will be additional financial costs due to the harassment. A woman student who has been sexually harassed can sue for:

- *Monetary damages:* Besides getting reimbursed for any out-of-pocket expenses, you can collect damages for all of your reasonably foreseeable losses due to the harassment, such as the loss of a job opportunity.[31] If the circumstances warrant it, you may also collect punitive damages and damages for mental anguish. Unlike the situation with the federal employment laws, none of these damages are expressly limited or capped.
- *Injunctive relief:* You can also ask the court to issue an "injunction," or court order, requiring the school to stop the harassment, change its policies, create and publicize new procedures, devise a training program for its employees, and take other similar steps.
- *Attorneys' fees:* If you win the case, you probably also will be able to require the school to pay your attorneys' fees.

OTHER LEGAL AVENUES

A student who has been sexually harassed in school has access to many of the same non–civil rights remedies that women harassed in the workplace have. (See the discussion of tort actions and criminal charges in the Sexual Harassment in Employment section above.) Moreover, if the case involves sexual abuse, molestation, or assault of a minor, child abuse and similar laws will be applicable.

Students may have one additional avenue of recourse available, and it applies whether the harasser is a teacher or a student. Some colleges and public school systems have enacted disciplinary codes that make sexual harassment, "hate speech," and "discriminatory harassment" a violation of school policy. Under such codes, for example, a male student who sexually harassed a young woman might be suspended or even expelled if the incident was repeated or particularly severe. Unfortunately, not too many schools have adopted such policies yet because the constitutionality of at least the hate speech codes has been called into question.[32] In any case, you may find some additional avenues for action in your school's personnel policies or student code.

SEXUAL HARASSMENT IN HOUSING

What Is Sexual Harassment?

As with education and employment, sexual harassment is all too frequent in housing. Low-income women in public housing are especially vulnerable to demands that they grant sexual favors in exchange for being moved up on the long waiting list for vacancies, getting necessary repairs made, or avoiding eviction. Even with private housing, however, it is not unusual for women to experience sexual harassment from resident managers, groundskeepers, or landlords.

Unlike the situation in education, though, in the area of housing, courts don't seem to have any questions about whether hostile environment claims are valid. Thus, there needn't be any refusal to rent, a rent increase, an eviction, or any other economic loss for you to have grounds to complain.[33] It is enough that your ability to exercise your right to enjoy your home is substantially reduced by the harassment. As with hostile environment claims in the workplace, the harassment must be repeated or severe.[34] Repeated catcalls in the parking lot by the groundskeeper, or a resident manager who enters women's apartments "for repairs" without notice, are examples of this kind of harassment.

Sexual harassment is illegal if it is done by the landlord or anyone over whom the landlord has supervisory responsibility. This would include resident managers, maintenance workers, and repair contractors. Similarly, sexual harassment by a real estate agent or mortgage lender ("You can have the house/loan if you sleep with me") in a real estate transaction is also recognized.[35] In addition, under a special anti-intimidation provision of the law, tenants or neighbors who harass you can be individually liable, even though they don't have any connection to the landlord (see discussion below). As with the laws governing employment and education, retaliation for filing a complaint is a separate violation of the law.

Legal Options, Complaint Procedures, and Remedies

CIVIL RIGHTS LAWS[36]

The federal Fair Housing Act, called Title VIII,[37] is particularly broad in scope. It covers all publicly subsidized housing as well as almost all[38] private housing. It prohibits discrimination in the sale and rental of housing because of a person's race, color, national origin, sex, religion, disability, or familial status (presence of children). Most states have their own similar fair housing laws that you can use to build your case.[39]

Moreover, because of our country's disgraceful and often violent history of racial segregation, the federal law also contains two provisions that specifically prohibit any person from attempting to intimidate, coerce, harass, or interfere with another's enjoyment of her or his housing rights on the basis of race, sex, and other characteristics. Because sexual harassment is clearly discrimination and harassment based on sex, it fits easily within the federal law's anti-intimidation provisions.[40] The first provision, which is aimed at the harasser directly (whether he is a landlord or a neighbor), can be used by itself or as an additional ground for a private lawsuit.[41] The second provision covers intimidation and harassment only if force or a threat of force is involved.[42] In the latter case, the harassment is a criminal offense and can be prosecuted only by the U.S. Department of Justice.

Your options and the process for filing a complaint have some things in common with education complaints and some things in common with employment complaints. For instance, as with complaints about harassment in school, you can either try an administrative process first or go directly to court; it's your choice.[43] But, if you decide to file a complaint with HUD first, it will defer to your local human rights agency, if there is one, to handle the complaint (just as with complaints about workplace harassment).

The deadlines for filing complaints about housing discrimination are much more generous than those applicable to other kinds of discrimination. If you go directly to court, you need only file your complaint within two years of the date when the sexual harassment occurred. If you choose HUD's out-of-court procedure, your complaint must be filed within one year after the harassment occurred. If you decide to file a complaint with HUD and later decide to file a lawsuit because HUD (or the local agency to which the complaint was referred) hasn't acted yet, you don't endanger the timeliness of your lawsuit. The court's clock stops while you are pursuing your complaint through HUD.

If you want to get your case decided or settled without going to court, HUD offers an administrative procedure that can resolve your case much more quickly and inexpensively than litigation. Once you file your complaint, HUD (or the local agency to which the complaint was referred) has 100 days to decide whether your case has merit. If it decides in your favor, it will issue what is called a "charge" of discrimination. If it decides against you, it will dismiss your complaint, and your only option then is to hire a lawyer and sue in court.

During this 100-day period, the agency will investigate your complaint and try to settle it informally. If you can get the harasser/landlord to agree to a settlement using this informal "conciliation" process, that ends it (unless the harasser/landlord breaks the agreement, which means you must take additional legal steps). If the landlord won't settle, yet the agency agrees that you've been discriminated against and issues the charge of discrimination, you then have two choices about how to proceed.

First, you can have the case decided in a formal hearing by a HUD administrative law judge (ALJ). With this procedure, the ALJ must hold the hearing no later than 120 days (four months) after the charge was issued, and must render a decision within 60 days (two months) after the hearing ends. If the ALJ decides in your favor, you can get all the damages you'd be entitled to get in court, except for punitive damages. This decision becomes final unless the Secretary of HUD modifies it within 30 days. If you are dissatisfied with the ALJ's decision, you can appeal it on limited grounds first within the agency and then to a federal appeals court. Your second option after a charge is issued is to skip the ALJ and go to court. If you choose this option, you will be represented by the U.S. Department of Justice, and you can get all of the damages you would otherwise have been able to get had you gone directly to court in the first place.

Several kinds of injuries may result from having been sexually harassed in housing. For instance, if a resident manager harasses you so much that you feel compelled to move, your financial losses would include at the least moving expenses and possibly the additional cost of a higher rent. If you get evicted from subsidized public housing because you won't sleep with the project manager, you could collect compensation for your eviction losses as well as the amount of the rent subsidy. Finally, the physical and emotional damage from being harassed is also compensable. The damages available in court for victims of housing discrimination are quite comprehensive:

- *Monetary damages:* Besides getting compensated for any actual economic losses, you can collect damages for the emotional distress and humiliation that accompany the harassment. If the violation was intentional, such as when the landlord was the harasser, you might also be able to collect punitive damages.
- *Injunctive relief:* You can also seek an "injunction," or court order, requiring the landlord to stop the harassment, make operational changes, train employees, or take other preventive steps.
- *Attorneys' fees:* If you win, you can collect your attorneys' fees and legal costs from the defendant.[44]

OTHER LEGAL AVENUES

On January 27, 1992, a group of women in California won the largest settlement ever recorded for a case of sexual harassment in housing. In that case, a resident manager of an apartment complex was accused of harassing several tenants by demanding sexual favors, grabbing their breasts, entering their apartments, and verbally harassing them, among other things. Fifteen women and twenty-five children sued. Besides claiming violations of the federal and state fair housing laws, they sued for breach of contract and several torts. In addition, the Justice Department sued and requested large fines. The landlord eventually consented to settling the two suits—for more than $1.65 million in damages, fines, and attorneys' fees! The attorney who represented the victims credited the win to the fact that the women got organized, collected evidence, and were willing to fight back.[45]

As this landmark case illustrates, there are several grounds for challenging sexual harassment in housing in addition to the civil rights laws—grounds for which damages can be unlimited. Besides suing for breach of contract and many of the torts previously discussed, the women in this case sued for trespass, conversion (stealing), and retaliatory eviction (being evicted for complaining about discrimination). In this last situation, when a landlord seeks to evict a tenant in retaliation for complaining about harassment, the tenant can use the harassment as a defense.[46] If a woman feels forced to move to avoid the harassment, she may also be able to sue for constructive eviction (conditions were so bad it was the equivalent of being evicted). Depending on the facts, a woman may also be able to file criminal charges for offenses such as breaking and entering or sexual assault—the women in California have also filed rape charges against the harasser.

Finally, renting and selling homes are businesses. Therefore, victims may be able to use their state law against unfair trade practices. Under these laws, damages are typically tripled in order to take the profit out of illegal business conduct. Another business-related remedy would be to seek revocation of a realtor's real estate license or a landlord's housing license.[47]

SEXUAL HARASSMENT ON THE STREET

For women, sexual harassment on the street is so pervasive that it seems like just another part of the landscape. The same catcalls, whistles, leers, sexually abusive comments, demands for sex, and grabbing that occur at work, at school, and in housing seem to be multiplied tenfold on the street. Women, according to some men, don't belong *there* either. On the street, however, it is not a rent increase, bad grade, or demotion that is being threatened. Instead, most women feel that their personal safety is what is at risk with street harassment.[48]

Parodoxically, although the street is where sexual harassment occurs most often and can be most threatening, it is also the place where women have the fewest legal remedies. The federal government has not declared the streets a place where women should expect to be free of discriminatory harassment. Nor have most states. Still, there are a few possibilities for legal recourse open to you.

If you are physically harassed—grabbed, pinched, or rubbed

up against—and you can identify the assailant, you can probably bring criminal charges for assault. Most states also make sexual "contact" against the victim's will a misdemeanor sexual offense. If you want to bring such charges, however, be aware that several things may get in your way. First, since men do this anonymously, it will be rare that you will be able to identify a street harasser. In fact, it is because they are anonymous that they feel freer to harass. Second, even if you can identify and locate the harasser after the incident, the police and the prosecutor may not take the charge seriously, and therefore will refuse to arrest or prosecute. Under criminal law, you are just a "witness" to the crime, and have no decision-making power over whether the police or prosecutor does anything. Third, in some states, unwanted sexual contact is only an offense if the harasser had a particular motive, such as sexual arousal, for the touching; this may be inapplicable or hard to prove. Finally, if you succeed in pressing your case, the harasser probably won't go to jail, but he may have to hire a lawyer, pay a fine, and worry about having a sexual offense record—things he's not likely to soon forget.

For verbal and other kinds of harassment, the legal options are few. If the same neighbor harasses you every day as you walk past his house, you may be able to use the antiharassment provision of the federal housing law (see above) to take him to court. Some states and localities have enacted "hate-violence" laws that provide separate, harsher penalties for assaults, property damage, and harassment or intimidation that occur *because of* the victim's race, religion, color, and so forth. A few of these statutes also include "sex" as a protected category. The constitutionality of such laws, however, is now in doubt.[49] Some states and localities have laws against threatening, stalking,[50] and similar behavior. Although such laws were often originally intended to protect battered women, they may also be usable against some harassers. Check with a local battered women's shelter to find out about these laws and whether they might apply to what happened to you. If so, again, you may be able to bring criminal charges. You may even be able to get a restraining order (a type of injunction) against the harasser that would prohibit him from coming near you.

Finally, if you have the time and the inclination, you may want to consider taking the harasser to small claims court for intentional infliction of emotional distress or some similar tort. Small claims court is usually less formal than other courts and you don't need a lawyer, but you still have to prove the elements of your case. Identifying the harasser, of course, may be a problem. Ask the street harasser his full name—you'd be surprised how many men will tell you. If men in a passing car harass you, try to get the car's license number to track them down. If men on a worksite or driving a company vehicle harass you, talk to the employer, find out the harasser's identity, confront the employer, and demand action. If you aren't satisfied with the response, consider taking both of them to small claims court— the harasser for intentional infliction of emotional distress and his employer for negligent supervision.

CONCLUSION

The law isn't always the right solution for everyone. Knowing it is there and what it covers, however, gives you leverage and widens your options for responding to sexual harassment. Whatever you do, try to confront and challenge sexual harassment whenever it happens, whenever you can. If all of us fight it together, men will finally have no choice but to stop it.

RESOURCES FOR ACTION: FURTHER READING AND ORGANIZATIONS

The following list of resources is by no means exhaustive but will give you a good start in learning more about sexual harassment, your legal rights, and effective defense strategies. Some of the books contain extensive bibliographies and lists of organizations. The organizations can link you with their local chapters or other local resource groups that deal with sexual harassment.

BOOKS

Backhouse, Connie, and Leah Cohen. *Sexual Harassment on the Job: How to Avoid the Working Woman's Nightmare.* Englewood Cliffs, NJ: Prentice-Hall, 1981.
A perceptive analysis of sexual harassment, including case studies, action plans, and a brief historical overview.

Backhouse, Connie, et al. *Fighting Sexual Harassment: An Advocacy Handbook.* Boston: Alyson Publications/Alliance Against Sexual Coercion, 1981.
Practical advice from the Alliance Against Sexual Coercion for women who are harassed and for social service workers whose clients are dealing with harassment (founded in 1976, the Alliance was one of the first women's groups formed specifically to address sexual harassment).

Barreca, Regina. *They Used to Call Me Snow White . . . But I Drifted.* New York: Penguin Books, 1991.
An insightful (and funny) discussion of gender, power, and humor, including women's use of humor to deflect sexual harassers.

Bart, Pauline, and Patricia O'Brien. *Stopping Rape: Successful Survival Strategies.* Elmsford, NY: Pergamon Press, 1985.
A first-rate analysis of self-defense tactics that work, based on women's experiences in actual assaults.

Bravo, Ellen, and Ellen Cassedy. *The 9 to 5 Guide to Combatting Sexual Harassment: Candid Advice from 9 to 5, the National Association of Working Women.* New York: John Wiley & Sons, 1992.
One of the best practical guides for women facing sexual harassment on the job.

Brownmiller, Susan. *Against Our Will: Men, Women, and Rape.* New York: Simon & Schuster, 1975.
The classic, in-depth exploration of the role of sexual assault in society.

Caignon, Denise, and Gail Groves, eds. *Her Wits About Her: Self-Defense Success Stories by Women.* New York: Harper & Row, 1987.
Women's own stories of confronting, escaping, and surviving rapists in many different situations.

Community Action Strategies to Stop Rape. *Rape Prevention Workshops: A Group Leader's Guide.* Columbus, OH: Women Against Rape, 1980.
The original instructor's guide outlining confrontation techniques to stop street harassers and other rape-prevention strategies; available from The Feminist Institute, P.O. Box 30563, Bethesda, MD 20814.

Coverdale-Sumrall, Amber, and Dena Taylor, eds. *Sexual Harassment: Women Speak Out.* Freedom, CA: Crossing Press, 1992.
A powerful collection of women's first-person accounts of sexual harassment, with more than seventy-five contributors.

Delacoste, Frederique, and Felice Newman, eds. *Fight Back! Feminist Resistance to Male Violence.* Minneapolis: Cleis Press, 1981.
Essays, stories, and defense strategies from women who have faced rape, battering, incest, and harassment.

Dworkin, Andrea. *Letters from a War Zone: Writings, 1976–1989.* New York: E. P. Dutton, 1989.
A collection of essays on sexuality, sexual violence, and the realities of women's lives.

Dziech, Billie Wright, and Linda Weiner. *The Lecherous Professor: Sexual Harassment on Campus.* Chicago: University of Illinois Press, 1990.
A well-researched examination of the extent and effect of sexual harassment in academic settings.

Eskenazi, Martin, and David Gallen. *Sexual Harassment: Know Your Rights!* New York: Carroll & Graff, 1992.
A useful overview, with essays by Anita Hill and Catharine MacKinnon, as well as a state-by-state listing of Equal Employment Opportunity Commission offices.

Farley, Lin. *Sexual Shakedown: The Sexual Harassment of Women on the Job.* New York: McGraw-Hill, 1978.

One of the first political, economic, and historical analyses of sexual harassment in the workplace, including information on feminist efforts to stop harassment.

Gutek, Barbara. *Sex and the Workplace: The Impact of Sexual Behavior and Harassment on Women, Men, and Organizations.* San Francisco: Jossey-Bass, 1985.
A discussion of research findings on male and female perceptions of harassment and the effects of harassment on women.

Jaggar, Alison M., and Paula S. Rothenberg. *Feminist Frameworks: Alternative Theoretical Accounts of the Relations between Women and Men,* 2nd ed. New York: McGraw-Hill, 1984.
A collection of classic essays on gender, race, class, and power; contributors include Audre Lorde, Adrienne Rich, Barbara Ehrenreich, and dozens more.

Lindemann, B., and D. Kadue. *Sexual Harassment in Employment Law.* Washington, DC: BNA, Inc., 1992.
Intended primarily for lawyers, this handbook offers a detailed description of the statutes, case law, and legal procedures regarding sexual harassment on the job.

McAllister, Pam. *You Can't Kill the Spirit.* Philadelphia: New Society Publishers, 1988.
A history of women's creative, nonviolent, direct-action strategies for social change, from as far back as 1300 B.C.

McAllister, Pam. *This River of Courage: Generations of Women's Resistance and Action.* Philadelphia: New Society Publishers, 1991.
An examination of nonviolent action by women in many different cultures, against many forms of injustice.

McCann, Nancy Dodd, and Thomas A. McGinn. *Harassed: 100 Women Define Inappropriate Behavior in the Workplace.* Homewood, IL: Business One Irwin, 1992.
The results of an innovative research survey evaluating women's perceptions of a wide variety of sexual harassment situations.

MacKinnon, Catharine A. *Sexual Harassment of Working Women.* New Haven: Yale University Press, 1979.
The ground-breaking legal and political analysis that first defined sexual harassment as a form of illegal sex discrimination.

Medea, Andra, and Kathleen Thompson. *Against Rape, A Survival Manual for Women: How to Avoid Entrapment and How to Cope with Rape Physically and Emotionally.* New York: Farrar, Straus and Giroux, 1974.
A useful overview of sexual assault, street harassment, and basic self-defense techniques.
Morrison, Toni, ed. *Race-ing Justice, En-gendering Power: Essays on Anita Hill, Clarence Thomas, and the Construction of Social Reality.* New York: Pantheon Books, 1992.
An excellent, thought-provoking collection of essays on the sexual and racial repercussions of Anita Hill's testimony before the Senate Judiciary Committee.
National Gay and Lesbian Task Force. *Organizing Against Violence.* Washington, DC: NGLTF, 1992.
An excellent resource manual on how to document and counter hate crimes, organize an antiviolence project, and more.
Paludi, Michele A., ed. *Ivory Power: Sexual Harassment on Campus.* Albany: State University of New York Press, 1990.
An analysis of harassment in university settings; includes a bibliography and list of organizations.
Paludi, Michele A., and Richard Barickman. *Academic and Workplace Harassment: A Resource Manual.* Albany: State University of New York Press, 1991.
A review of research on sexual harassment, as well as individual, institutional, and legal strategies for dealing with harassment.
Petrocelli, William, and Barbara Kate Repa. *Sexual Harassment on the Job.* Berkeley: Nolo Press, 1992.
A comprehensive and easy-to-understand manual on the laws and legal procedures concerning workplace harassment; also contains guidance about lawyers, a summary of state antidiscrimination laws and an extensive list of helpful organizations.
Sanford, Linda Tschirhart, and Ann Fetter. *In Defense of Ourselves: A Rape Prevention Handbook for Women.* Garden City, NY: Doubleday & Co., 1979.
Sound, practical self-defense information for women, including clear photographs of basic kicks and other techniques.
Schwemm, Robert G. *Housing Discrimination: Law and Litigation.* New York: Clark Boardman Callaghan, 1990.

Detailed coverage of housing discrimination law and legal procedures, in a looseleaf format that is updated periodically; available in law libraries.

Siegal, Deborah L. *Sexual Harassment: Research and Resources*. New York: National Council for Research on Women, 1991.
An excellent summary of current research on the incidence and effects of academic and workplace harassment; includes lists of researchers, organizations, and expert witnesses.

Spender, Dale. *Man Made Language*. London: Routledge and Kegan Paul, 1980.
Insightful feminist analysis of gender and power in the use of language.

Tannen, Deborah. *You Just Don't Understand: Men and Women in Conversation*. New York: Ballantine Books, 1990.
An analysis of the gender-based patterns of everyday language and miscommunication between women and men.

U.S. Merit Systems Protection Board. *Sexual Harassment of Federal Workers: An Update*. Washington, DC: U.S. Government Printing Office, 1987.
Summary of findings from the second major survey on sexual harassment in the federal workforce.

Wagner, Ellen J. *Sexual Harassment in the Workplace: How to Prevent, Investigate, and Resolve Problems in Your Organization*. New York: AMACOM, 1992.
Advice for corporate managers and personnel officers, from the American Management Association.

Walmesley, Claire. *Assertiveness: The Right to Be You*. London: BBC Books, 1991.
A good primer on assertiveness skills, on and off the job.

Warshaw, Robin. *I Never Called It Rape: The Ms. Report on Recognizing, Fighting, and Surviving Date and Acquaintance Rape*. New York: Harper & Row, 1988.
A comprehensive report on acquaintance rape, including research results and risk-reduction strategies.

Webb, Susan L. *Step Forward, Sexual Harassment in the Workplace: What You Need to Know*. New York: Mastermedia, 1991.
A basic guide, including information on workplace training sessions on sexual harassment.

Williams, Randall, and Lyn Wells. *When Hate Groups Come to*

Town: A Handbook of Model Community Responses. Atlanta: Center for Democratic Renewal, 1984.

A practical manual on community-organizing strategies to counter the Klan and other hate groups, useful for women who are organizing community projects to stop street harassers.

Women's Legal Defense Fund. *Sex Discrimination in the Workplace: A Legal Handbook.* Washington, DC: WLDF, 1988.

A short, well written summary of federal, state, and local antidiscrimination laws and procedures.

ORGANIZATIONS AND SERVICES

9 to 5 (National Association of Working Women)
614 Superior Ave., NW, Cleveland, OH 44115
216-566-9308
Provides written materials on sexual harassment in the workplace, as well as a hotline (800-522-0925) for information, advice, and referrals.

American Arbitration Association
140 West 51st St., New York, NY 10020
212-484-4000
Offers mediation and arbitration services through local offices around the country; if calling for a referral, ask for individuals and groups with experience in mediating sexual-harassment settlements.

American Association of University Women
1111 16th St., NW, Washington, DC 20036
202-785-7744
AAUW's Legal Advocacy Fund addresses sexual harassment in higher education, while its Educational Fund addresses harassment of students in grades K through 12.

Center for the Prevention of Sexual and Domestic Violence
1914 North 34th St., Suite 105, Seattle, WA 98103
206-634-1903
Provides information and strategies for women dealing with harassment or sexual abuse by members of the clergy.

Center for Women in Government
135 Western Ave., Draper Hall, #310, Albany, NY 12222
518-442-3900

Provides information on the legal rights of women who are state government employees, including procedures for legal action against harassment on the job.

Center for Women's Policy Studies
2000 P St., NW, Suite 508, Washington, DC 20036
202-872-1770
Publishes reports and action guides for women on academic and workplace harassment.

Coalition of Labor Union Women
15 Union Square, New York, NY 10003
212-242-0700
Offers legal referrals for union women and publishes sample workplace policies and contract language on sexual harassment.

D.C. Rape Crisis Center
P.O. Box 21005, Washington, DC 20009
202-232-0789
Provides confrontation-training workshops for women, as well as managers' and employees' harassment-prevention seminars for corporations, government agencies, universities, and nonprofit organizations in the Washington metropolitan area.

Equal Rights Advocates
1663 Mission St., Suite 550, San Francisco, CA 94103
415-621-0505
Offers basic legal information, advice, and referrals in Spanish and English.

Federally Employed Women (FEW)
1400 Eye St., NW, Suite 425, Washington, DC, 20005
202-898-0994
Provides information on the legal rights of women who are federal employees and the special procedures required for legal action against harassment in the federal workforce.

Fund for the Feminist Majority
1600 Wilson Blvd., Suite 704, Arlington, VA 22209
703-522-2214
Provides information on sexual harassment, referrals, and a sexual harassment hotline (703-522-2501).

Klein Associates, Inc.
One Kendall Square, Suite 2200, Cambridge, MA 02139
617-577-1513

Provides consulting services for corporations and other organizations on the design and analysis of sexual-harassment surveys and the development of policies, complaint procedures, and training programs.

National Council for Research on Women
47–49 East 65th St., New York, NY 10021
212-570-5001
The Council's Sexual Harassment Information Project provides guides to research on harassment and referral lists of researchers, organizations, and expert witnesses.

National Organization for Women Legal Defense and Education Fund
99 Hudson St., 12th Floor, New York, NY 10013
212-925-6635
Supplies lawyer referrals and technical-assistance materials for attorneys handling harassment cases.

National Women's Law Center
1616 P St., NW, Suite 100, Washington, DC 20036
202-328-5160
Provides advice and information on all forms of sexual harassment; especially knowledgeable about harassment in education.

The Nile Consulting Group
8714 Hayshed Lane, Suite 301, Columbia, MD 21045
410-997-8448
Conducts seminars on preventing sexual harassment for government, corporate, and nonprofit organizations.

Pacific Resource Development Group
4044 NE 58th Street, Seattle, WA 98105
800-767-3062
Publishes *The Webb Report*, a monthly newsletter on sexual harassment in the workplace; also provides training videotapes, instructors for corporate harassment-prevention seminars, and investigators for sexual-harassment complaints.

Society of Professionals in Dispute Resolution
815 15 St., NW, Suite 530, Washington, DC 20005
202-783-7277
Provides referral lists of trained mediators and dispute-resolution organizations across the country.

U.S. Department of Labor, Women's Bureau
200 Constitution Ave., NW, Washington, DC 20210
202-523-6665

Offers a detailed list of resources on sexual harassment, including organizations, court cases, and training materials.
Wider Opportunities for Women
1325 G St., NW, Washington, DC 20005
202-638-3143
Advocates for rights of women workers, particularly women in nontraditional occupations and trades.
Women's Legal Defense Fund
1875 Connecticut Ave., NW, Washington, DC 20009
202-986-2600
Provides information and advocates for improved legislation on sexual harassment and other forms of discrimination.
W.R.A.T.H. (Women Refusing to Accept Tenant Harassment)
607 Elmira Road, Suite 299, Vacaville, CA 95687
707-426-9014
Provides guidance and action plans for women dealing with sexual harassment of tenants.

1. Sexual Harassment:
The Beginning of the End

1. Deborah L. Siegal, *Sexual Harassment: Research and Resources* (New York: The National Council for Research on Women, 1991), 2.
2. John Lancaster and Ann Devroy, "Head of Navy Quits in Tailhook Scandal," *The New York Times*, 27 June 1992.
3. Siegal, *Sexual Harassment*, v.
4. Siegal, *Sexual Harassment*, 10; and Daniel Goleman, "Sexual Harassment: It's About Power, Not Sex," *The New York Times*, 22 October 1991.
5. "Fighting Back," *Essence* (August 1992), 128.
6. Siegal, *Sexual Harassment*, 2–3, 20.

2. What's Going On Here?
Why Do Men Harass Women?

1. "Rape: The Macho View," *Psychology Today* (April 1987), 12. For a full report of this study, see Donald L. Mosher and Ronald D. Anderson, "Macho Personality, Sexual Aggression, and Reactions to Guided Imagery of Realistic Rape," *Journal of Research in Personality* 20 (March 1986), 77–94.
2. See table accompanying John Lancaster, "Navy Probe Faults at Least 70 Officers," *The Washington Post*, 3 June 1992, citing data from the U.S. General Accounting Office on sexual harassment at the U.S. military academies; and U.S. Merit Systems Protection Board, *Sexual Harassment in the Federal Government: An Update*, 30 June 1988, 2, 11.
3. Ellen Bravo and Ellen Cassedy, *The 9 to 5 Guide to Combatting Sexual Harassment: Candid Advice from 9 to 5, the National Association of Working Women* (New York: John Wiley & Sons, Inc., 1992), 64.
4. Cheryl Benard and Edit Schlaffer, "The Man in the Street: Why He Harasses," in Allison M. Jaggar and Paula S. Rothenberg, eds., *Feminist Frameworks*, 2d ed. (New York: McGraw-Hill, 1984), 71.
5. Ibid.

6. Ibid.
7. Barbara Meyer Wertheimer, *We Were There: The Story of Working Women in America* (New York: Pantheon Books, 1977), 82.
8. Elizabeth Fox-Genovese, *Within the Plantation Household: Black and White Women of the Old South* (Chapel Hill, NC: University of North Carolina Press, 1988). For a powerful account of one woman who fought back, see Melton A. McLaurin, *Celia, A Slave* (Athens, GA: University of Georgia Press, 1991). Celia, a slave in Callaway County, Missouri, was repeatedly raped by her owner, bore him two children, and eventually killed him in self-defense, in her own cabin. The state of Missouri convicted Celia of murder and hung her in December 1855, at the age of nineteen.
9. For a useful discussion of the history of sexual harassment—including Alcott's experience and the story of Carrie Davies, an eighteen-year-old housemaid in Toronto in 1915 who shot her harassing employer in self-defense and was acquitted—see Constance Backhouse and Leah Cohen, *Sexual Harassment on the Job* (Englewood Cliffs, NJ: Prentice-Hall, Inc., 1981), 46–64.
10. Ibid., 59.
11. *The Factory Girls' Album*, Exeter, New Hampshire, 31 October 1846; reprinted in Philip S. Foner, ed., *The Factory Girls* (Chicago: University of Illinois Press, 1977), 80–81.
12. Letter from "A Factory Girl in the Nashua Corporation," *The Nashua Gazette*, Nashua, New Hampshire, 1 October 1846; reprinted in Foner, *Factory Girls*, 83.
13. Sarah G. Bagley, *Voice of Industry*, Lowell, Massachusetts, 15 May 1846; reprinted in Foner, *Factory Girls*, 166–67.
14. Wertheimer, *We Were There*, 238–40.
15. Maud Nathan, *The Story of an Epoch-Making Movement* (New York: Doubleday, 1926), 7; quoted in Mary Bularzik, *Sexual Harassment in the Workplace* (Somerville, MA: New England Free Press, 1979), 7.
16. Rose Cohen, *Out of the Shadow* (New York: George Dovan, 1918), 851; quoted in Bularzik, *Sexual Harassment*, 11.
17. Michael Hiley, *Victorian Working Women* (Boston: David R. Godine, 1980), 31–32, quoting the diary of Arthur Munby for Saturday, 16 August 1862.
18. Hiley, *Victorian Working Women*, 32.

3. THE ROOTS OF SUCCESSFUL RESISTANCE: CIVIL RIGHTS, SELF-DEFENSE, AND NONVIOLENCE

1. Langdon Davis, "A History of Nonviolence" (INVERT monograph, no year), 3–4.
2. Dale Spender, *Women of Ideas*, 3d ed. (London: Pandora Press, 1990), 737.
3. Aldon D. Morris, *The Origins of the Civil Rights Movement* (New York: Free Press, 1984), 218–21. See also Doug McAdam, *Freedom Summer* (New York: Oxford University Press, 1988) and Taylor Branch, *Parting the Waters: America in the King Years 1954–63* (New York: Simon & Schuster, 1988).
4. Interview with Rosa Parks, in Henry Hampton and Steve Fayer, *Voices of Freedom* (New York: Bantam Books, 1990).
5. Morris, *Origins*, 51.
6. These criteria are a modified version of the standards set forth in Community Action Strategies to Stop Rape, *Rape Prevention Workshops: A Group Leader's Guide* (Columbus, OH: Women Against Rape, 1980).
7. For example, for a revealing anthropological analysis of the unwritten "laws" that govern the behavior of waitresses, bartenders, and customers in a typical bar, see James P. Spradley and Brenda J. Mann, *The Cocktail Waitress* (New York: John Wiley & Sons, 1975).
8. Marty Langelan, "Thinking About Tactics: Basic Elements of Nonviolent Actions" (working paper, Nonviolence Collective, Washington Peace Center, 1990).
9. Barbara Deming, "On Revolution and Equilibrium," in Jane Meyerding, ed., *We Are All Part of One Another: A Barbara Deming Reader* (Philadelphia: New Society Publishers, 1984), 176–77. This analysis of the forcefulness of the confrontation dynamic draws heavily on Deming's discussion of the role of nonviolent force in campaigns for social justice.

4. CONFRONTATION: STOPPING HARASSERS ON THE JOB AND ON THE STREET

1. For white women, there is one caveat attached to this guideline. Many white women have been conditioned by racism to

view all African-American men as potential assailants; some also react the same way to Hispanic, Asian, or Arab men. Racism leads white women to overestimate the danger they face from men of color and underestimate the very real threat from white males. *Most rapists are of the same race and social class as their victims.* A white woman whose "instincts" automatically set off her alarms every time a man of color approaches is likely to be reacting to her own learned racism, not to the reality of the situation.

2. See, for example, M. J. Horowitz, *Stress Response Syndromes* (New York: Jason Aronson, 1976), and L. Terr, "Chowchilla Revisited: The Effects of Psychic Trauma Four Years After a School Bus Kidnapping," *American Journal of Psychiatry* 140 (1983), 1543–50.

3. For two interesting discussions of male/female language differences, see Deborah Tannen, *You Just Don't Understand: Men and Women in Conversation* (New York: Ballantine Books, 1990), and Dale Spender, *Man Made Language* (London: Routledge and Kegan Paul, 1980).

4. Benard and Schlaffer, "Man in the Street," 71.

5. WHEN CHILDREN ARE THE TARGET: KIDS WHO DEFEND THEMSELVES

1. For more information on incest and child sexual abuse, see Ellen Bass and Louise Thornton, *I Never Told Anyone* (New York: Harper Colophon Books, 1983); Christine Coutois, *Healing the Incest Wound: Adult Survivors in Therapy* (New York: W. W. Norton, 1988); Linda Gordon, *Heroes of Their Own Lives* (New York: Penguin Books, 1988); Florence Rush, *The Best-Kept Secret: Sexual Abuse of Children* (Englewood Cliffs, NJ: Prentice-Hall, 1980); and Diana E. H. Russell, *The Secret Trauma: Incest in the Lives of Girls and Women* (New York: Basic Books, 1986).

2. The D.C. Rape Crisis Center teaches "Staying Safe" classes for children throughout the Washington, D.C., school system and has published a booklet for children and their parents, *Staying Safe—Sexual Assault: How to Protect Yourself,* by I. Nkenge Toure and Elizabeth Ozer. Copies are available ($3) from the Rape Crisis Center, P.O. Box 21005, Washington, DC 20009.

6. WHEN THE JOB BECOMES A MISERY: CONFRONTING HARASSERS AT WORK

1. Interview with Sarah Burns, in Siegal, *Sexual Harassment*, 21–22.

7. DEEP IN HOSTILE TERRITORY: CONFRONTING HARASSERS IN MALE-DOMINATED JOBS

1. Siegal, *Sexual Harassment*, 16–17.
2. Ibid., 15.

8. NOT ALL MEN HARASS: MEN AS ALLIES FOR WOMEN

1. An earlier version of this story and statement appeared under the title "Stolen Glances/Lost Love" in the newsletter of the National Organization for Changing Men, *Brotherbond* 5 (May 1987), 1–3.
2. Portions of this list are derived from Bill Moyers et al., *The International Day of Nuclear Disarmament Handbook*, and *The C.D. Handbook of the National Lesbian and Gay March on Washington*.

9. CONSTRUCTION WORKERS, SUBWAY CREEPS, AND OTHER DAILY HAZARDS: CONFRONTING HARASSERS IN THE COMMUNITY

1. Katha Pollitt, "Hers," *The New York Times*, 12 December 1985.

12. CONFRONTING RAPISTS: SELF-DEFENSE IN A SEXUAL ASSAULT

1. Susan Brownmiller, *Against Our Will: Men, Women, and Rape* (New York: Simon & Schuster, 1975). See also Community Action Strategies to Stop Rape, *Freeing Our Lives: A Feminist*

Analysis of Rape Prevention (Columbus, OH: Women Against Rape, 1978).

2. For more information on self-defense, contact your local rape crisis center. The following books are also useful: Pauline B. Bart and Patricia H. O'Brien, *Stopping Rape: Successful Survival Strategies* (Elmsford, New York: Pergamon Press, 1985); Frederique Delacoste and Felice Newman, eds., *Fight Back! Feminist Resistance to Male Violence* (Minneapolis: Cleis Press, 1981); Denise Caignon and Gail Groves, eds., *Her Wits About Her: Self-Defense Success Stories by Women* (New York: Harper & Row, 1987); Andra Medea and Kathleen Thompson, *Against Rape* (New York: Farrar, Straus and Giroux, 1974); Linda Tschirhart Sanford and Ann Fetter, *In Defense of Ourselves* (Garden City, New York: Doubleday & Company, 1979); and Robin Warshaw, *I Never Called It Rape: The Ms. Report on Recognizing, Fighting, and Surviving Date and Acquaintance Rape* (New York: Harper & Row, 1988).

13. THERE IS STRENGTH IN NUMBERS: THE POWER OF GROUP CONFRONTATIONS

1. Annie McCombs spent thirteen years working on the waterfront as a deckhand; she has since earned a paralegal degree and is currently writing and studying literature. She claims to believe that male supremacy will be destroyed in her lifetime (however, she does wonder how long she'll have to live to make this true). Annie dedicates this story to the memory of Cheryl Parker, who showed her that confronting sex discrimination could be effective, empowering, and sometimes even fun.

APPENDIX B: YOUR LEGAL OPTIONS: SEXUAL HARASSMENT AND THE LAW

1. The law also prohibits sexual harassment against men. However, because the reality is that the vast majority of cases involve harassment of women by men, the pronouns and examples in the text speak in terms of male harassers and female victims.

2. Sexual harassment was legally recognized first in the workplace. The legal approach developed there has since served as the model followed in the areas of education and housing. Be-

cause the law developed for workplace harassment has been extended (almost wholesale) to these other areas, basic legal concepts are explained just once, in the Sexual Harassment in Employment section of this appendix, and key differences from the employment setting are noted in the other sections.

3. Evidence of a woman's "sexually provocative" language and dress can be relevant to the issue of "unwelcomeness." See Meritor Savings Bank, FSB v. Vinson, 477 U.S. 57, 106 S.Ct. 2399, 2406-07 (1986).

4. 29 CFR § 1604.11(a).

5. See Broderick v. Ruder, 685 F.Supp. 1269 (D.D.C. 1988).

6. Meritor Savings Bank, FSB v. Vinson, 477 U.S. 57, 106 S.Ct. 2399, 2406 (1986) ("The correct inquiry is whether . . . [the woman] by her conduct indicated that the alleged sexual advances were unwelcome, not whether her actual participation in sexual intercourse was voluntary").

7. See Bell v. Crackin Good Bakers, Inc., 777 F.2d 1497, 1503 (11th Cir. 1985) (woman not required to show the harassment had sexual overtones because her claim was not for "sexual harassment" but rather harassment because she was a woman [implying that nonsexual, antiwoman harassment isn't encompassed within claims for "sexual harassment"]; see also McKinney v. Dole, 765 F.2d 1129 (D.C. Cir. 1985) and Lipsett v. Univ. of Puerto Rico, 864 F.2d 881 (1st Cir. 1988).

8. See Robinson v. Jacksonville Shipyards, Inc., 760 F.Supp. 1486, 1526 (M.D.Fla. 1991) ("A pre-existing atmosphere that deters women from entering or continuing in a profession or job is no less destructive to and offensive to workplace equality than a sign declaring 'Men Only' ").

9. Henson v. Dundee, 682 F.2d 897, 902 (11th Cir. 1982).

10. Wyerick v. Bayou Steel Corp., 887 F.2d 1271, 1275 (5th Cir. 1989).

11. See, e.g., Rabidue v. Osceola Ref. Corp., 805 F.2d 611, 626 (6th Cir. 1986) (Keith, J., dissenting); Ellison v. Brady, 924 F.2d 872 (9th Cir. 1991).

12. Title VII makes it unlawful for an employer "to discriminate against any individual with respect to his compensation, terms, conditions, or privileges of employment, because of such individual's race, color, religion, sex, or national origin." 42 U.S.C. § 2000e-2(a)(1).

13. For example, although federal law requires fifteen employ-

ees, some state laws require far fewer. Space limitations prohibit a review of each state law and the differences in coverage or remedies available, if any, from federal law. For a complete listing, see W. Petrocelli and B. Repa, *Sexual Harassment on the Job* (Nolo Press, 1992).

14. If the harasser is a government official, an employee of an organization that receives federal financial assistance, or the employee of a government contractor, there are additional federal civil rights laws that may apply: the Equal Protection Clause of the Fourteenth Amendment to the U.S. Constitution, Executive Order 11246 (prohibiting discrimination by federal contractors), and § 1983 of the Civil Rights Act of 1871, 42 U.S.C. § 1983 (prohibiting state officials from depriving citizens of their federal civil rights).

15. 29 CFR § 1614.105(2)(1).

16. Federal employees must follow a slightly different procedure, which requires that agency and EEOC procedures be exhausted before suing. Check with your agency's EEO officer for further information.

17. If you weren't hired because of sexual harassment in the hiring process, you can collect compensation for the actual value of the lost opportunity, minus the amount you earned from finding another job. This is tough, but not impossible, to prove.

18. The availability of damages for sex discrimination is the result of new federal legislation passed by Congress in 1991. Civil Rights Act of 1991, P.L. 102-166, 102d Cong., 2d Sess., 105 Stat. 1071 (1991). As of this writing, another proposal is pending that would eliminate the $50,000–$300,000 damage cap and bring remedies for sex discrimination into line with remedies available for race discrimination.

19. Consumer beware! Working out how attorneys' fees and other litigation expenses are to be handled if you win and if you lose can be tricky. For guidance on this, see W. Petrocelli and B. Repa, *Sexual Harassment on the Job*, Chapter 9 (Nolo Press, 1992), and K. Ostberg, *Using a Lawyer . . . And What to Do if Things Go Wrong* (Random House, 1985) (available in bookstores or from HALT, 1319 F St., NW, #300, Washington, DC 20004).

20. What is the difference between offering a woman one hundred dollars in exchange for sex and offering a woman a promotion in exchange for sex? Is there any reason why sexual

harassers in the workplace shouldn't be criminally prosecuted for soliciting prostitution? Although the author does not know whether anyone has ever tried this, prostitution laws would seem to apply.

21. This law (Title IX) also covers *employment* discrimination by schools against their employees. Thus, teachers and other school employees can use this law to complain about sexual harassment by colleagues and superiors.

22. Franklin v. Gwinnett County Public Schools, _ U.S. _, 112 S.Ct. 1028 (1992).

23. In 1992, an appellate court in Pennsylvania held that neither school officials nor a school district could be held liable for the repeated sexual assaults of some students by others inside the school, and in early 1993, the U.S. Supreme Court let that decision stand. D.R. by L.R. v. Middle Bucks Area Vocational Technical School, 972 F.2d 1364 (3d Cir. 1992), *cert. den'd*, _ U.S. _ (Jan. 19, 1993). For arguments in favor of recognizing student-to-student harassment, see *Sexual Harassment Between Peers Under Title VII and Title IX: Why Girls Just Can't Wait to Be Working Women*, 16 Vermont L.Rev. 303 (1991); J. Strauss, *Peer Sexual Harassment of High School Students: A Reasonable Student Standard and an Affirmative Duty Imposed on Educational Institutions*, 10 L.& Inequality 163 (1992).

24. No court to date has expressly held that students may sue educational institutions using a hostile environment theory, though they have come very close. See Moire v. Temple School of Medicine, 613 F.Supp. 1360 (E.D. Pa. 1985), *aff'd*, 800 F.2d 1136 (3d Cir. 1986) (hostile environment claim possible under Title IX, but the facts don't support it in this case); Franklin v. Gwinnett County Public Schools, _ U.S. _, 112 S.Ct. 1028, 1037 (1992) (citing a hostile environment case for the proposition that, as under Title VII (employment), sexual abuse of a student by a teacher is sex discrimination); Lipsett v. Univ. of Puerto Rico, 864 F.2d 881 (1st Cir. 1988) (holding that hostile environment claims brought against educational institutions by school *employees* are valid under the Title IX (education) provisions that prohibit employment discrimination by schools). But, one court has expressly disallowed hostile environment claims against schools. Bougher v. Univ. of Pittsburgh, 713 F.Supp. 139, 144 (W.D.Pa. 1989), *aff'd on other grounds*, 882 F.2d 74 (3d Cir. 1989).

25. J. Gross, "Schools Are Newest Arena for Sex-Harassment Cases," *New York Times*, at A1(N) (March 11, 1992).

26. Because most schools are publicly funded or indirectly receive federal funds, the Equal Protection Clause of the Fourteenth Amendment to the U.S. Constitution and § 1983 of the Civil Rights Act of 1871 (prohibiting state officials from depriving citizens of their federal civil rights) may also apply.

27. Title IX mandates that no person "shall, on the basis of sex, be excluded from participation in, be denied the benefits of, or be subjected to discrimination under any education program or activity receiving Federal financial assistance." Education Amendments of 1972, 20 U.S.C. § 1681(a).

28. Besides exempting wholly private schools, the law also contains a few exceptions for religious and military schools and organizations such as the Boy Scouts and Girl Scouts.

29. This long-standing, expansive view of the law's coverage came to a screeching halt in 1984 when, in the case of Grove City College v. Bell, 465 U.S. 555, 104 S.Ct. 1211 (1984), the Supreme Court held that only the specific program that received the direct or indirect funds must comply with the law. Congress overruled this overly narrow interpretation and restored the law to its pre–*Grove City* status when it adopted the Civil Rights Restoration Act of 1987, P.L. 100-259, 100th Cong., 2d Sess., 102 Stat. 28 (1988). Section 908 of that law states that if any part of an educational institution receives federal assistance, *all* of its operations are subject to the law.

30. Minnesota has a state law against sexual harassment in schools, and California is reported to be considering legislation that would make sexual harassment of students by students grounds for disciplinary action such as suspension or expulsion. J. Gross, "Schools Are Newest Arena for Sex-Harassment Cases," *New York Times*, at A1(N) (March 11, 1992).

31. Up until very recently, monetary damages were not available. A 1992 Supreme Court case changed that. Franklin v. Gwinnett County Public Schools, _ U.S. _, 112 S.Ct. 1028 (1992).

32. See Doe v. Univ. of Michigan, 721 F.Supp. 852 (E.D.Mich. 1989), holding that UM's code against discriminatory harassment was too vague and overbroad to square with the First Amendment. Even more damning, however, is a recent Supreme Court case that calls the constitutionality of all hate-

violence statutes into question. The case is R.A.V. v. St. Paul,
_ U.S. _, 112 S.Ct. 2538 (1992), holding that a local hate-
violence ordinance violated the First Amendment because it
penalized only certain kinds of "speech" based on its content.
33. See, e.g., Gnerre v. Mass. Comm'n Against Discrimination,
402 Mass. 502, 524 N.E.2d 84 (Mass. 1988); New York, by
Abrams v. Merlino, 694 F.Supp. 1101 (S.D.N.Y. 1988).
34. But compare Shellhammer v. Lewallen, 1 Fair Hous.-Fair
Lend. ¶ 15,472 (W.D. Ohio 1983), aff'd without op., 770 F.2d
167 (6th Cir. 1985) (hostile environment should be judged from
the particular plaintiff's point of view), with Gnerre v. Mass.
Comm'n Against Discrimination, 402 Mass. 502, 524 N.E.2d 84
(Mass. 1988) (hostile environment should be judged from a reasonable person's point of view).
35. See, e.g., New York, by Abrams v. Merlino, 694 F.Supp.
1101 (S.D.N.Y. 1988).
36. If the harassment occurs in public housing, the Equal Protection Clause of the Fourteenth Amendment to the U.S. Constitution and § 1983 of the Civil Rights Act of 1871 (prohibiting
state officials from depriving citizens of their federal civil rights)
may also apply.
37. 42 U.S.C. §§ 3601 et seq., amended by the 1988 Fair Housing Amendments Act, P.L.100-430, 100th Cong., 2d Sess. (1988).
38. The law exempts from its coverage single-family houses
that are for sale by the owner, live-in landlords of very small
apartment buildings, and a few others. Even these owners, however, can be liable for discrimination under certain conditions.
See 42 U.S.C. § 3603(b).
39. See, e.g., Chomicki v. Wittekind, 128 Wisc.2d 188, 381
N.W.2d 561 (Ct. App. 1985).
40. See, e.g., Grieger v. Sheets, 689 F.Supp. 835 (N.D.Ill. 1988).
41. See 42 U.S.C. § 3617.
42. See 42 U.S.C. § 3631.
43. You can also pursue both at once, but if you reach an
agreement, start a hearing, or get a decision using the HUD
procedure, your lawsuit will end. Similarly, if your lawsuit goes
to trial before HUD has acted, your complaint with HUD will
be terminated.
44. Except for punitive damages, all of these same remedies are
available from the ALJ using HUD's administrative process.
45. The settlement of the two cases, Fiedler v. Dana Properties,

No. S 89-1396 LKK (E.D. Calif.) and U.S. v. Dana Properties, No. S 90-0254 LKK (E.D. Calif.), was reported in Bulletin #9 of Prentice-Hall's *Fair Housing–Fair Lending Reporter*, ¶ 9.1, at 1–2 (March 1, 1992).

46. Barela v. Superior Court, 30 Cal.3d 244, 636 P.2d 582 (1981).

47. *Home Is No Haven: An Analysis of Sexual Harassment in Housing*, 1987 U. Wisc. L.Rev. 1061, 1084–85 (1987).

48. Women are right to feel this way. Sexual harassment is often used by rapists as a way to "test" potential victims; women who respond passively are viewed as easy prey.

49. See n. 32 supra concerning the *R.A.V.* case. Statutes that impose stiffer penalties for hate-motivated crimes are also currently being reviewed by the Supreme Court.

50. Antistalking laws typically prohibit malicious and repeated following or harassing of another person that poses a "credible threat" of violence. See "Anti-Stalking Laws Top List of New Legislation," *Washington Post*, at A7 (June 29, 1992).